OIL PRIVATIZATION, PUBLIC CHOICE AND INTERNATIONAL FORCES

Oil Privatization, Public Choice and International Forces

Stephanie M. Hoopes
Lecturer in International Relations and Politics
School of Social Sciences
University of Sussex

First published in Great Britain 1997 by

MACMILLAN PRESS LTD
Houndmills, Basingstoke, Hampshire RG21 6XS and London
Companies and representatives throughout the world

A catalogue record for this book is available from the British Library.

ISBN 0–333–65072–7

First published in the United States of America 1997 by
ST. MARTIN'S PRESS, INC.,
Scholarly and Reference Division,
175 Fifth Avenue, New York, N.Y. 10010

ISBN 0–312–15975–7

Library of Congress Cataloging-in-Publication Data
Hoopes, Stephanie M.
Oil privatization, public choice and international forces /
Stephanie M. Hoopes.
p.   cm.
ISBN 0–312–15975–7
1. Petroleum industry and trade—Government policy—Great Britain.
2. Privatization—Great Britain.   I. Title.
HD9571.6.H66   1996
338.2'7282'0941—dc20   96–10361
                                                        CIP

This book is printed on paper suitable for recycling and made from fully managed and
sustained forest sources.

10   9   8   7   6   5   4   3   2   1
06   05   04   03   02   01   00   99   98   97

Printed in Great Britain by
The Ipswich Book Company Ltd
Ipswich, Suffolk

Contents

List of Figures

List of Tables

List of Abbreviations

AOPEC	Arab Organisation of Petroleum Exporting Countries
b/d	barrels per day
BGC	British Gas Corporation
BNOC	British National Oil Company
BP	British Petroleum
CBI	Confederation of British Industry
CPRS	Central Policy Review Staff
DEn	Department of Energy
EC	European Community
EMS	European Monetary System
GDP	Gross Domestic Product
GNP	Gross National Product
IEA	International Energy Agency
IPE	International Political Economy
MMC	Monopolies and Mergers Commission
MP	Member of Parliament
NCB	National Coal Board
OECD	Organisation of Economic Cooperation and Development
OPEC	Organisation of Petroleum Exporting Countries
PAC	Public Accounts Committee
PM	Prime Minister
PSBR	Public Sector Borrowing Requirement
TUC	Trades Union Congress
US	United States
UKCS	United Kingdom Continental Shelf

1 Introduction

Privatisation in Britain has been heralded by British politicians, the press and political observers alike as a radical break in government policy – not only for the British government, but for any government. Privatisation is in stark contrast to the trend, especially since the Second World War, of government growth. A major part of the government's sales were its oil assets – Britoil, Enterprise Oil and Wytch Farm, and a majority shareholding in British Petroleum – sold within a 10-year period, 1977–87, reversing a policy which had lasted 73 years. Control of energy resources has traditionally been a source of power for states; yet the sale of Britain's oil assets, vital resources in an oil-dependent world, passed without much opposition or even much notice. In this book I seek to explain why the government pursued this seemingly irrational policy. This first chapter reviews traditional international relations and domestic politics perspectives and previous attempts to explain the retrenchment of government, and then establishes a public choice theory approach with several modifications to existing models to explain Britain's oil sales.

STATE POWER AND NATURAL RESOURCES

Ever since Thucydides wrote *The History of the Peloponnesian War*, scholars of politics have asserted that states seek to maximise their power and that natural resources are an essential component of that power (Gilpin, 1986, pp. 308–9; Carr, 1964, pp. 114–29). Continuing in this vein, international relations scholars of the realist tradition assume that the state is the key unit of analysis, that states seek power, and that states behave rationally (Keohane, 1986b, p. 7). Realists and neorealists contend that states try to enhance the power and material well-being of their inhabitants and, therefore, as Stephen Krasner (1985a) asserts, 'states want power and control as much as wealth' (p. 3). One of the primary means to power is control of material resources. Robert Keohane, in his seminal work *After Hegemony* (1984a), argues that power is based on the control of material resources; similarly, G. John Ikenberry and Charles A. Kupchan (1990) assert: 'Power is directly related to the command of material resources' (p. 3).

1

Of all a state's resources, most scholars agree that raw materials are among the most important. Keohane (1984a) lists raw materials ahead of other sources including capital, markets and competitive advantage in the production of highly valued goods (p. 32). Similarly, Krasner (1978) argues that raw materials are intimately connected with the effective functioning of the economy, the well-being of individual citizens and the national defence (p. 52). More narrowly, of the raw resources, energy is often cited as the most important for a state to control. Thucydides even mentioned the importance of energy resources, though he was referring to wheat for fuelling soldiers' bodies. More recently, Susan Strange (1988) explained energy's economic importance:

> For all developed economies, whether planned, mixed or market-oriented, energy is a vital factor of production. The basic industries in every modern economy ... all need large inputs of energy, whether this comes from oil, coal, gas or nuclear power. Nor can any modern economy function without transport. Road, rail, sea and air transportation are all heavy users of energy. And when there is a breakdown in the supply of power to homes and factories, a modern society comes almost to a standstill (p. 186).

Henry Kissinger highlights the political and military as well as the economic importance of oil, though specifically to the United States:

> The [1973–74] energy crisis has placed at risk all of this nation's objectives in the world. It has mortgaged our economy and made our foreign policy vulnerable to unprecedented pressures ... it has also profoundly affected our national security by triggering a policy crisis of global dimensions (as quoted in Strange, 1988, p. 201).

Most importantly, in terms of the focus of this study, realists argue that a state's immediate response to a threat to those resources is to increase direct control. Strange (1988) points out that this was certainly the case for oil:

> After the first OPEC price rise, other states' concern with this new *problematique* of security – how to secure supplies of energy for the country's industry and transportation systems – led, as we saw, to greater state intervention in markets and to much greater diversity of state policies towards energy sources other than oil (p. 202).

While there are numerous means of control, Yair Aharoni (1986) suggests that the most effective is state ownership. He argues that state-owned companies allow governments to exert more control over resources as well as to provide invisible methods to pay largesse to different constituents.

State-owned industries also permit politicians to dispense political patronage and to carry out projects which might not otherwise win legislative approval. As state-owned companies also have a degree of autonomy, politicians can claim that they are free of blame if a project fails, while they are well positioned to take credit for any successes (p. 38). Aharoni also argues that oil ownership, in particular, enables governments to reduce dependence on multinational companies, to develop the understanding necessary to check multinational companies' activities, and to insure inexpensive and reliable crude oil supplies (p. 103; also see Suleiman and Waterbury, 1990, p. 18).

The evidence supports this view of power-maximising states as, in fact, most states became directly involved in the oil industry during the decade following the 1973–4 oil crisis. Over half of the world's state-owned oil companies existing today were created between 1970 and 1982. In addition, states without oil (such as Japan and Germany) became more involved by negotiating long-term oil contracts directly with oil producing countries (*Financial Times*, 1992). Britain conformed to this pattern by creating a state-owned oil company in 1976.

Confounding traditional realists' understandings of states and power, however, a year later, in 1977, the British government began selling its oil assets, with a tranche of British Petroleum (BP) shares reducing the government's holding from 68 per cent to 51 per cent. By 1987, the British government had sold the production portion of the British National Oil Company (BNOC), now known as Britoil, and abolished BNOC's trading operations; it had forced the British Gas Corporation (BGC) to sell all its oil assets (now known as Enterprise Oil and Wytch Farm) and had completely divested its holding in BP. In so doing, scholars and critics have argued, the British state reduced its control over a vital resource and a essential means to power. At the time, David Heald (1981) maintained: 'Through privatisation measures, the government is reducing its leverage over the oil sector' (p. 107). Similarly, Michael Webb (1985) argued: 'The privatisation of energy industries reduces the scope for the direct involvement of government in their decision taking' (p. 31).

PARADOX OF EXPLAINING STATE RETRENCHMENT

Britain is not the only country to undertake such sales, which are part of a phenomenon coined more broadly as privatisation, and defined by John Vickers and Vincent Wright (1989), as 'that wide range of policies designed to reduce the scope, limit the functions and generally weaken the influence of the public sector' (p. 3). Since the early 1980s, plans have been made for privatisations in industrialised and developing countries and by liberal as well as conservative governments, including Turkey, Nigeria, Argentina, Mexico, Pakistan, India, Malaysia, Cuba, Mozambique, New Zealand, Belgium, Austria, Sweden, the Netherlands, Germany, France, Spain, Italy and eastern Europe. In fact, *The Economist* remarked in 1975, 'Everybody's Doing It' (as quoted in Suleiman and Waterbury, 1990, p. 3).

The development of privatisation challenged scholars' view of the state in domestic politics as well as international relations. For example, most scholars agreed with Joseph Schumpeter's view (1952) that the further expansion of public bureaucracies was 'the one certain thing about our future' (p. 294). Many theorists have been unable plausibly to explain the retrenchment of the state at all, as Paul Starr (1990) points out:

> Whether or not the current turn towards privatisation discloses a general failure of government, it certainly discloses a general failure of social theory. From the 1950s through the 1970s, theorists of the most diverse persuasions assumed that growing welfare and regulatory states in the West and entrenched communist states in the East were accomplished facts, unlikely to be reversed or undone (p. 22).

Despite these problems, or possibly because of them, there have been numerous attempts to explain privatisation. Before continuing, I briefly review a few of these explanations.

State autonomy theorists maintain that states in their mutual interest always prefer to control vital resources. The adoption of a policy not in the state's interest can only be explained by the success of 'powerful' private actors in influencing an 'uncohesive state' (Nordlinger, 1988, pp. 881–3; also see Krasner, 1978; Nordlinger, 1981). In other words, states with regimes that allow private actors access to the policy-making process are forced to give larger shares of both sovereign largesse and entrepreneurial concessions to interest groups (Vernon, 1971; Moran, 1974; Nelsen, 1991). Merrie Gilbert Klapp (1987) uses this type of argument for explaining British oil policy. She argues that the British state's oil asset sales resulted because a 'weak' British state succumbed to shipping and fishing groups as well as multinational oil companies. The evidence on privatisation, however, shows that the initiative for the sales came from the political leaders themselves, and not from strong interest groups. In fact, most current accounts of privatisation, from Europe to Africa, describe the obstacles leaders must overcome to implement their privatisation goals rather than interest groups persuading the government (for example, *Financial Times*, 24 June 1993 and 1 September 1993). State autonomy theorists therefore have great difficulty in explaining why a state would *choose* to sell and give up control of a natural resource.

Many theorists try to explain the overall retrenchment of growth with systems level solutions. Most of these types of theories identify one independent variable, such as technology, economic growth, the demands of interest groups or voters, or financial capacity. They suggest that a reversal of one or another of such external influences will cause a change in the trend of government growth (Hood, 1991, pp. 43–56). While parsimonious, systems approaches do not explain why the government retrenches in some sectors and not others. More sophisticated systems approaches, such as a 'super auto reversible' model which has the benefit of incorporating several levels of variables, still cannot explain why privatisation occurs in both industrial and developing countries (Hood, 1991, pp. 56–9), but the levels of variables offer some insight as to how to organise complex solutions.

Elite theory explains why privatisation originates from a government despite little popular demand for the policy. Elite theorists argue that the top governmental positions, and therefore the national agenda, are controlled by a homogeneous elite, and that privatisation was proposed because it met elite goals of greater technological efficiency and was consistent with their ideological beliefs (McAlister and Studlar, 1989, p. 160, Table I; Aharoni, 1986, p. 393). Elite theorists, though, have trouble explaining why the state ever nationalised industries in the first place, or why they are selling them at one specific point in time.

The ideological aspect of the elite's argument has emerged as the conventional wisdom. While troublesome to scholars, the 'man on the street' in Britain easily explains privatisation as an ideological and party-driven policy: the Labour Party with their socialist ideology nationalised Britain's industries, and the Conservatives under Margaret Thatcher, with their belief in free markets and private enterprise, privatised Britain's industries (Aharoni, 1986, p. 317; Pliatsky, 1989, p. 107; Moore, 1990, p. 2). More sophisticated accounts similarly claim that change in ideology is linked to change in state-ownership. Joel Wolfe (1991), for example, measured the correlation between the change in state-ownership and the ideology of the government in power, and postulates there is a strong relationship. On closer examination, however, this theory does not hold, even in Britain where privatisation is strongly associated with Thatcher's Conservative ideology. In fact, both Conservative and Labour governments undertook nationalisation at various points in this century, primarily to aid industries which were in real financial trouble (Abromeit, 1988, p. 69). The rationale for nationalisation and higher correlation, therefore, is between economic need and financial assistance rather than ideology. As regards privatisation of the oil assets, a Labour government was actually the first to privatise with the sale of BP shares in 1977. The evidence also shows a pragmatic evolution of a privatisation programme under the Conservative government after 1979.

Pluralists argue that the form which state-owned companies take and, ultimately, their very existence is the product of struggles between state bureaucracies and interest groups (including the managers of the state-owned companies) vying for control and benefits. In this view, shifts in institutional links and relative power or political interests affect the performance or role of the state-owned companies, and relegate the role of the politician to that of merely a bystander or referee. In the case of the oil asset sales, however, only the oil private-sector companies were passively interested in privatisation. The management of BNOC and BGC were actively opposed, and the civil servants were only facilitators. The primary promoters of privatisation were, in fact, the politicians. More sophisticated neo-pluralist arguments (Richardson and Jordan, 1979; Richardson, 1993) still cannot explain change (Dowding, 1991), but may be useful in understanding the form privatisation took once underway, as civil servants and state-enterprise managers were front-line actors and interested parties. But little work has been done to explain who these actors were and why they influenced the various privatisation outcomes. What the (neo)pluralist appoach does offer, though, is the recognition that the managers of state-owned industries are a force in their own right and that the civil service were players, while the pluralist view ignores the fact that the major source of privatisation in this case was the politicians.

In conventional public choice models political actors are typically characterised as having self-interested reasons for favouring expanded government (Niskanen, 1971; Dunleavy, 1991, pp. 154–61; Starr, 1990, p. 35), yet governments do shrink as well as grow and departments expand and contract (Rose, 1984, p. 44). While the budget-maximising model, for example, provides a strong explanation for the growth of government, it has traditionally been unable to explain state retrenchment (Downs, 1957; Niskanen, 1971). Starr (1990) sums up the problem:

> If there are self-interested reasons for political leaders, bureaucrats, and voter coalitions to favour expanded government, we need to understand how privatisation ever arrived on the political agenda at all (p. 35).

Traditional demand-side public choice explanations, such as the median voter model, fail to explain the adoption of a policy which continued to be supported only by the minority of the electorate, as privatisation was.

Using a less traditional supply-side public choice approach, Mariusz Mark Dobek (1993) argues that privatisation was a politically motivated vote-maximising policy aimed at expanding the pro-Conservative constituency. Rather than following public opinion as the traditional median voter model predicts, Dobek's theory turns the model around and suggests that the Conservatives were attempting to lead or influence public opinion (p. 27). While there is some evidence that privatisation provided modest electoral gains over time, there were initially no direct electoral advantages, primarily because those who benefited were already Conservative supporters (McAlister and Studlar, 1989, pp. 170–4). Thus, demand and supply-side explanations highlight the diversity of approaches to privatisation, but they fail to provide a convincing explanation of Britain's oil asset sales.

In summary, while none of the existing theories provides a satisfactory explanation of privatisation in general or the British government's sale of oil assets in particular, many offer important insights. I address these advantages further in the next section, and suggest an alternative approach to this apparently theoretically perplexing set of events.

DEVELOPING A FINER GRAIN APPROACH

Except for the 'super auto reversible' model, all the theories discussed above focus on only one aspect of the sales process. This, I argue, limits the power of explanation. The systems approaches, as well as macro level (and first principles) public choice theories, propose one explanation and use sweeping assumptions to explain policy change, and are therefore too simplistic to explain specific policies, much less variations of policy types between sectors. As such, from the broad theoretical perspective, policy outcomes appear 'irrational', yet smaller scale theories have not provided satisfactory explanations either. To explain government retrenchment, even in one sector, it is necessary to examine separately each factor that contributes to the ultimate decision. While the broad outcome may appear at first to be irrational (or at least difficult to explain), by examining the individual parts so that each can be understood in rational terms, the whole can also be understood. Institutional public choice models provide a vehicle for this approach, as they provide a means to gain a detailed account of one group of actors or one aspect of decision making and thus provide a means to analyse each of the pieces which make up this case. Though there are many strands of public choice theory, the fundamental principles are that the individual is the central unit of analysis and that individuals are rational actors who therefore act to maximise their own utility according to the constraints they face (Frey, 1984, pp. 201–2). The focus of public choice theory is the political individual: the voter, the member of an interest group, the politician and the bureaucrat. No institutional public choice models fit this case precisely, however, so I offer variations of existing models or suggest new ones to help explain the privatisation of oil in Britain. And then, though there is little precedent, I reassemble these individual analyses into the whole.

One of the pieces often excluded from analyses of domestic policy making is the international level. Privatisation, though, cannot be disconnected from the international environment. This point is highlighted with the case of oil which, as an internationally traded commodity and the basis of a country's economic and military security, is also undisputedly a matter of high politics. And as academics in international relations know, these factors are crucial: in fact, there is a genre of international relations literature called the 'second-image reversed' which examines the impact of international level independent variables upon domestic political processes (Gourevitch, 1978). The focus of this literature, however, has been on foreign policy issues (Rosenau, 1969; Allison, 1971; Frieden, 1991; Hill, 1983; Putnam, 1988), primarily trade (Lake, 1988; Avery, 1993; Milner, 1988; Rogowski, 1990; Katzenstein, 1978; B. Cohen, 1989). Public choice theories traditionally fit into the category of domestic policy-making analyses and tend to ignore the international arena or at best consider international factors as secondary or contextual (Frey, 1984, p. 200; Moyer and Josling, 1990). There are, however, a few notable exceptions which suggest that public choice theory can incorporate factors as wide ranging as international and domestic (Odell and Willett, 1990; Schonhardt-Bailey, 1991), and that public choice theory can be used for a complex and international case such as the sale of British oil assets.

The need to extend the range of analysis beyond that of the national government or the domestic economy has been recognised (Keohane, 1984b, p. 15; Gourevitch, 1978, pp. 906–7; and Allison, 1971), and there have been many attempts to combine levels of analysis (Rosenau, 1969; Putnam, 1988; Palan, 1990; Ikenberry, Lake and Mastanduno, 1988; Milner, 1989; B. Cohen, 1989). None so far, however, has accomplished the task with parsimony and accuracy. A drawback to incorporating international level factors, as well as the domestic, is that it makes data collection and analysis unwieldy. While not exclusive to public choice theory, no effort to construct a general theoretical model has produced a parsimonious or even useful construct (Rosenau, 1990; Palan, 1990). Simpler models, primarily two-level games, treat the state as a unitary actor and thereby ignore some of the most important domestic variables (Putnam, 1988; Avery, 1993; Guerrieri and Padoan, 1989; Knopf, 1993). The insight of quite modest attempts to include additional factors, such as Vicki Golich's analysis (1992) of United States and European collaboration in the aircraft industry, suggest that further efforts will be productive.

The two dimensions to the approach are illustrated graphically, the combination of constraints and options with a Venn diagram (see Figures 1.1 and 1.2) and the levels of analysis with a funnel (see Figure 1.3). At each level of analysis, both the options available and the constraints to the main actors are analysed, as illustrated with a Venn diagram. The circles 1, 2 and 3 represent constraints and structures to policy choices while the points A, B and C represent three of the infinite number of policy options on the plane of the Venn diagram, see Figure 1.1. Only in the area in which the parameters all overlap is a given policy option possible: the points in the overlap are the possible combinations of policies which could

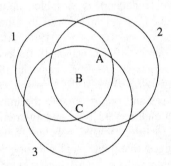

Figure 1.1   Policy Parameters, Time T_1

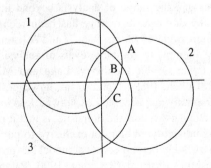

Figure 1.2   Policy Parameters, Time T_2

be implemented for that given level of analysis. As shown in Figure 1.1, at one point in time T_1, circles 1, 2 and 3 overlap so that policies A, B and C are all possible. While the policy options remain in place, constraints and structures change over time, altering what is possible – limiting options in some cases while opening up new possibilities in others. Thus Figure 1.2 illustrates time T_2 in the future when the circles have moved so that of these three options, only policy B is possible.

The second dimension to this book's approach, the levels of analysis, is illustrated with a funnel (see Figure 1.3). The circles of the funnel represent the area of overlap in the Venn diagrams at a given level which in succession narrow the range for the level below. The examination of influences in this study will be conducted on four levels, starting first with the international environment, followed by the nationalised oil companies, then the civil service (or governmental bureaucracy) and finally the British political process. Each level has the potential to make a contribution to the final outcome. But it is only from the overlap of levels that the ultimate policy outcome can be understood.

STRUCTURE OF THE BOOK

This book examines the British government's sale of its oil assets, some of the most important early privatisations. Instead of focusing on oil across countries, or on all privatisations within one country, this study focuses on a single sector, with the aim of understanding all the details and gaining the full flavour which is often lost in larger studies. The corresponding

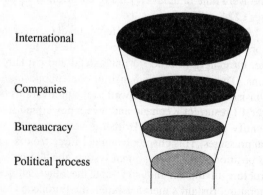

International

Companies

Bureaucracy

Political process

Figure 1.3   Layers of Constraints to Policy Making

challenge, therefore, is to make sure that the conclusions here are not so specific that they pertain only to this case, but rather are transferable to other countries or other policy sectors.

In terms of methodology, the primary source of material for this study was a series of 54 interviews with Department of Energy and Treasury civil servants, Labour and Conservative ministers, and BNOC, BP and BGC executives (see list in Appendix III). In addition to the interviews, I used a number of other sources including company annual reports, government publications, *Hansard Parliamentary Debates* and the memoirs of some of the key figures, as well as systematic searches for relevant articles in *The Times, The Sunday Times, The Financial Times, The Independent, The Guardian, The Economist* and the *Petroleum Economist*. MORI and Gallup public opinion polls also proved extremely useful both for what was recorded and what was not.

To outline the book briefly, after developing the theoretical perspective and summarising the general case in this first chapter, in Chapter 2 I give a brief historical overview of the British government's involvement in the oil industry. This begins with the government's initial investment at the turn of the century in the Anglo-Persian Oil Company, as British Petroleum was then known, and continues through changes in demand, Britain's withdrawal from the Middle East, and the discovery of oil in the North Sea. Throughout the chapter emphasises the British government's policy towards oil and means to control supply.

Turning to the specifics of this case, Chapter 3 examines the details of the sale of Britain's oil assets; how they evolved from the first sale of BP shares in 1977 to three further tranches as well as the sales of Britoil, Enterprise Oil and Wytch Farm. The sales were completed between 1977 and 1987 and were nine in number, raising £8.5 billion for the Treasury at a cost of over £224 million.

The next four chapters focus on a different level of analysis, identifying the key actors and attempting to define the 'rules of the game' in which they operate, ultimately in order to understand and explain their actions and decisions. This is a modified institutional public choice approach which emphasises the constraints as well as the motivations of actors.

In Chapter 4 I resurrect Keohane and Nye's power and issue models in order to identify areas where the British government was susceptible to international pressures. This chapter examines three factors, two suggested by Britain's position in the international system, the international economy and the structure of the oil industry; and the other suggested by neo-liberalist literature, Britain's membership in the European Community and the International Energy Agency. The focus of the investigation is on whether and how these factors affected the British government's decision to sell its oil assets.

In Chapter 5 I analyse a group of public sector employees, the managers of state-owned companies. Though often listed in the literature on privatisation as a possible obstacle to privatisation, little work has been done to explain why or how these managers opposed privatisation. Using the different reactions of the managers of BP, BNOC and BGC, I compare how organisational autonomy, financial independence and success in achieving the company's mission affected the managers' response to privatisation proposals.

In Chapter 6 I explore alternatives to budget-maximising theories to explain why civil servants in the Department of Energy did not resist privatisation collectively, but rather accepted or aided it at the individual level. I focus on the importance of work tasks, career-maximising strategies, the flexibility of the British bureaucratic structure and the strength of the departments to explain their actions.

Next, in Chapter 7, after establishing that public demand for privatisation was weak, I examine the supply-side of the British political process. The two primary factors I identify are the role of policy entrepreneurs and strategies for party political advantage. I examine the calculation politicians made, both personally as policy entrepreneurs of privatisation, and also in party political terms, including the distribution of costs and benefits to opponents and supporters over the short and long term, and the position and intensity of party members' attitudes towards privatisation.

Finally, in Chapter 8, I reconsider the basic question: why would a government (or anyone) sell an asset? I review the implications of the findings for the international level and the domestic level, and the calculus of the three sets of actors – the managers of the state-owned companies, the civil servants and the politicians. Next I consider the broader ramifications of the empirical findings for other privatisations and for better government. Finally, I conclude with a discussion on the findings of this case as a whole.

2 The Build-up of the British Government's Involvement in Oil

The sale of the British government's oil assets occurred at the end of a long history of government involvement in the oil industry. This chapter provides an overview of how the government came to own oil assets and sets the stage for the government's decision to sell them. The two consistent factors in the government's involvement in the oil industry from 1914 to the mid-1980s were its investment in BP and its reliance on private international oil companies. The circumstances for the government's policy changed considerably over time. From the turn of the century through the Second World War, oil was primarily a military fuel. During this period, the industry was dominated by a few large international oil companies. The end of the era was marked by the decline of Britain's influence in the Middle East in the 1950s. During this time, the government became the major shareholder in the Anglo-Persian Oil Company (APOC) which became the Anglo-Iranian Oil Company (AIOC) in 1935 and finally British Petroleum (BP) in 1954.

After the Second World War, there was a surge in demand for oil as non-military uses were developed. This increased demand, along with the rise of the Organisation of Petroleum Exporting Countries (OPEC), greatly altered the environment in which British energy policy was made. These changes were also part of the impetus that led to the discovery of oil in the North Sea in 1969, which in turn created a new set of concerns and opportunities for the British government.

Circumstances continued to change through the 1970s and 1980s. There was an increase in domestic production in the wake of price rises and corresponding increases in company profits and government tax revenue. Most notably, this period is marked by the lack of major supply problems in Britain.

THE BEGINNINGS OF ANGLO-PERSIAN AND THE MAJORS

In the early 1900s oil became an issue for the British government, not for economic reasons (coal was still the dominant fuel for transportation and industry), but because oil had been proven to be the technically superior military fuel, in terms of efficiency, transportation and storage. A faster and more powerful fleet was vital for the Navy as it entered an arms race with Germany (Lesser, 1989, pp. 25–6; also see Churchill, 1923, pp. 129, 134). Reliance on oil presented risks because Britain believed its largest suppliers, the American Standard Oil Company and Royal Dutch Shell, had a virtual monopoly on the industry worldwide. There were no established sources of oil either in the British Isles or the empire, with the exception of Burmah Oil operating in India. Hard smokeless coal, on the other hand, was in abundant domestic supply. The concerns also had two political dimensions: the monopoly situation was in part feared because Shell was thought to be under the control of the Germans, although this later proved to be untrue; in addition, most of the regions where oil was found were politically unstable. The Foreign Office, therefore, was particularly interested in oil ownership as a means to help stabilise and control the politically sensitive and strategically important area of Persia then under threat from Russian intervention (*Statist*, 30 May 1914; McBeth, 1985, p. 8; *Hansard Parliamentary Debates (Commons)*, 17 July 1913, 17 June 1914, 29 June 1914 and 7 July 1914; Geoffrey Jones, 1981, p. 12; *Economist*, 20 June 1914).

Britain's First Investment in Oil

The government sought to have a wide geographical distribution of sources of oil, independent oil competition and supplies from areas under British control (*Hansard Parliamentary Debates (Commons)*, 17 July 1913). The young, privately held Anglo-Persian Oil Company provided a means to address these problems and was eager to have government investment. The company saw that, in addition to direct financial investment, the government could guarantee to purchase APOC's oil, thereby alleviating concern for sales channels for its production, which was a real problem at the time because of stiff competition from Standard Oil and Shell. The development of the APOC–British government partnership took 11 years to consummate, from its first loan application in 1903 to May 1914 when the government finally agreed to become a partner in APOC. Over 50 per cent of APOC's shares remained in private hands, and the company's articles of association limited the government's role to appointing two directors to the board and a veto power. In the next few years, as APOC's financial demands rose, the government's shareholding increased to two-thirds but their role remained the same, as confirmed in a letter from the Treasury signed by John Bradbury in May 1914 (see Appendix II).

The government's decision to invest was not reached without controversial parliamentary debates. Winston Churchill, as First Lord of the Admiralty, was one of the strongest advocates. He argued that the government's investment in APOC:

> has not only secured to the Navy a very substantial proportion of its oil supply, but has led to the acquisition by the government of a controlling share in oil properties and interests which are at present valued at scores of millions sterling, and also to very considerable economies, which are still continuing, in the purchase price of Admiralty oil (Churchill, 1923, p. 13).

The opposition included economists deprecating naval expenditure, members of mining constituencies and oil executives objecting to a national inroad upon their monopolies, Conservatives disapproving of state trading, and partisan opponents denouncing the project as an unwarranted gamble with public money. There were also those who objected to the reallocation of a Naval budget surplus to finance the investment, and the avoidance of proper parliamentary debate (Churchill, 1923, p. 172; Ferrier, 1982, pp. 169–70; *Hansard Parliamentary Debates (Commons)*, 17 June 1914). Surprisingly, there was little opposition from the coal industry. This was primarily because they were dominating domestic energy consumption (oil supplied less than one per cent), increasing profits and providing progressive working conditions. Their view, therefore, was that the oil industry in general and APOC in particular did not represent a substantial threat to their interests (PEPIG, 1936, pp. 115–16; Mitchell, 1984, p. 304; Buxtem, 1978, pp. 155, 162–3; Gregory, 1968, pp. 97–177; Jevons, 1969, pp. 694–5).

Controversy over APOC's finance continued as a major point of contention between APOC and the government throughout their relationship. APOC's continual pressure on the Treasury for more capital helped to bring the matter of government ownership of APOC to the fore in the early 1920s and again in the mid-1950s. The issue was brought to a head by APOC itself when the board proposed in July 1921 that the company merge with Royal Dutch/Shell. APOC argued that Britain would benefit because for the first time a majority of Shell (50.2 per cent) would be British held, and the Treasury would save money at a time when cash demands were heavy (Corley, 1988, pp. 291–6). The government, however, rejected the idea – on purely political grounds. As the President of the Board of Trade explained, the government simply could not face a lobby of those opposed to monopolies (Corley, 1988, p. 297; Ferrier, 1982, p. 250).

Shell and Burmah Oil continued to push the idea, which was given a brief reprieve with the enlistment of Winston Churchill, then out of government, to lobby for them. Churchill was persuasive with the Prime Minister on the financial side: APOC's profits had declined by a third since 1920–1 and the dividend was halved, so a sale would bring the hard-pressed Treasury a welcome windfall of £20 million. When an election was announced, however, Churchill withdrew from the negotiations. With opposition from the Admiralty (because 40 per cent of naval fuel was supplied by APOC) and the Labour Party, the idea was again defeated in Cabinet at the beginning of 1924 (Corley, 1988, pp. 298–306; Barnes and Nicholson, 1980, pp. 346–7). A revealing indicator is the flurry of questions (over 20 during the decade) the issue received in the House of Commons.

A second set of deliberations occurred in the 1950s. Though the government had just reconfirmed its existing arrangement with AIOC (which APOC became in 1935) in a letter from the Treasury on 12 April 1951, signed by Edward Bridges (see Appendix II), there were rumours in 1953 that they wanted to sell their 56 per cent shareholding. Though a buyer – an insurance company – was even specified, nothing happened. The rumours re-emerged in 1957 and five questions were asked in the House of Commons about the government's holding in AIOC. But when Burmah Oil, who thought they had a verbal agreement for the right of first refusal on BP shares, asked the Chancellor, he denied that the government was considering a sale (Corley, 1988, p. 284). Nothing further transpired.

DECLINE IN BRITAIN'S CONTROL OF OIL, THE RISE IN DOMESTIC DEMAND

Circumstances began to change with Britain's withdrawal from the Middle East and its declining position as a great power. As such, the government became less able to protect BP's interests in the Middle East. The limits to British government assistance were first realised in the Iranian crisis in 1950 and were made more evident by the Suez crisis in 1956. At the same time, demand for oil in Britain was growing.

The First Iranian Crisis

As a symbol of imperialism and a valuable national asset, AIOC became the focus of the Iranians' wrath following a coup by the nationalists led by Mohammed Mossadegh in 1950. The first directive of the new leader was to nationalise AIOC (Inglis, 1977, pp. 34–6; Anderson, 1969, pp. 46–8;

Terzian, 1985). Although AIOC had received extensive diplomatic assistance in Persia, there was a limit to what the British government could now do. Once Mossadegh was overthrown in 1953, Britain was unable to reserve AIOC's pre-eminent position. Britain and the United States, as the home governments of the oil companies based in the Middle East and the largest consumers of Middle East oil, actively worked to install a more sympathetic government in Teheran, conveyed a BP executive. The most visible action was an embargo against Iranian oil exports. At the same time, a voluntary committee of oil companies and consumer countries was created to coordinate supply so that the oil for the Korean War was not interrupted. So while Iranian output dropped from 660 000 barrels per day (b/d) in 1950 to 20 000 b/d in 1952, world production actually increased over the same time period, from 10.9 million b/d to 13.0 million b/d (*Financial Times*, 19 October 1987; Terzian, 1985, p. 13; Yergin, 1991, p. 464).

The resolution of the crisis left the Iranian oil assets redistributed. The assets remained in the possession of the National Iranian Oil Company, and production was allocated to a consortium of international companies, of which AIOC was only one. Control of production was divided so that AIOC received 40 per cent, the Aramco partners – Jersey, Socony, Texaco and Standard of California – plus Gulf received 8 per cent each, Shell received 14 per cent, and the French company CFP received 6 per cent (Anderson, 1969, pp. 58–9). Although the Iranians rejected any compensation to the British, the other members of the consortium paid AIOC $90 million for the 60 per cent rights the company was said to be giving up (Yergin, 1991, p. 478).

The Suez Crisis

The decline of Britain's role in the Middle East and ability to provide assistance for BP (as AIOC became in 1954) was further marked by the Suez crisis of 1956. The canal was British owned and vital to Europe (in 1955, for example, two-thirds of Europe's oil passed through the canal). On 26 July 1955, Colonel Gamal Abdel Nasser of Egypt announced its expropriation. The implications were spelled out by the Foreign Minister, Anthony Eden: 'We could not live without oil and … we had no intention of being strangled to death.' Nor could Britain's fragile balance of payments position afford the loss of foreign earnings from the canal. In addition, a defeat would have had a demoralising effect on Britain's already eroding international prestige (Eden, 1960, p. 401). Britain could not defend the Suez canal, however, and the United States was not prepared to take over control of the canal or to aid in its defence. The British, French and Israelis felt they were left with no option but to attack Egypt on their own, which proved to be disastrous. Without the backing of the United States, in the form of additional oil supplies or finance, Europe was left on the verge of an energy crisis. A full-scale war was averted, however, when the United States negotiated British and French withdrawal in exchange for desperately needed supplies (Engler, 1961, p. 261; Yergin, 1991, pp. 489–90).

The crises, and most importantly their associated costs, initiated the withdrawal of British forces from the Middle East which was to be completed by 1971. In terms of BP's relationship with the government, the crisis marked a change in what the government was able to offer, namely the protection of BP's Middle East operations (Chester, 1983, pp. 98–9; Engler, 1961, pp. 260–4). The other far-reaching implication, a BP executive affirmed, was that the Iranian crisis combined with the Suez crisis provided the impetus necessary to push BP to develop into a fully integrated oil company.

A False Sense of Security

Remarkably, the growth of the oil industry and the fall of oil prices during the 1950s and 1960s overshadowed the crises and lulled oil consumers into a dependence on oil. With prices falling and fresh oil discoveries being made, there was a new sense of consumer confidence, minimising the need for governments to take security measures. The government continued to rely on the private oil industry and the BP through the post-Second World War period. Though the government responded to the increasing importance of oil by forming governmental committees and bureaus, these were uncoordinated and located in various departments (Ferrier, 1982, pp. 223, 247).

Despite the changes of government and corresponding political ideologies, government relations with BP remained virtually the same. As part of a post-war reconstruction programme, the Labour government embarked on a series of nationalisations, but BP was conspicuously not part of the programme and ministers did not seek to increase their control over AIOC in any way (*Hansard Parliamentary Debates (Commons)*, 22 December 1920). In fact, the government protected both the domestic coal industry and the oil companies until 1960. Thereafter, the government continued to allow the major oil companies to command the best terminal and storage facilities and to maintain their exclusive contracts with most filling stations (Hartshorn, 1962, pp. 236–7; Newman, 1934, pp. 439–40; PEPIG, 1936, p. 116).

The British government's confidence in the existing relationship with BP was illustrated by its lack of concern in 1969 when its holding dropped below 50 per cent to 48.2 per cent for the first time since 1914.

According to BP's 1969 annual report, BP had issued new shares to the Distillers Company in exchange for Distillers' chemicals and plastics interests (also see Fraser and Wilson, 1988, p. 51; Anderson, 1969, p. 20). The impact, however, was slight. As James Callaghan pointed out: 'Well, I let BP fall below 51 per cent when I was Chancellor and nobody made a row' (Benn, 1989, p. 647). In fact, the reduction went virtually unnoticed in the House of Commons, where the Treasury merely made a statement that the government would not restore the holding back above the 50 per cent mark. No other questions or statements were raised in Parliament about the government's holdings until one in 1971 and then not again until 1974, when the obvious questions following the oil crisis were raised (*Hansard Parliamentary Debates (Commons)*, 24 October 1967).

BRITAIN'S VULNERABILITY AND SUBSEQUENT SEARCH FOR OIL INDEPENDENCE

Though Britain realised its vulnerability in terms of oil after the Suez crisis, it was the 1973–4 oil embargo which critically altered the government's approach to energy. In response to the embargo, the British government sought new means to address security of supply, including the creation of the Department of Energy and the British National Oil Company. In so doing, the government was greatly aided by the discovery of oil in the North Sea and the increase in the price of oil which made production there financially feasible.

The 1973–4 Oil Crisis

When AOPEC, the Arab members of OPEC, enforced an oil embargo against the United States and the Netherlands, the effect on Britain was a dramatic increase in oil prices in the 1970s (see Figure 2.1) causing severe economic damage and political disruption, both of which were exacerbated by a coal miners' strike in 1974. The 1973 oil crisis proved to be a test of the government's reliance on BP and the private oil companies.

The issue of the government's reliance came to a head in December 1973 when the Prime Minister, Edward Heath, asked Shell and BP to supply more oil to Britain. Eric Drake, then chairman of BP, refused the Prime Minister even though the government was its largest shareholder. Drake argued that to favour Britain could cause retaliation from other governments, and possibly even nationalisation of BP operations in those

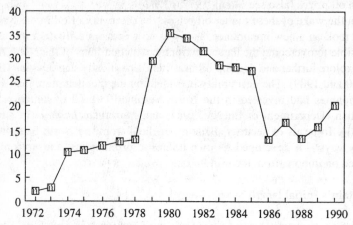

US dollar per barrel

Source: BP Statistical Review of World Energy, 1991.

Figure 2.1   Price of Crude Oil

countries. Therefore, as a director of the company entrusted with the welfare of all stockholders, Drake argued that he could not comply with the government's request. If the government were to pass the appropriate laws, Drake said, BP would, of course, comply. Heath, however, did not take that route and BP's directors were left to make decisions in the company's best interest (also see Arnold, 1978, p. 36; and Maull, 1977, p. 272). Shell also refused, although 40 per cent British owned, a Treasury civil servant explained, citing the interests of its Dutch shareholders who comprised the other 60 per cent of the company (Yergin, 1991, pp. 261–4; Arnold, 1978, p. 36). At the time, as one Conservative remarked, 'Heath and half the government were amazed with BP's response.' A Department of Energy minister remarked:

> Heath was horrified in 1974 to have no control over the company during the oil crisis. I inherited that cannon. The resulting feeling was that the country had to have control over its own oil.

The crisis also forced Britain to decide whether to show solidarity with the EC, which it had just joined, or to keep its status as a friendly country in the eyes of the Arabs. The decision was neatly taken care of by the oil companies. Working together, they provided a mechanism for oil sharing, ostensibly by refusing to favour one country over another; their incentive of course, as one Treasury civil servant pointed out, was profit from the high oil prices (also see Maull, 1977, p. 271).

In the wake of these higher oil prices, the discovery of oil in the North Sea took on a new importance, as it was now economically desirable and feasible to overcome the harsh environmental conditions of the North Sea to explore further and develop oil in Britain's politically stable region (BP, 1990 and 1989). The desirability is evident by the fact that more than 150 companies had invested in the North Sea by 1980, 82 of which were British (Department of Energy, 1984; and *Petroleum Economist*, April 1981). In terms of security, Britain benefited from the North Sea oil in two ways – it developed its own domestic oil supplies, and no longer relied on imports from the Middle East.

Britain's Initial North Sea Strategy

The first commercial gas discovery in the North Sea was made in 1965, and oil was discovered in November 1969. Further discoveries, advances in offshore technology and vast amounts of investment made it possible for the first oil to reach the British shore on 18 June 1975. During the next decade, Britain shifted from being a major oil importer to being a net oil exporter (see Figure 2.2), and from being dependent on the Middle East to being self-sufficient in oil from in its own backyard. Figure 2.2 shows

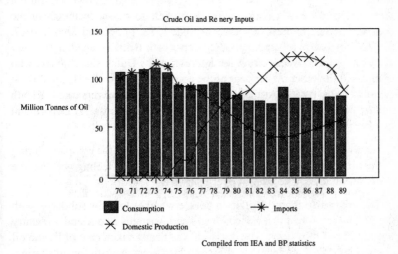

Compiled from IEA and BP statistics

Figure 2.2   UK Oil Supply and Demand, 1970–89

imports continued, this is because industrial economies use several kinds of crude oil. The high quality of the North Sea oil also made it a profitable export when cheaper lower grades could be used instead (BP, 1980, 1989 and 1990). By 1983 Britain was the sixth largest oil producer in the world, ahead of countries like Kuwait and Libya. The overall UK energy supply situation also improved with North Sea oil production and the change in energy demand after the 1973 oil crisis. There was an overall energy surplus by 1980, with the decrease in the demand for oil and coal accounting for the majority of the decline, while demand for gas actually increased slightly and nuclear stayed the same (see Figure 2.3).

The gross value of oil and gas from the United Kingdom Continental Shelf (UKCS), the British portion of the North Sea, rose from £6.3 billion in 1979 to £18.8 billion in 1983, and as a proportion of GNP from 2.5 per cent to 5.3 per cent. Tax revenues from companies operating in the North Sea rose from £562 million in 1978–9 to £8.9 billion in 1983–4 (*Economist*, 12 May 1984). In perspective, the contribution to GDP was always less than that of many other industries, such as construction and agriculture, and the North Sea's direct effect on jobs was small because oil and gas were highly capital-intensive industries. However, much of the capital invested in the North Sea came from abroad and thus was an addition to Britain's economy (*Economist*, 23 January 1982).

The Establishment of the Department of Energy

In 1973 the House of Commons Public Accounts Committee (PAC) issued a report which criticised the government for giving away too many

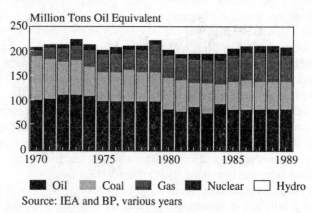

Figure 2.3   UK Energy Consumption by Energy Type, 1970–89

benefits associated with North Sea oil. With pressure mounting during the coal miners' strike and the 1973 oil crisis, the Conservative government created the Department of Energy (DEn) in January 1974, consolidating divisions and bureaus spread across at least three departments previously managing energy matters. The new department was given a high profile with the appointment of Lord Carrington, the Tory Party chairman, as the Secretary of State (Inglis, 1977, p. 49; *Economist*, 12 January 1974; Cosgrave, 1985; Hennessy, 1989, pp. 432, 445–8).

The DEn was an agency which spent a low proportion of its total budget on salaries because its primary task was to channel funds to other public sector organisations, namely the nationalised energy industries (Dunleavy, 1989a, pp. 254–5; Dunleavy, 1989b, p. 400; also see McInnes, 1991, p. 21). The DEn also raised large amounts of finance. In 1983, for example, the receipts from royalties in the North Sea were almost £2 billion according to the department's supply estimate, dwarfing the department's total budget, which for the same year was £50 million. As a new department with a small staff, the DEn had difficulty establishing its position versus the Treasury and the Central Policy Review Staff (CPRS) who had already established their credibility in energy matters. The DEn's public reputation was also tarnished by mistakes such as the £44 million overpayment in grants to oil companies in 1979 and the poor administrative handling of the coal miners' strike in 1980 (Thatcher, 1993, pp. 140–1; Ham, 1981, pp. 40–1; Blackstone and Plowden, 1990, pp. 80–3). Civil servants argued, however, that by the mid-1980s, the department was in better command of the energy control apparatus, including taxation, subsidies and grants, licences, the nationalised industries, safety and shadow prices. The issue of the poor quality of the DEn staff, however, was raised again in November 1990 after the Piper Alpha disaster when the Cullen Report severely criticised the department for major safety failings. As a result, the DEn was stripped of its responsibility for offshore safety to the benefit of the Health and Safety Executive (*Financial Times: North Sea Letter*, 14 November 1990). In 1993, the DEn was amalgamated into the DTI.

The other notable feature about the department was its lack of consumer or environmental orientation. There were no divisions within the department with such responsibilities. Though recognised by energy ministers, this was not seen as a problem, in part because consumers and environmentalists were dealt with as they affected other aspects of the department's business, such as oil production. In addition, especially in the early days of North Sea development, production was given highest priority (also see McInnes, 1991, Figures 1–6).

The nationalised industries were the most important feature of the department. On the one hand they were the means to control the energy sectors, but on the other they were semi-independent organisations in competition with each other. They were so powerful, however, that the DEn was unable to make them cooperate or coordinate strategies (Heald, 1989, p. 103). For example, there was a committee of the planning directors for each industry, but as one executive who attended the only meeting between 1980 and 1982 explained, 'we couldn't agree on anything ... no one wanted to reveal numbers or plans'. In terms of finance, only the coal and nuclear industries were largely dependent on the department. Electricity and gas had been raising an increasing proportion of their revenue from customers and thus were able to repay government debt and make net contributions to government funds (Likierman, 1988, p. 34). The largest net earners under the control of the department, however, were the oil and gas industries. Therefore, despite the fact that one civil servant claimed the 'touchstone' of the department's policy was security of supply, the department had few means of direct control over that supply. Efforts to even articulate the DEn's policy were hampered by the persistent change in factors such as the price of oil. In the end, one civil servant lamented, it was impossible to say anything except in generalities, or as one nationalised industry executive said, 'the department might have argued that there was a policy, but had no means to implement it'.

The Department of Energy's Influence in the Oil Industry

The DEn's primary means of controlling oil exploration and development in the North Sea were discretionary licences and taxation. The DEn was also responsible for the offshore-supply industry, depletion policy and recording statistics. The discretionary system allowed the government to discriminate between applicants on the basis of their contributions to the North Sea development and Britain's economy, a DEn civil servant explained, as well as to favour British companies. The Treasury preferred an auction system to raise more money up front, which was tried in the fourth round in 1971 where 15 blocks were sold for £37 million and again in the eighth round in 1983 where seven blocks were sold for £33 million. With these exceptions, the discretionary system prevailed because, as a DEn civil servant explained, the government decided that the control which ensued from awarding licences was more valuable than the extra cash an auction might raise (also see: Turner, 1984, p. 95; *Petroleum Economist*, June 1982, p. 253 and March 1983, p. 100). For example, the government used licences as a carrot in the participation negotiations.

When the threat of withholding licences from uncooperative companies was carried out in the fifth licensing round, in the words of one DEn civil servant, 'the government's negotiating position was boosted enormously'.

Of all the government's means, the tax regime affected the oil companies the most; it was a major factor in their exploration and development calculations. In 1964 the private oil companies were granted long concessions, low tax rates and few regulations to entice them to explore and develop the North Sea. In fact, once oil was discovered, risk was reduced and the future gains became apparent, the government began to raise taxes and increase the level of regulation. Shifts in the price and demand for oil changed the bargaining position of ministers and the companies over time. Under the first licensing round the government charged 12.5 per cent in royalties and the standard corporate tax, which was 53.75 per cent at the time. Taxes were increased and added over time: in 1975 the Oil Taxation Act was passed which limited tax loopholes and created a new Petroleum Revenue Tax of 45 per cent, which was raised to 75 per cent by 1982. The Supplementary Petroleum Duty (later replaced by the Advance Petroleum Revenue Tax) was added in 1981 and was set at 20 per cent (Nelsen, 1991, pp. 20, 55, 91; *Petroleum Economist*, April 1982, p. 133; and Turner, 1975, p. 93). Changes continued in the early 1980s. As the price of oil began to fall, the DEn was in a disadvantageous position, oil companies' profits fell and North Sea production approached a natural decline. To induce private oil companies to develop smaller, marginal fields, the type of fields thought to be remaining, the government made new tax concessions. Once the price of oil began to increase after the 1986 low, however, investment picked up slowly, and the bargaining positions reversed (*Petroleum Economist*, July 1982, September 1982, April 1983 and April 1986; *Economist*, March 1983).

Because of its crucial impact on the energy industry, the Department of Energy also built up an expertise in taxation, which was utilised by the unusual practice of advising the Treasury. Civil servants explained that the DEn was included in the oil taxation system because the Treasury needed their knowledge. Because of their different objectives, there were obvious disagreements over the tax rates. According to civil servants, the Treasury wanted higher tax revenues, while the DEn was concerned that higher taxes might discourage investment and cause consumer criticism.

The DEn's responsibilities also included depletion policy, the offshore-supply industry and the maintenance of energy statistics, but these were considered secondary functions compared to issuing licences and taxation. In terms of depletion policy, according to civil servants, the Treasury and the oil companies wanted oil produced as fast as possible to maintain revenues, while some in the DEn were concerned with security of supply and wanted to spread the production of oil further into the future. Though options were discussed, no restrictions were placed on production.

The most successful division was that of the Off-shore Supplies Office (OSO). The Department of Energy took over the OSO, created by the DTI in 1973 – and where much of the hard work had already been done – to ensure Britain's share of the offshore oil supply industry (all the equipment and services needed for oil exploration and development). The DEn devoted much time and effort to the challenge though and was proud of the results: by the early 1980s, 73 per cent of offshore-supply contracts (in terms of value and including British subsidiaries of American and French companies) went to British companies, compared with almost none in the mid-1970s (*Economist*, 12 May 1984; and Jenkin, 1981, pp. 63–4, 73, 82).

In addition, the DEn maintained sophisticated energy statistics, but according to a DEn civil servant, few outside the department ever used them. So that when Nigel Lawson proposed to end the practice in the early 1980s, there was little objection (Lawson, 1992, p.163). At the same time, the IEA was starting to compute similar statistics across countries.

The Role of the Private Oil Companies

Despite the crises of the 1950s and 1960s and the plethora of companies that were attracted to the North Sea, the government continued to rely on the majors, and through the discretionary licence system ensured that production was concentrated in the hands of the majors. As shown in Figure 2.4, the seven major oil companies controlled at least 50 per cent of North Sea oil throughout its development (DEn, 1984 and 1991). From the DEn's perspective, it sought to include in the development of the North Sea as many companies as were capable. As one civil servant explained, the rationale was 'the larger the array [of oil companies], the more ideas and thinking, the larger the pay-off'. The small companies, however, could not meet the capital costs of developing new finds, and thus the majors were favoured. Initially, BP and Shell controlled 20 per cent and 15 per cent of the North Sea respectively, and the five American companies controlled much of the remainder. Over time, however, smaller companies increased their portion from 10 per cent in 1975 to 25 per cent by the early 1980s (DEn, 1984 and 1991; and Arnold, 1978, p. 42; *Economist*, 18 March 1989).

The government had, in fact, always been dependent on the private oil industry. According to one civil servant: 'Despite upheavals going

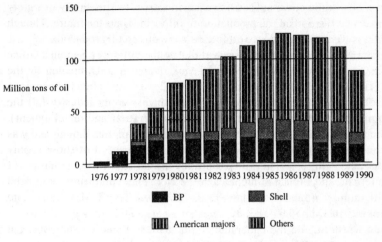

Source: Department of Energy, Development of Oil and Gas
Resources of the United Kingdom, various years.

Figure 2.4   North Sea Oil Production by Company, 1975–89

back to Suez, the oil industry always managed to deliver the oil – much
more so than anyone gave them credit for in advance.' Another pointed
out that 'the department tended to look after the interests of the oil companies; it was the tradition'. Through informal and formal channels at all
levels, DEn civil servants frequently spoke with the oil companies. As a
result, most civil servants were sympathetic to or at least understood the
private oil companies' positions. The DEn civil servants were proud of
these good relationships. The ultimate manifestation of the DEn's
concern for oil companies was their strategy of guarding against excessive governmental interference; it was thought that too much interference
would force the companies to go elsewhere. According to one civil
servant:

> The government was continually turning the screw tighter to see what
> happened until finally in 1981 they went too far and there was a down
> turn [in development], and the policies were then reversed.

As another civil servant explained, 'the department was too soft sometimes [on the oil companies] ... but in the end, we still had to work with
them'.

   There was also a healthy dose of scepticism about the oil companies
evident among civil servants in the DEn. One civil servant explained that

the oil companies 'could say they were mindful of the national interest, but they were also commercial and we couldn't change that'. The civil servant argued that the participation agreements (discussed below) were therefore necessary to override those commercial obligations. Another simply explained, 'oil companies have different interests than the government and the population'.

The government devised two specific means of control, participation agreements and assurances, as well as BNOC. Participation, as originally planned by the Labour government, was a full partnership arrangement whereby a national oil company would participate in the exploration and development, contribute 51 per cent of the expenditure and then receive 51 per cent of the production and profits. The Treasury argued that it could not fund the 51 per cent investment, and the private oil companies argued that they had already invested a substantial amount of capital in the North Sea on the understanding that there would be no government interference (*Times*, 12 August 1974, p. 1; and *Hansard Parliamentary Debates (Lords)*, 23 July 1975; H.Wilson, 1979, p. 40). Taking into account these obstacles, another concept of participation was developed: cooperation with a national oil company. The national company would have the right to take at market price up to 51 per cent of a company's oil production, with government assurances that the companies would be no better off and no worse off by the arrangement (Baker and Daniel, 1983, p. 149). In practice this meant that the national oil company could buy up to 51 per cent of a company's production at market price, thereby nominally controlling 51 per cent of UK oil, and then immediately resell it, sometimes even back to the same company. One DEn civil servant described the arrangement: 'On the surface it looked good, but it was really a bit of a wrangle [illusion] ... and didn't do much.'

Even though the concept proved to be relatively innocuous, long negotiations ensued during the 1970s in which the government used leverage over the companies needing loan guarantees or other assistance. It took a year of negotiations before an agreement was reached with BP on 25 January 1976 at a meeting between the Prime Minister, the Secretary of State for Energy and the chairman of BP (H.Wilson, 1979, p. 42). Agreement with the other major international oil companies proved more difficult; newspaper accounts from *The Times* reveal that the Chairmen of Exxon and Shell were vocally antagonistic. Agreements were only achieved, explained DEn civil servants and ministers, after the government showed its willingness to withhold licences from a company refusing to cooperate.

Another means of control, company 'assurances', was enacted in conjunction with the participation agreements. These assurances followed a similar arrangement to the one outlined in a letter from BP to the DEn obtained by the *Financial Times*. The letter stated that BP would cover any short-term gap which stopped short of a major international crisis (defined as a 7 per cent cut in supply) as long as there was 'no legal or governmental constraint on its ability to raise prices as a necessary means of recovering costs'(*Economist,* 12 May 1984.) For a price all companies would guarantee supply, at least in a short-term crisis. According to DEn civil servants, these assurances were the government's main means of securing energy supplies after BNOC was split and Britoil was sold in 1982.

The Creation and the Role of the British National Oil Company

With the 1973 oil crisis, the government began to consider the idea of a national oil company. The participation arrangements made a national oil company of some sort necessary. The thinking began under the Conservative government, according to BNOC and BP executives, but it was the Labour government elected in 1974 which debated more extreme options, including making BP into a fully national oil company and allowing only British companies into the North Sea (also see Hamilton, 1978, p. 16).

The option of transforming BP into a fully government-owned company was made more plausible by a chance happening. In January 1975, the government increased its stake in BP from 48 per cent to 68 per cent as part of a deal to aid the financially troubled Burmah Oil. An original shareholder in BP, Burmah Oil maintained a 20 per cent stake. Under the government's scheme to help the financially troubled company, Burmah sold its holding to the Bank of England (while the Treasury held the original shares) for £179 million. According to the BP Annual Report, by March 1976, the shares were valued at £447 million. The Burmah shareholders sued the Bank of England for improper proceedings, but eventually nothing was proved (*Economist*, 11 December 1976, p. 119; and Benn, 1990, p. 75). The increased holding also spurred questions in the House of Commons, but the government responded that a decision had not yet been made, and implied that the government was considering the sale of the shares. Ironically, the suit against the government prevented the sale of those shares for several years.

Instead of nationalising BP, a new entity was created in 1976, the British National Oil Company (BNOC), by Labour Party ministers who had been debating the merits of a National Hydrocarbons Corporation inside the party since 1967 (Hann, 1986, p. 254). The arguments for and against BNOC were similar to those made about the government's initial investment in APOC. According to a BNOC executive, advocates argued that BNOC would defend against the tyranny of the existing large corporations, and provide general benefits to Britain's economy (also see *Hansard Parliamentary Debates (Lords)*, 23 July 1975). The existence of national oil companies in other democracies including France, Canada and Italy, according to DEn civil servants, diffused the accusations of extreme socialism. The opposition included the coal industry which feared that government support would divert their customers to oil, Conservatives against government involvement in industry and the oil companies who believed that BNOC would impede their development of the North Sea at a crucial time (Inglis, 1977, p. 52; Shelbourne, 1981, p. 3). Yet, as one BP director said:

> We are in partnership with governments of all political complexions all over the world. We are unlikely to be frightened off by anything the Labour government has in mind. In any case our investment [in the North Sea] is now too big. It would be too late to stop [producing] even if we wanted to.

Opponents' fears were highlighted because BNOC was created partly under the direction of two Labour leaders, whom DEn civil servants and BNOC executives described as strongly believing in state-ownership – Tony Benn, Secretary of State for Energy from 1976–9, and Tommy Balogh, a former Member of the Economic and Financial Committee of the Labour Party and Minister of State in the DEn from 1974–5 and deputy chairman of BNOC from 1976–8.

BNOC was created to serve two sometimes contradictory roles. First it was an information-gathering, monitoring and advisory agent. Second it was a commercial oil production and trading company (Vickers and Yarrow, 1988, p. 323). BNOC thus had the dual role, as BNOC and BP executives explained, of competing against private oil companies in the North Sea as well as advising their regulators, and many saw these functions as contradictory. One BNOC executive found that fear of a 'spy in the camp' was second only to fear of technical incompetence as reasons why private companies did not want to work with BNOC. The management argued that BNOC was not a regulatory agency, only an adviser to the government, and a 'Chinese Wall' had been erected between the operations side and the rest (*Sunday Times*, 21 May 1978; House of Commons Nationalised Industries Select Committee, 1977–8, p. 43).

The production side of BNOC started off with the oil assets of the National Coal Board, and soon thereafter BNOC purchased 80 per cent of the Burmah Oil Company's North Sea oil fields (Vickers and Yarrow, 1988, p. 320; R. Bailey, 1978, p. 328). The government also favoured BNOC by granting the company further substantial UKCS acreage in the fifth and sixth rounds (1976 and 1979). By 1982 BNOC had obtained production interests in nine North Sea oil fields and one gas field and was responsible for 7 per cent of all North Sea oil production (Webb, 1985, p. 29).

On the trading side, from the beginning BNOC activated the participation agreements with the oil companies giving it access to over 51 per cent of North Sea oil. This was unexpected by many; as one DEn civil servant explained:

> There were some ministers and certainly a lot of officials who thought BNOC would never in a million years think of exercising the options. They thought we would just have them there in case there was some crisis and then you could exercise the option ... Whereas [BNOC Chairman Frank Kearton], backed by Tony Benn, was going to exercise the options right away and get in the oil industry and get some clout ... Kearton was not just going to sit there and be a front man, he wanted a real job to do. At that time, ownership of oil, even if you paid market price for it, gave you clout. To have control of basically 50 per cent of UK oil was something.

As another DEn civil servant simply stated: 'The oil companies were surprised. The oil companies were always surprised though.' By 1981, with its own production, participation oil and royalty in kind, BNOC controlled up to 60 per cent of North Sea oil. Even after the production assets were sold in 1985, BNOC still controlled 30 per cent of North Sea oil (*Financial Times*, 15 July 1985, p. 4; *Hansard Parliamentary Debates (Commons)*, 15 July 1985; Shelbourne, 1981, p. 6; Webb, 1985, p. 29). As one BNOC executive explained:

> by 1979, BNOC was the largest crude oil wholesaler, a very important source for non-Arab refineries. We were making decisions about where oil should go, on our own or with the government.

Like many nationalised companies, BNOC soon found the government's financial control a severe constraint to expansion. The financial provisions for BNOC were established in the Oil and Pipelines Act 1975. Through the National Oil Account (NOA) BNOC received funds for business transactions, but at the same time was obliged to submit, on a daily basis, all sums received. To give itself more financial freedom, in June 1977, BNOC completed arrangements to raise $825 million through advance oil sales. This money was used to repay the loans from the National Loans Fund, thus significantly reducing BNOC's interest payments, and partly to finance new UKCS expansion. As one executive described it:

> The turning point for BNOC was when we convinced major bankers to loan us the $825 million, which was basically a forward sale of oil. Banks found BNOC had an entirely sensible business plan – went ahead and did the deal. The oil companies couldn't understand. The banks played a role in persuading the oil companies to stop whinging and go on with the game in town. The loan enabled BNOC to pay its own way, and not take away from money spent on hospitals etc., and helped to reduce the PSBR.

The finance also led the way for BNOC to expand outside the United Kingdom for the first time – in Dubai, Indonesia, the Republic of Ireland and France (Britoil, 'Offer for Sale', 1982, p. 6).

With so much oil under its control, BNOC grew into the position of being a price setter for North Sea oil. The price BNOC paid for its North Sea oil participation was set each quarter by BNOC with input from Energy and Treasury ministers. Ultimately, however, BNOC was too small to be a world price leader. With the development of the spot market in the early 1980s and the drop in the price of oil in 1984, it became apparent that BNOC could at best only effect short-term prices (*Economist*, 5 January 1985; *Hansard Parliamentary Debates (Commons)*, 18 December 1984). One DEn civil servant explained, the government's aim was to smooth the jagged price fluctuations and, according to a BNOC executive, the government's instructions were to avoid short-term vacillations. The most serious costs of past crises were those imposed by rapid and significant changes in the price of oil which have been only loosely linked to the scale of reductions in supply (Smart, 1985, p. 157; *Petroleum Economist*, October 1982, p. 398; IMF, 1990; BP, 1990; DEn, 1990). Thus, it was argued that there were benefits to controlling the price, as explained in 1984 by the Minister of State for Energy, Alick Buchanan-Smith:

> It is a small sum to pay in relation to the more general benefits and in relation to the higher cost to the economy which would be caused by the short term destabilisation of prices (*Hansard Parliamentary Debates (Commons)*, 18 December 1984).

While a distinct entity, BNOC also gave the DEn additional clout and control of the North Sea. BNOC reinforced the DEn's taxation expertise, as the DEn was responsible for calculating and collecting BNOC's royalties, except for those paid in kind from 1977 to 1985 which BNOC then disposed of under the direction of the DEn. BNOC also made participation possible which, as already discussed, gave the DEn considerable leverage over private sector companies in the North Sea.

BGC as a Player in the North Sea

The government also owned the British Gas Corporation (BGC) which evolved into an active player in oil exploration and production in the North Sea. The 1948 Gas Act nationalised over 1000 town gas works and created the Gas Council. In the 1950s, according to BGC executives, the Gas Council was an ailing business and there was even talk of winding it down (also see Jewers, 1983). With the possibility of finding gas in the North Sea in the 1960s, however, the Council's prospects improved. Its functions were extended by the Gas Act of 1965 and the Council began to explore on and offshore in order to gain some direct control of the primary resources on which they depended as well as to learn first hand the technology, the difficulties and the costs of exploration and development work (House of Commons Energy Select Committee, Wytch Farm Memo, 1981–2, p. ix; Pearson, 1981, p. 98). Gas was discovered in 1966 and brought onshore the following year. In 1968 the Council's first field became operational, and in 1969 it signed an industrial contract for the sale of gas to ICI. Under the Conservative government, the Gas Act 1972 consolidated the Gas Council into the British Gas Corporation (BGC), and in 1976 Denis Rooke became its chairman and a forceful defender of the corporation.

While the Labour government never considered giving BGC the role of national oil company, the corporation was able to remain active in the oil industry until 1982, building up a sizeable portfolio which included interests in over 25 offshore fields and the Wytch Farm onshore field. The government had numerous opportunities to limit BGC's expansion into oil, but declined on each occasion. The first opportunity was when BNOC was created and the Petroleum and Pipelines Act 1975 specified that BNOC should receive the oil assets of the BGC (R. Bailey, 1978, pp. 328–9; *Hansard Parliamentary Debates (Commons)*, 13 March 1984). BGC argued that it was impossible to know beforehand which fields were going to yield oil or gas, and in many cases they were found together. Department of Energy civil servants, however, pointed out that some distinction could be made initially because gas fields were predominantly located in the south North Sea while oil is found in the north. However, BGC's arguments prevailed, as a BNOC manager explained: 'Rooke fought a rearguard action ... He won the battle at the time because there was no one at BNOC yet to fight on the other side.' A second opportunity occurred when BGC's petroleum production licence covering the Wytch Farm onshore oil field came due in 1974. Instead of cancelling the contract, the DEn reapproved the licence for a further 40 years (House of Commons Energy Select Committee, Wytch Farm Memo, 1981–2, p. xxiii). The Labour government, in addition, encouraged BGC's exploration and development efforts by favouring applications for North Sea licences where BGC was a partner.

Did Ownership Make a Difference in the 1979 Oil Crisis?

In 1979 Britain had the benefit of North Sea oil for the first time during a world oil crisis. Although the worldwide supply disruptions in the spring of 1979 and then again in 1980 were not as great as during the 1973–4 crisis, the price of oil rose quickly. With North Sea supplies, Britain did not have to worry about serious shortages of oil. While the price increase was harmful to industry, it made high cost North Sea oil exploration more profitable, as well as increasing Treasury revenues.

The crisis, however, caused a relative scarcity of petrol during the summer of 1979. The irony of having North Sea oil production in full swing at the same time that apparent supply shortages were occurring at British garages was not lost on the British public and, according to a DEn civil servant, caused Energy Secretary David Howell considerable political embarrassment (also see Hann, 1986, p. 258). Howell's emergency plan included taking North Sea oil royalties in kind rather than cash, increasing production incentives by suspending gas flaring restrictions, announcing a bigger licensing round, and ordering companies operating in the North Sea to cut exports from Britain – essentially using the participation agreements that the previous Labour government had enacted (Redwood, 1984, p. 106).

These measures were not enough to abate the crisis. The problem was not a lack of oil, however, but the inability to shift supply destinations quickly because long-term supply contracts were the norm. As a BNOC executive pointed out, not even the state-owned BNOC could redirect its short-term supply (also see *Daily Telegraph*, 22 May 1979 and 6 June 1979). The disruptions soon stopped and the problem of short-term flexibility was solved, not by BNOC, but by competition between suppliers, the development of a spot market in Rotterdam, and the subsequent shift from long-term to short-term contracts (Yergin, 1991, pp. 718–19, 767–8). Thus, the increasing competitiveness of the oil industry, rather than BNOC and governmental directives, overcame the supply problem.

CONCLUSION

The two consistent factors in the government's involvement in the oil industry from 1914 to the mid-1980s were its investment in BP and its reliance on private international oil companies. Since the government agreed in May 1914 to become APOC's major shareholder, its role was limited to appointing two directors to the board and a veto power. Despite its holding in BP, the government relied primarily on private oil companies for supplies during the First and Second World Wars and to meet the increase in demand for oil in the post-war era, to develop the North Sea and to ensure oil supplies to Britain in a crisis.

Despite this consistency, there were many circumstances that changed. First, Britain's dependence on oil expanded from purely military needs to economic needs and became a vital input into the country's economy in the post-Second World War era. Second, the British government's ability to protect BP's interests in the Middle East decreased. And third, Britain's oil sources changed from foreign to domestic. With the discovery of oil in the North Sea and self-sufficiency by 1980, the government gained a new means of leverage over the oil industry.

To adapt to these changes, the British government created the DEn in 1974 and the BNOC in 1976 and allowed BGC to evolve into an active player in the North Sea. The DEn's primary means of controlling the oil industry were discretionary licences and taxation. The DEn was also responsible for the offshore-supply industry, depletion policy and recording statistics. BNOC was a production company, the recipient of the government's participation oil and thus a major oil trader, as well as an advisory agent to the government. BGC, with a monopoly over the British gas supply, also discovered, developed and produced oil in the North Sea. Ultimately, however, the government continued its reliance on the private oil companies for the development of the North Sea and for security of supply. The seven major oil companies, in fact, developed a majority of North Sea oil. Security was insured through participation agreements which gave the government the ability to control up to 51 per cent of all production, and assurances which guaranteed that the private companies would supply in a crisis, provided they could charge the necessary price to cover any costs.

The sale of the government's oil assets ended one of the two consistent factors in the British government's long involvement in the oil industry, investment in BP. The sales, however, forced a continued reliance on the second, the private oil companies. In the next chapter I examine the specific details of how the government executed these sales, and then I turn to why.

3 The Sequencing of the Oil Asset Sales in Britain

The sale of Britain's oil assets occurred during a ten-year period, 1977–87, and involved nine separate sales, with sizes ranging from just over £200 million for Wytch Farm to £5.5 billion for the last tranche of BP shares. The government received £8.5 billion in total for the sales, the biggest yield from any single industry sector in the privatisation programme (Vickers and Yarrow, 1988, p. 316). The costs of the privatisation are conservatively estimated at £223 million. See the summary in Table 3.1.

Though privatisation is often described as a Conservative government phenomenon, the sales actually started in 1977 with the Labour government's sale of shares in British Petroleum. Starting here is crucial for a full understanding of the development of privatisation in Britain. The Conservative government's sales are more widely known, though it is often overlooked that they began with two BP share sales which further reduced the government's holding in BP. In addition to BP, the Conservative government sold the production operations of BNOC as Britoil and BGC's oil assets as Wytch Farm and Enterprise Oil. Britoil was sold in two tranches, 51 per cent in 1982 and the remainder, except for one 'golden share', in 1985. The golden share was only later withdrawn after being tested in 1988 when Britoil was the subject of a takeover bid. The Conservative government sold British Gas's onshore oil field, Wytch Farm, and created Enterprise Oil with its offshore oil fields and then sold the fields as a functioning entity. The oil sales were completed in 1987 when the government sold its remaining shares in BP. This last sale was complicated by the fact that not only was this sale the biggest ever share offering at the time; it also coincided with the October 1987 stock market crash.

Because many of the details of these sales have not previously been recorded in scholarly works on privatisation, although they are often listed, much of the information in this explanatory chapter is based on first-hand interviews. The review of these sales provides a useful prelude to the subsequent chapters.

Table 3.1 Proceeds and Costs from Oil Asset Sales

	Proceeds (£ millions)	Costs (£ millions)	Remaining Government Shareholding (%)
British Petroleum			68
June 1977	535	20	51
November 1979	290	9.6	46
July 1981	15	7	39
September 1983	565	9.4	31.5
October 1987	5500	137.1	0
BNOC			100
November 1982	549	11.9	48.8
August 1985	450	15	0
British Gas's oil assets			
Wytch Farm			
May 1984	215	2.7	N/A
Enterprise Oil			
June 1984	392	10	N/A
Total	8511	222.7	0

BRITISH PETROLEUM – THE FIRST SALE

Although privatisation as a phenomenon is commonly attributed to Margaret Thatcher, it was a Labour Cabinet which made the first major sale in 1977 by selling part of the government's holding in BP, reducing its stake in the company from 68 to 51 per cent. Pressure for the sale stemmed from the government's severe balance of payments deficit in the wake of the 1973 oil crisis and mid-1970s global recession. The British government was twice forced to request a loan from the International Monetary Fund (IMF), in November 1975 and in the summer of 1976. The IMF pressured the government to reduce its public sector borrowing requirement (PSBR), suggesting targets of between £6.5 and 7 billion for 1977–8 compared with the government's own estimate of £11.2 billion (*Economist*, 6 December 1975 and 11 December 1976; de Vries, 1985, pp. 464–8, 471; and Barnett, 1982, p. 102).

The Chancellor Denis Healey lamented that the problem for the Labour Cabinet was that 'almost all of the spending cuts ran against the

Labour Party's principles, and many also ran against ... campaign promises' (Healey, 1989, p. 401). The Cabinet was split over how to proceed, and selling BP shares provided a ready solution (*Economist*, 4 December 1976, p. 15; Callaghan, 1987, p. 435; and Barnett, 1982, p. 104). Joel Barnett (1982), then the Chief Secretary of the Treasury, explained:

> If the money could be found elsewhere, all the better ... it was much more sensible to raise £500 million [actually £535 million] in this non-deflationary way, rather than to have to cut the borrowing requirement with deflationary measures such as expenditure cuts or tax increases (p. 108).

Later, he explained in our interview: 'We couldn't worry about the future, it was the immediate cash advantage that was essential, even though in the long run the revenues might have been better.' Even Tony Benn, the staunchest advocate of retaining the full shareholding, finally admitted that letting the sale go ahead was preferable to further spending cuts (Benn, 1989, pp. 647, 653; Benn, 1990, pp. 14, 102).

Instead of counting this sale as revenue, the British government established the accounting practice of recording asset sales as negative expenditure. Due to the accounting procedure, Treasury ministers and civil servants explained, the sales enabled the British government to lower the PSBR by £535 million more than they might otherwise have done without further domestic spending cuts. (For further discussion, see Chapters 4 and 7.) The decision to accept the accounting for the BP share sale as negative spending was not seen as very important; at the time no one foresaw the precedent that would be set. As one senior Treasury civil servant explained, it was a very pragmatic decision. The matter was discussed in the Treasury, and the solution adopted was based on the fact that the recently acquired BP shares from Burmah Oil were recorded as positive spending, and therefore the sale of BP shares should count as negative spending.

The argument then became one of how much to sell and how much to cut. Without much disagreement, the Cabinet decided to retain a 51 per cent holding, limiting potential charges from the left that they had relinquished control of a major state asset. Tony Benn was the only minister who seemed to realise the political problems the choice might cause Labour later on. After the sale, as recorded in his diary (1990):

> We have handed some of the most valuable assets of this country to the Shah [The National Iranian Oil Corporation was reported to be trying to

buy 1 per cent of BP shares], to the Americans and to private share-holders, and I am ashamed to be a member of the Cabinet that has done this ... We have provided a blueprint for selling off public assets in the future and we will have no argument against it. It is an outrage (p. 175).

The logistics of the sale were complicated, however, by the legal action from the Burmah Oil shareholders against the Bank of England. Although their claim was weak, the government had to proceed with the possibility that they could lose the suit. As a result the government could only sell the shares held by the Treasury, and not those of the Bank of England (*Economist*, 11 December 1976; Benn, 1990, p. 75).

Though the government did not consult BP before the announcement of the sale, they left BP to make the sale arrangements. Because it was at the time the biggest share sale ever, 25 per cent of the shares were offered in the United States in order to avoid flooding the British market. Expanding into the United States was also important, BP executives explained, because they thought that it would reduce the United States government's resistance to BP's development plans in Alaska. In late June 1977, 17 per cent of BP's shares, 66.8 million ordinary stock units of £1 each, were offered for sale at the price of 845p each. Because the offer was fully sub-scribed in Britain, the allocation to investors in the United States was in the end reduced from 25 per cent to 20 per cent. Preference was given to applications from occupational pension funds, BP employees and sub-underwriters. The government's holding was reduced to 51 per cent, of which 30.87 per cent was held by the Treasury and 20.13 per cent by the Bank. The sale raised £535 million for the Exchequer. The costs for under-writers and advisers, for this first sale, were estimated at £20 million (Fraser and Wilson, 1988, pp. 51–2).

In 1979, a Conservative government led by Margaret Thatcher was elected, and soon began further sales of oil assets. As Tony Benn had foreseen, Chancellor Geoffrey Howe justified the sales by claiming that 'the government was following the example set by the previous adminis-tration' (as quoted in Fraser and Wilson, 1988, pp. 51–2; also see Yarrow, 1989, p. 309; Vickers and Yarrow, 1988, p. 324; Brittan, 1984, p. 109). The government subsequently sold a 5.17 per cent tranche of BP stock in November 1979, which reduced the government's holding below the 50 per cent mark to 45.83 per cent. Just over 80 million shares of 25p each were sold in November 1979 at a price of 363p per share. The offer was again oversubscribed and considered a success, raising £290 million. The estimates for the costs of the sale ranged from the government's estimate of £5.2 million to the Public Accounts

Committee's (PAC's) estimate of £14 million (Mayer and Meadowcroft, 1985, p. 48; TUC, 1985, p. 19).

The government's holding was further diluted in August 1980 to 44.61 per cent as the result of the purchase by BP of Selection Trust. The government's holding was again reduced (to 39.04 per cent) in July 1981 when the government ministers opted not to subscribe to a BP rights issue. Instead, the government sold their entitlements to the 100 million shares to other shareholders at a 15p premium of 290p per share compared to the rights issue price of 275p. The sale overshadowed the British stock market for the month of July, and net proceeds for the government were £8 million; £15 million total for the sale minus BP's expenses of £7 million (Fraser and Wilson, 1988, pp. 52–3; *The Times*, 17 July 1981 and 14 July 1981).

None of these sales required legislation because they involved a publicly traded company so they were not seen as a major policy departure either by the public or by the politicians who later became privatisation advocates (Lawson, 1992, p. 200). BP receipts, though, were always included in what the Conservatives later referred to as their 'privatisation programme'. This programme received an enormous boost in September 1983 when the government sold a further 130 million ordinary shares of 25p each of BP at a minimum tender price of 435p each. The sale was fully subscribed and raised £565 million, with a government estimate of £9.4 million for the costs (Fraser and Wilson, 1988, p. 53; Mayer and Meadowcroft, 1985, p. 48; TUC, 1985, p. 19).

THE BRITOIL SAGA – 1982–8

Upon entering office, the Conservative government carefully considered what to do with BNOC, by gathering information and gauging public opinion. The chairman of BNOC, Frank Kearton, meanwhile, made it clear that he wanted to retire as soon as possible. He was replaced by an interim chairman, Ron Utiger, because, according to BNOC executives, the government had not yet decided what its policy was going to be (also see *The Times,* 31 May 1980, p. 19). In May 1980, nine months later, Philip Shelbourne, a merchant banker from Samuel Montague who had been working on privatisation ideas with the Department of Energy (DEn), was appointed the chairman of BNOC, marking the beginning of the government's change in policy towards the company. According to BNOC executives, given his background, the new direction for the company was obvious – privatisation in one form or another. In 1982, BNOC became the largest privatisation yet undertaken in Britain.

The delay from the date of Shelbourne's appointment to the sale of the first tranche of Britoil occurred because privatisation was not a clear choice. Other issues demanded the government's attention, including BNOC's special privileges, and other options, such as the forward sale of oil, a bond issue or an investment trust, were presented as alternatives (Redwood, 1984, pp. 106–7). As Sir Alistair Morton, then deputy chairman of BNOC, explained:

> The 'granny bonds,' or certified certificate bonds would be sold through the post office. The post office called one day and said we can't do this, it will take us two years to train our staff. The Treasury never understood this option, and it wasn't much discussed ... a second option was an investment trust which would be managed by BNOC into perpetuity, in which shares in the trust would be sold to investors and pay dividends based on the income of the trust ... [Secretary of State for Energy, David Howell] never seemed to understand these proposals.

Privatisation of BNOC was first set back in 1980 when a bill submitted by Howell, giving the government the authority to sell BNOC, was not given parliamentary time. The following year, the new Secretary of State for Energy, Nigel Lawson, was almost thwarted, as Howell had been, by the lack of legislative time. Lawson had prepared two privatisation bills, one for BNOC and one for BGC's oil fields, but the Cabinet ruled that there was only time for one. Instead of choosing one or the other, Lawson combined both measures into a single bill (Webb, 1985, p. 33; Lawson, 1992). While the combination of the two bills meant presentational changes, it did not affect the timing or the outcome of either of the privatisations.

The question then became how to sell BNOC. The BNOC board, management and even Shelbourne opposed splitting the company, which entailed selling the production portion to the private sector and retaining the trading operations in government ownership. According to Shelbourne, they argued that a whole company would be stronger, provide balance to the majors in the North Sea, and offer better value for the shareholders. One board member who strongly advocated keeping the company whole was Sir Denis Rooke, chairman of BGC, whose primary concern was the precedent such a split might create for the future treatment of BGC's oil and gas operations.

Yet no one persuasively suggested how the government could regulate a private company trading state oil. Though there were plans for this function to be leased out to BNOC they were not well developed. Thus, as one BNOC executive summed it up:

BNOC had been through the difficult times. We had begun to gain the grudging respect of the industry, and were making a lot of money. We had shown we could be useful, and had reconciled our different roles. We were just beginning to gain an identity. To be faced with going private was exciting and scary, but to be faced with splitting was very sad. But I think if we were honest, we had to realise that it was quite difficult to put it [the trading side] in the hands of a private entity. So, in objecting to the split, in some senses we were objecting to privatisation.

Another reason the government wanted to retain the trading portion was to counter criticisms that it was relinquishing control of an important national asset (Keegan, 1989, p. 96; Baker and Daniel, 1983, p. 153; Hann, 1986, pp. 258–9). In our interview, Shelbourne explained that, in the end, he convinced the board members that the government was the majority share-holder and it could do with the company what it wanted. Only three BNOC board members remained opposed, two trade unionists and Sir Denis Rooke. BNOC was thus split; the production operations became Britoil and the trading operations remained BNOC.

Lawson agreed a minimum tender price with the consultation of Dundas Hamilton, a stockbroker whose firm had no connection with the issue, who was appointed the government's independent adviser on pricing. This was the first time the government had used an independent adviser. Nigel Lawson (1992) explained:

It was, quite simply, designed to provide an extra line of defence against a possible investigation by the parliamentary watchdog, the Public Accounts Committee (PAC), the most powerful of all the Select Committees, which was by this time becoming restive at the apparent underpricing of privatisation issues and consequent loss to the taxpayer (p. 220).

The government also responded to concerns over the future of Britoil – that it remain British and independent – by creating a special share, which became known as a 'golden share'. In a letter to the chairman of Britoil, Nigel Lawson stated that the government might:

wish in the relevant circumstances to use its voting rights of the Special Share to ensure that control of the Company remained in the hands of an independent Board of Directors (Britoil, 1982, pp. 16–17).

This sentiment was reinforced both in the Britoil prospectus and in Britoil's articles of association.

The government then sold 51 per cent of Britoil in a share offering on 19 November 1982. The share price was expensive for BNOC's high debt/equity ratio compared to other large oil companies, and because the new corporation was unable to retain either the £219 million of profits or the £127 million remaining in the National Oil Account. The sale resulted in near disaster as a sudden collapse in the price of oil just before the sale made Britoil even less attractive to investors. In addition, the sale was limited to Britain and was not offered in the largest stock market, the United States (Britoil, 1982, p. 71). Of the 255 million shares of 10p each on offer at a price of 219p, only 69.7 million were taken up (27 per cent of the shares put up for sale), mostly by private investors and Britoil employees. The underwriters were forced to take up the remaining 73 per cent or 185.3 million shares. Because it was underwritten, the government received its guaranteed £549 million. The cost estimates ranged from £17 million by the National Audit Office (NAO) to £12.5 by the Public Accounts Committee and £11.3 million by the government (*Financial Times*, 31 October 1987, p. 6; *Petroleum Economist*, November 1982, p. 449 and December 1982, p. 510; Fraser and Wilson, 1988, pp. 28–9; Mayer and Meadowcroft, 1985, p. 48; TUC, 1985, pp. 22–3).

The undersubscription of the Britoil offer served as a good lesson in many respects. First, it made the Public Accounts Committee realise that underwriting served an important purpose, and was not just a way to give money to friends in the City as Labour claimed. And second, it demonstrated that an independent price adviser was helpful in deferring blame for an undersubscribed sale (Lawson, 1992, p. 221). In fact, both practices were repeated in subsequent privatisations.

The government sold its remaining 48.8 per cent interest in Britoil in August 1985, and retained only its golden share. In contrast with the first issue, the 1985 sale was straightforward and was oversubscribed. Shelbourne described it as simply 'marvellous'. The government reserved a portion of the 243 million shares at a price of 185p for the markets in the United States, Canada and Europe, but the majority (over 40 per cent) was sold to British institutional investors. The government's gross proceeds were £450 million, and the *Financial Times* estimated the costs at £15 million (Fraser and Wilson, 1988, pp. 28–9; Mayer and Meadowcroft, 1985, p. 48).

While Britoil proved it could survive on its own, BNOC could not. Because the government continued to insist that the company operate on the basis of long-term contracts in an effort to achieve the unstated policy of stabilising oil prices, BNOC was forced to sell on the spot market at a loss. With the decline in oil prices in 1984 and 1985 this practice quickly became both expensive and politically embarrassing. As one Treasury civil servant revealed:

> It is obviously very painful for the Treasury to have a body in the public sector buying oil at $28.65 and selling at a lower price; it gives us very great pain, be assured of that.

From the point of view of BNOC, the government made too much over these losses because the price set by BNOC was the price the government used as a tax reference point, the higher BNOC's price in a declining market, the less the government lost in terms of revenues. In fact, three-quarters of the losses were gained back through taxes which were based on (this higher) price of oil. A BNOC executive explained:

> the sums involved were small compared to the total size, £12 million out of billions per year traded. BNOC had always made a small profit. It must have been embarrassing though for politicians to ask Parliament for money to cover the losses.

The costs were magnified because BNOC was required under the Oil and Gas (Enterprise) Act 1982 to submit a Supplementary Estimate to Parliament for funds to cover any losses, which is what happened in 1984. The request led to an urgent enquiry by the House of Commons Select Committee on Energy. As conditions worsened, BNOC lost more money, and had to repeat the process again later that year, thus making the loss of money a public embarrassment to the government. The losses totalled £11 million in 1984 (BNOC, *Annual Report and Accounts*, 1984, pp. 3–4; *Petroleum Economist*, January 1985, p. 24, and April 1985, p. 114; *Hansard Parliamentary Debates (Commons)*, 18 December 1984, 13 March 1985, 14 May 1985 and 15 July 1985).

Because there was no saleable entity, legislation was introduced in March 1985 to abolish BNOC and replace it with a regulatory agency which would retain three of BNOC's functions:

- custody of participation agreements;
- disposal of oil received as royalty in kind; and
- management of the government's pipeline system (Vickers and Yarrow, 1988, pp. 321–2).

The government's reasons were summarised by then Minister of State for Energy Alick Buchanan-Smith:

> We have made changes because circumstances have changed. The situation is not the same as it was in the early 1970s, either in relation to the

oil market or to the structure of the oil industry. The Bill is a reflection of the changes. What might have been appropriate 10 years ago is not necessarily appropriate today (*Hansard Parliamentary Debates (Commons)*, 15 July 1985).

The Oil and Pipelines Bill was enacted on 30 October, and BNOC was formally dissolved in March 1986, and it was replaced by the Oil and Pipelines Agency (OPA), newly created within the DEn.

The story of Britoil and BNOC did not end in 1985. The government's one remaining tie to Britoil, its golden share, again ensnared the government in the company's affairs in late 1987 when BP initiated a takeover bid for Britoil. The government issued contradictory statements, and thus caused great uncertainty at the time. Prime Minister Margaret Thatcher initially stated: 'I understand that it is a commercial transaction, and it is not for us to interfere' (*Hansard Parliamentary Debates (Commons)*, 10 December 1987). It was revealed a few days later that Atlantic Richfield (Arco) had also begun acquiring stock in an effort to take over Britoil. The government then seemingly reversed its position on 18 December 1987 with a statement from the Treasury confirming that the government would use its golden share to prevent a takeover of Britoil (*Hansard Parliamentary Debates (Commons)*, 16 December 1987 and 11 January 1988; Fraser and Wilson, 1988, p. 30).

Ministers did not reveal how they would use the golden share, if at all, even to the Britoil management. Thus neither Britoil nor the bidders, BNOC and Britoil executives complained, knew whether or how the government would prevent a transaction (also see Britoil, 1988, p. 10). From the accounts given by Britoil executives, it appears that Arco was intimidated by the golden share while BP was not, which explains why Arco agreed to sell its shares in Britoil to BP in January 1988. Then, with over 50 per cent of Britoil's shares, BP made an offer for the outstanding shares at 500p per share. As Britoil chairman Philip Shelbourne pointed out, this offer was attractive to Britoil shareholders as many had bought their shares in the first issue at a price of 218p per share. In fact, the Britoil share price had never risen above its issue price until the takeover bid.

According to some accounts, BP had acquired as much as 80 per cent of the Britoil stock. With such a high acceptance rate by the shareholders, the government had little choice but to allow the sale to proceed. On 23 February 1988, the Chancellor announced that the government would not use its veto power in exchange for certain assurances from BP regarding employment, exploration and development of Britoil's assets, Britoil's Glasgow base, and the composition of the Britoil board (Fraser and

Wilson, 1988, p. 30; *Hansard Parliamentary Debates (Commons)*, 8 February 1988 and 23 February 1988).

THE SALE OF BRITISH GAS'S OIL ASSETS

The government faced its toughest opposition to privatisation from BGC. Like BP, BGC was a large well-established company and also had the advantage of having a natural monopoly on gas. BGC was also headed by a strong and politically well connected chairman, Denis Rooke, who was determined to keep BGC's operations intact. Secretary of State for Energy Nigel Lawson, however, was determined to minimise Rooke's power, and took measures to do so, such as appointing three new board members. Lawson (1992) recalled: 'These three eminent businessmen could not be pushed around by anyone. They also kept me better informed than my officials were usually able to do' (p. 214). Not surprisingly, therefore, the BGC sales were different from the others. The government's tactic was to strip away oil assets, leaving BGC's gas-related organisation and staff intact. The onshore oil assets of Wytch Farm were sold in a trade sale, while the offshore assets were transformed into a new company, Enterprise Oil, and sold in a tender offer. Together, the sale of these assets accounted for roughly 10 per cent of total British oil production (Webb, 1985, p. 33).

Wytch Farm

The management delayed the sale of Wytch Farm for two years and seven months after the issue of the first directive, and it was in fact the longest of all privatisations to be completed. The first oil asset sale did not need new legislation as the field under consideration, Wytch Farm, was an onshore oil field and, therefore, was covered under the Gas Act 1972. The Act allowed the Secretary of State to direct the corporation to dispose of any assets held by them (Gas Act 1972, S. 7(2)(a); British Gas Corporation, *Annual Report and Accounts*, 1981–2, p. 18; *Hansard Parliamentary Debates (Commons)*, 13 March 1984). As with the BP sale, it was left to BGC to make arrangements for the disposal, beginning with an invitation to tender in July 1982. The management of BGC argued against the sale publicly and privately and was unhelpful in the government's efforts to gain information and slow to act on decisions. One obstacle was price: BGC estimated that Wytch Farm was worth £450 million, while Wood Mackenzie and Company, a stockbroker firm, gave an independent valuation of £165.5 million. The bids received reflected Wood Mackenzie's estimate and did not exceed £160 million. The BGC management nevertheless argued that a great loss would occur if the assets were sold so cheaply (Gas Act 1972, S. 7(2)(a); British Gas Corporation, *Annual Report and Accounts*, 1981–2, p. 18; *Hansard Parliamentary Debates (Commons)*, 13 March 1984).

The management also argued that the government's directive was a punishment for success. Since BGC discovered Wytch Farm itself, and because it was one of their most successful finds, they could not perceive legislative reasons why the government was forcing them to sell one of their most significant achievements (Jewers, 1983; *Guardian*, 10 June 1983). The management argued that the sale would harm the national interest; specifically, the sale would damage BGC's standing as a free partner in exploration and development for hydrocarbons; it would endanger BGC's ability to bring a sufficient level of expertise and knowledge to the negotiation of gas contracts; it would cost the taxpayers money because a forced sale was unlikely to realise the full value of the assets; and it would threaten environmental disruption as the buyer would not necessarily have the same high level of commitment to solving environmental problems as BGC (House of Commons Energy Select Committee, Wytch Farm Memo, 1981–2, pp. xxi–xxii).

Despite BGC's protests, Lawson announced in March 1983 that it would be commercially justifiable and in the national interest to proceed (*Hansard Parliamentary Debates (Commons)*, 13 March 1984). BGC was ordered to sell its 50 per cent share in Wytch Farm to the Dorset Group, a consortium of five independent British companies. Due to further complications and delays, the sale did not go through though until May 1984, over a year later. The Group agreed to pay £85 million up front, and an additional £130 million when production reached 20 000 b/d – production was then under 4500 b/d, but was predicted to reach 40 000 b/d (*Petroleum Economist*, June 1984). The government's costs for the sale were £98 388, but the cost to BGC was about £1.75 million, which was met out of the proceeds of the sale (TUC, 1985, p. 13; *Hansard Parliamentary Debates (Commons)*, 8 June 1984).

Enterprise Oil

As with Wytch Farm, BGC was opposed to the sale of their offshore oil assets. Their biggest complaint was the loss of revenue without compensation. In the 1984 *Annual Report and Accounts*, the company complained that the sale had 'an adverse effect on its [BGC's] financial position which will continue to be felt into the future' (p. 5). By this time, however, BGC was earning huge profits which, as a Treasury civil servant and BGC executive pointed out, the government was having difficulty extracting from the corporation. The sale of assets was thought to be a means to capture some of the profits. The government sought to facilitate the transaction (and avoid problems such as those with Wytch Farm) by enacting the Oil and Gas (Enterprise) Act 1982 which gave the Secretary of State for Energy clear authority to sell BGC's offshore oil assets, Enterprise Oil.

While the idea of a straight trade sale was initially considered (*Financial Times*, 18 June 1984, 28 June 1984 and 29 June 1984, p. 22), the option was rejected for three reasons, according to civil servants and a business executive. First, based on the assumption that the private bidder would have been an American company, the government feared a political reaction to a transfer of oil assets overseas. Second, the DEn saw the opportunity to create an independent British oil company. Third, based on the assumption that the assets would be bought in part for tax relief (due to offsetting allowances) Treasury civil servants argued that the operation's oil exploration activities would accrue to the purchaser and tax avoidance would reduce the Treasury's net gain. Therefore, though several international companies approached the government to buy the blocks, they were turned down.

A directive from the Secretary of State for Energy in August 1982 required BGC to dispose of its interests in five UKCS blocks. These blocks were incorporated on 26 November 1982 under the name British Gas North Sea Oil Holdings Limited, and started trading on 1 May 1983, while remaining a subsidiary of BGC. In September 1983, all the directors of British Gas North Sea Oil Holdings Limited resigned, and ownership was transferred to the Secretary of State, without compensation to BGC. The name was changed to Enterprise Oil Limited, and two managers, one from the DEn, were appointed to oversee the assets and build a company organisation. In late October 1983, a second batch of BGC oil assets, interests in 20 UKCS blocks, were incorporated under the name British Gas North Sea Oil Exploration Acreage Limited. On 20 December 1983, these assets were acquired by Enterprise Oil but remained under the control of the Secretary of State for Energy, again without compensation to BGC. Enterprise was re-registered as a public company in April 1984 (Enterprise Oil, 1984, pp. 1, 19; BGC, *Annual Report and Accounts*, 1982–3, p. 5, and 1984, p. 5; *Financial Times*, 26 October 1983; Enterprise Oil, *Annual Report and Accounts*, 1984, p. 8).

As a privatisation candidate and a new company, Enterprise Oil faced three risks, as pointed out in the prospectus. First, the 1983 Labour Party

Conference had passed a resolution to re-nationalise Enterprise Oil. Second, while the oil business in general was risky, Enterprise Oil was in particular handicapped by the mature stage of its fields which were set to decline after 1987, and could not guarantee new discoveries. Third, as a newly created company, Enterprise Oil had no track record.

These difficulties were addressed in a number of ways. The government made it clear that they would have no continuing involvement in Enterprise following the sale offer. In all other respects, the government confirmed that Enterprise Oil would be treated in the same way as any other private sector oil company. The new team set out a business strategy for Enterprise Oil which took into consideration Enterprise's mature asset base. To give further credibility to the company, the government agreed to contribute the earnings from the fields since they began trading as an entity in May 1983, giving the company a significant cash resourcing, £70 million, with which to proceed. Lastly, although the company did not have a history, the government attracted qualified oil professionals with individual track records who, as one of the early members conveyed, were able to set up a respected team.

Enterprise did not have much trouble finding qualified personnel, as recent takeover victims such as Gulf and Getty provided a large pool from which to choose. Once organised, the company grew quickly, in 1983 there were only eight employees; by June 1984 there were 48, and by December 1984 there were 90 staff. Having agreed to the government's objectives, given up their previous jobs and put their names on the prospectus, the management as well as the government had a stake in the success of Enterprise Oil as an independent entity (Enterprise Oil, 1984; *Financial Times*, 18 June 1984 and 13 December 1983). In the end another measure was added, a special share, to ensure the continued independence of Enterprise for a limited period. The share was held by the Secretary of State for Energy and was scheduled to be redeemed on 31 December 1988. With this special share, as explained in the *Offer for Sale*, the government had the ability to out-vote all shareholders in the event any person sought to exercise or to control the exercise of more than 50 per cent of the voting shares (1984, pp. 2, 43). The Enterprise management saw the special share as a necessary protection for an immature company. In order to give the government's policy of creating a new independent oil company the chance to work, they argued, the company needed some breathing space from predators.

Although nine paragraphs of the prospectus were devoted to the provisions of the special share, the circumstances in which it would be used were not clear. In fact, the government's intentions were stated more clearly in the *Financial Times*:

the only circumstances where the government would exercise its Golden Share powers would be if undesirable interests declared their intention of taking control. A straightforward build-up of shares in the company would not be legitimate grounds for government intervention (14 June 1984).

The proposed sale was well received by the City: the consensus was that Enterprise was worth the £520 million being tendered. By addressing the problems, spelling out the details in the prospectus and starting a promotional campaign, the new Enterprise Oil team overcame the potential price discounting sometimes encountered in the flotation of new companies (*Financial Times*, 5 July 1984). The issue was offered only in the United Kingdom, as the government was again sensitive to nationalistic feeling towards the North Sea. Enterprise, on the other hand, saw limiting the sale to Britain as a way of gaining favour with lenders in the City who they were sure to need in the future as the company required funds. There was, therefore, according to a DEn civil servant, no company push to expand the offering to Europe or the United States.

The entire shareholding in Enterprise Oil was put up for offer on 27 June 1984. Until then privatisations of ongoing companies had always been carried out in parts as a means to test the market and spread the risk. In part, due to the favourable reception from the City and in part due to the government's growing confidence and/or impatience with privatisation, the government decided to sell Enterprise Oil in one sale. This proved to be a problematic decision despite the consideration the government had given to Enterprise's weaknesses. Ultimately there are market forces that no government can control, such as the collapse of the spot market price for crude oil two days before the offering. This market fluctuation pushed the short-term value of the stock down. There was some discussion of delaying the issue, but there were too many forces moving the issue to the set date, including buyers having the funds available, the timeliness of the prospectus and the government's privatisation timetable. Since the issue had been underwritten, Enterprise was guaranteed to be sold and the government was guaranteed its money. Only the underwriters stood to lose. The government received its £392 million for the sale, while the cost estimates ranged from £9 million by the government to £11 million by the National Accounting Office (Fraser and Wilson, 1988, p. 34; *Economist*, 7 July 1984, p. 16; Mayer and Meadowcroft, 1985, p. 48; TUC, 1985, p. 25).

Though the Treasury received its money, there were many problems brought on by the decision to proceed with the sale. Due to the uncertainty in the oil market, investors were cautious and failed to subscribe fully to the issue. Interested stockbrokers waited to buy shares on the open market which was sure to be lower than the underwritten price. In fact, only 66 per cent of the shares were subscribed in the end. This provided a prime opportunity for a takeover bid, and just hours before the bidding closed, in an unexpected move, explained a DEn civil servant, Rio Tinto Zinc (RTZ, the British-based international mining and industrial group) subscribed to 49 per cent of the shares (also see Fraser and Wilson, 1988, p. 34).

The dilemma for the government was whether to support the principles of free enterprise *or* to support the strategy of creating an independent British oil company. RTZ had sought only 49 per cent of the shares for fear of invoking the government's special share, though 50 per cent had not been identified as a trigger (*Financial Times*, 29 June 1984). Alistair Frame, the chairman of RTZ, personally informed the Secretary of State for Energy, Peter Walker, of his company's intentions that day. As a major mining company, Frame explained, he decided that it was not worth ruining RTZ's relationship with the government with the takeover of Enterprise Oil. According to the Enterprise Oil management, Walker was furious anyway. Walker believed that government intentions were sacred. According to a DEn civil servant, he was determined that Enterprise should remain an independent company, with the full concordance of Enterprise Oil's executives.

On 28 June, Walker announced that, in keeping with the government's objective to make Enterprise Oil an independent British oil company, no bidder would be allotted more than 10 per cent of the shares in the offer. The City underwriters were thus left with 73 per cent of the 210 million Enterprise shares (*Financial Times*, 29 June 1984). RTZ tried yet again with a dawn raid on 2 July 1984 when trading began for Enterprise Oil shares on the London Stock Exchange and acquired another 5 per cent. Free trading in the market and little investor interest in the shares meant that by July 1984 RTZ was able to acquire 29.9 per cent of the shares (the maximum allowed by law) on the open market for 1p above the original offer price. Yet because of the government's golden share, RTZ lacked full control (Curwen, 1986, pp. 184–5; *Economist*, 7 July 1984).

The government's efforts to intervene in the market while simultaneously affirming its belief in free-market operations made it look inept. There was a strong case that RTZ, a well-managed international company, would be an ideal vehicle for expanding Britain's presence in the world oil industry (*Financial Times*, 29 June 1984). The oil assets of RTZ were estimated to be only one-third the size of those of Enterprise. Even with the combined assets, the RTZ oil company would not have been a dominant force in the North Sea compared to the majors (*Financial Times*, 3 July

1984). Enterprise, however, would have been controlled by a corporation larger than BGC, and one with international interests. The sale would have been merely the transfer of assets from one large corporation to another. A takeover by RTZ was not acceptable to a government determined to have an independent British oil company – even if that was not what the free market offered. With the government preventing any further acquisition of Enterprise shares, the matter ended when RTZ decided in December 1985 to transfer its holdings in Enterprise Oil to London and Scottish Marine Oil (LASMO) in exchange for a 25 per cent holding in LASMO (Fraser and Wilson, 1988, p. 34).

THE GOVERNMENT'S FINAL BP SALE

Though BP was not always considered a nationalised industry and therefore not truly part of the government's privatisation programme, it proved useful to the government in that context again in 1987. As Nigel Lawson (1992) explained:

> The postponement of the water flotation in July 1986 had created a gap in the privatisation timetable, and I had announced in March 1987 that it would be replaced with the sale of the government's remaining 31.5 per cent shareholding in BP (p. 757).

The last BP sale was publicly described as part of the government's policy to sell its minority shareholdings in companies as and when circumstances permitted. The government offered BP a golden share, but was turned down, leaving BP as one of the few privatised companies without one (*Hansard Parliamentary Debates (Commons)*, 18 March 1987; *Financial Times*, 19 March 1987; and Graham and Prosser, 1988, p. 429).

On the crest of a booming stock market, the government decided to sell all of its remaining shares, against the experience of Enterprise Oil and the advice of BP, who argued that three tranches would be more sensible, especially as the company needed to raise more capital itself through a share issue. One BP executive explained:

> We didn't believe the market had the capacity easily to accept all those shares. I don't think even they [ministers] would have tried to do it except that we had such a raging boom. BP shares were up to 440p. We would have much preferred three tranches. We decided to offer a new issue, and ride the back of the government. We needed to do a rights issue; it was just tactics that we did it with the government. The banking

advice at the time was if you want to do it, you need to wrap it all up and package it together. So we had to shift, being faced with a dead 'no' from the Lady – she was going to sell the whole lot. Then, if they believe they can sell, and the bankers believe it, why not get our rights issue too?

The combined shares made the £7 billion issue the largest ever attempted in the London market (*Financial Times*, 22 July 1987; *Hansard Parliamentary Debates (Commons)*, 21 July 1987 and 21–9 October 1987; Fraser and Wilson, 1988, pp. 53–5).

Another early point of conflict between BP and the government over the sale was over the sale's geographical allocation of shares. BP's strategic plan included international diversification of share ownership, with the goal of having 10 per cent of the shares held outside Britain by the end of 1987. In contrast, the government's policy objective was to maximise British equity ownership in order to confer benefits to voters and taxpayers and avoid accusations of losing national control. The government, however, realised that the inclusion of the United States market would ensure the largest return for the Exchequer; and in the end the government allocated over 24 per cent to the United States market, 8 per cent to Japan, and 5 per cent each to Canada and Europe (*Financial Times*, 30 January 1987).

The government sold 2194 million BP shares in October 1987. Of these, 1850 million were the government's 31 per cent stake in the company and the remaining 459 million were new share issues by BP. The government announced the fixed price of 330p per share on 15 October, just days before the October stock market crash. The impact of the crash was such that between 14 and 27 October, the *Financial Times* ordinary share index fell by 28 per cent, and the BP share price dropped 26 per cent, from 351p to 259p. The final date for applications for the government's offer was 28 October at which point only 70 million shares were applied for, 3 per cent of the total. Because the issue was underwritten, the government again received its full £5.5 billion; and because the government had bought BP's new issue shares outright, BP itself received £1.5 billion. The £114 million fee to the underwriters, though large, was worthwhile in this case as virtually all (97 per cent) of the shares were held by underwriters: 1179 million shares in Britain, 506 million shares in the United States, 160 million shares in Japan and 105 million shares each in Canada and Europe. The £23.1 million spent on advertising, however, had virtually no effect in the wake of the market crash (Fraser and Wilson, 1988, pp. 53–5; *Hansard Parliamentary Debates (Commons)*, 21 July 1987 and 21–9 October 1987;

Financial Times, 8 September 1988; *Sunday Times*, 4 December 1988; and *Financial Times*, 22 January 1988).

The decision to sell shares in the United States caused an unforeseen problem. As underwriters in the United States do not normally spread the risk of an issue to sub-underwriters, four American underwriters bore the whole of the BP issue themselves. The Americans, therefore, were understandably the ones who put the most pressure on the British government to withdraw the issue (*Financial Times*, 31 October 1987). Bending to pressure from the underwriters, the government finally agreed via the Bank of England to provide a floor price of 70p for the partly paid shares (compared to the partly paid flotation price of 120p per share).

The Bank, however, only had to buy back 38 million shares because the Kuwait Investment Office (KIO) purchased most of the outstanding BP shares at a few pence above the floor price. In fact, by November 1987 KIO had accumulated a 10 per cent stake in BP (nearly 600 million shares), but the KIO gave the government assurances that it was buying the shares only as an investment, and that it had no ambitions to control BP. By May 1988, though, KIO's stake had risen to 22 per cent of BP shares (*Financial Times*, 20 November 1987; Fraser and Wilson, 1988, pp. 55–6; *Hansard Parliamentary Debates (Commons)*, October 1987, 7 December 1988).

The government faced a difficult problem: Should it allow the free market to work or should it interfere and prevent a foreign entity from buying and controlling Britain's largest oil company? Instead of legislating, according to a BP executive, the government chose a less public route of referring the issue to the Monopolies and Mergers Commission (MMC). On 4 October 1988 the MMC ordered KIO to reduce its holdings in BP from 21.69 per cent to 9.9 per cent. Kuwait responded with threats of retaliation against the British government both financially and diplomatically, and also against British individuals, banks and companies. The Kuwait government stated that it would 'take all necessary steps to protect Kuwait's economic interests in Britain'. Kuwait had investments of $85 billion (£50 billion) overseas, and one-fifth of that was in Britain (*Financial Times*, 7 October 1988 and 10 October 1988).

BP was particularly concerned over how KIO would dispose of the shares. Although the British government extended the deadline for the reduction from one year to three, there was still a fear that KIO would dump the shares on the market or, worse, sell them to another company who might then vie for a takeover (*Financial Times*, 12 March 1988 and 17 December 1988). In January 1989, when KIO proposed a buy-back formula, BP was eager to accept. The government was kept informed, but was not a party to these negotiations. Nonetheless, in the final agreement, the government made a substantial contribution: BP agreed to buy back KIO's 11.7 per cent stake for £1.95 billion, and the government provided a refund of £458 million to KIO on Advance Corporation Tax payable on the sale of shares. KIO received 305p per share, 50p above the current BP share price, and made 16p per share profit at a time when other shareholders were still suffering a loss from the 1987 sale (*Financial Times*, 4 January 1989).

The sale was a boost to BP's independence, one of the BP management's primary objectives. BP chairman, Sir Peter Walters, told shareholders that the purchase of KIO's shares would remove any fears amongst potential investors that BP could have been influenced by a major shareholder which was also a member of OPEC (*Financial Times*, 1 February 1989). Once through this crisis, the BP management sought to distance itself again from the British government and present itself as a truly international company (*Financial Times*, 30 January 1989).

CONCLUSION

This chapter set out the specifics of how the British government sold its majority holding in BP, Britoil, Wytch Farm and Enterprise Oil in the space of 10 years, raising £8.5 billion against a minimum cost of £224 million. As the oil assets were some of the government's first privatisations, the process was a learning one, particularly regarding the extent to which the nationalised industry management would oppose the sales, the importance of safeguards such as independent pricing and underwriting, and the uncertainty of the markets. In the next four chapters, I examine the underlying reasons why the government sold these oil assets.

4 Constraints and Opportunities Presented by the International System

The importance of energy to a nation is most obvious at the international level. As a necessary input for both a strong military and a healthy economy, it is vital to the relative strength of a country. At this level, it is also most difficult to understand why a state would give up control of such a resource, especially for international relations scholars. Realists cannot comprehend a rational state relinquishing control. Even scholars of the interdependence school, though more accepting that other actors may be involved, find it puzzling, because of the economic implications for a country's economic competitiveness (Porter, 1990, pp. 546–7).

From the state level perspective, relinquishing control of a vital national resource appears irrational. An alternative vantage point provides some clarity. Using a variation of the 'second-image reversed' (Gourevitch, 1978), I consider the international factors that impact individual politicians making decisions. From this perspective, the international level is a set of parameters that individuals face, rather than an arena for monolithic actors. In order to make sense of this vast dimension, I resurrect Keohane and Nye's power and issue structure models (Keohane and Nye, 1979) to predict issue area vulnerability. Though many of their concepts already have been used, they have been adopted primarily by realists as aggregate power structure models designed to predict the general behaviour of states (Keohane, 1986b; Waltz, 1979; Grieco, 1988). The realists' variations have been constrained by many of their assumptions, most notably that the state is a unitary rational actor and therefore the only actor worth studying. Such a view prevents realists from predicting specific policy change or outcomes, which granted is often not their objective.

Some realists, however, have borrowed Keohane and Nye's issue model to explain a state's behaviour in specific issue areas. David Lake has developed the issue model in his book, *Power, Protection and Free Trade* (1988). He argues that: 'by examining the international economic structure, the position of a country within it, and the changes in the structure over time, it is possible to explain and predict trade strategies' (pp. 29–40). Though Lake's model cleverly combines the overall power structure model with the issue structure model, he gives his variation more credit than it deserves. Lake claims to explain specific trade policies from his two-dimensional model. Such precision is not possible, however, when domestic factors are not taken into consideration. For example, factors such as party in power, elections and legislative agenda, can alter the outcome in ways he is unable to predict from his overall structural or issue variables.

The importance of domestic variables is an old point of contention between the realist and the interdependence schools. In setting down the original tenets of realism, Kenneth Waltz (1954) acknowledged the role and linkage of domestic and international politics (with his three images), but ultimately he argued that all of importance could be derived from the structure of the international system (p. 230). While this might be plausible for explaining the outbreak of war, it is less true for predicting economic and social policy, or, as Keohane and Nye point out, 'Clearly there is a great deal of variance in international political behaviour that is not explained by the distribution of power among states' (Keohane and Nye, 1989, p. 261).

I propose to adapt Keohane and Nye's original model to the purpose it is most suited: to predict areas where change is likely to occur. Keohane and Nye's original premise is that the vulnerability of a country, 'the relative availability and costliness of the alternatives that various actors face' (p. 13), is linked to the degree and speed to which a country will change its policies. The issue structure model argues a similar connection for specific issue areas and therefore corresponding policies. The power of the models is decidedly less ambitious than what Keohane and Nye themselves had in mind, predicting regime change. The focus on regimes however raises unnecessary problems, such as defining regimes, and obscures the power that the structural models actually have. The limitation of the model, as Keohane and Nye themselves identify, is that the 'translation' of these constraints into domestic political reality is not taken into account (p. 18). Thus, I propose to use their model to identify initial structural constraints that Britain faced in the late 1970s and early 1980s – the time when the first privatisations occurred – in order to understand better the parameters British policy makers faced. In other words, I focus on the impact of international factors and their role in determining the *range* of policy options available to politicians of this particular case, oil asset sales. By identifying areas where Britain was most vulnerable, it is possible to assess where change is most likely to occur and why. Keohane and Nye implicitly recognised the advantages to this type of approach when they state: with 'the drawbacks of a single complex synthesis, it is better to

seek explanations with simple models and add complexity as necessary'
(p. 58). In subsequent chapters, I focus on how these parameters or constraints were translated into various domestic arenas.

Borrowing from Keohane and Nye's original variables, as well as some of
David Lake's interpretations, I present a two variable construct that analyses
countries' relative international positions for specific issues areas (see
Figure 4.1). The first variable is a country's overall power position. There are
many definitions of power and, as Keohane and Nye admit: 'Power has
always been an elusive concept' (Keohane and Nye, 1989, p. 11), though it is
generally accepted to be the ability of one actor to get another to do something that they otherwise would not do. While Keohane and Nye emphasise
that power is more than military might, they do not identify specific further
dimensions. Susan Strange, however, offers a useful view of power in her
book, *States and Markets* (1988), where she identifies and elaborates on four
specific aspects of power: security, production, credit and knowledge
(pp. 25–7). For this case study, I have roughly and crudely operationalised
power by combining relative indexes for these four dimensions of power:
countries' military expenditure (security), GNP per capita (production), allocation of IMF Special Drawing Rights (credit), and rate of literacy (knowledge). In these graphs I use measures for 1978 (Taylor and Jodice, 1983,
Tables 1.6, 3.6, C-39 and 5.3).

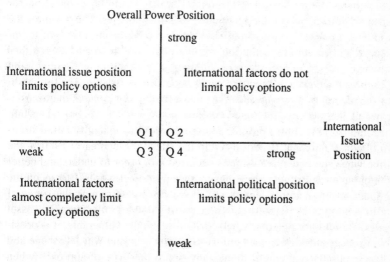

Figure 4.1　A Country's International Position

The second dimension, a sector specific economic variable, measures a country's position in a specific issue area. The key factor which determines a country's international issue position is the country's status in that sector relative to other countries, international organisations, multinational corporations or another international actor. For oil, I suggest this can be measured by the country's level of production as a percentage of world total (BP, 1990). For finance, I propose this can be measured as the sum of a country's total reserves and central government revenue (IMF, 1986).

The stronger the country is in terms of the specific economic issue and the more powerful overall, the more options are available to the country's policy makers and the less susceptible they are to international forces (Morse, as discussed in Gourevitch, 1978, p. 892), or in other words, domestic factors play a greater role in determining outcomes (quadrant 2). Conversely, the weaker the country's position, the fewer policy options are available and the more its policy makers are constrained by international factors (quadrant 3). When a country's position is weak either in overall power or on a specific economic issue, the policy options available are limited unless the strength of the country's stronger position compensates to provide additional options or alternatives (quadrants 1 and 4). It is important to note that Figure 4.1 is used only as an analytical framework as, inevitably, economic and political issues are linked and reinforce each other. OPEC serves as one such example.

Examples for specific issues and countries from 1976 and 1980 help to illustrate the relative strengths and weaknesses of different countries' positions. On the issue of oil (see Figure 4.2), Britain's position was strong in 1980 because its own oil production was increasing and would soon surpass domestic consumption. With its substantial overall power position, Britain was well placed in terms of sovereignty over its oil policy (quadrant 2). Britain's options were limited only by the countries with a stronger international position, in this example, the United States. Saudi Arabia was also in a strong oil position as the world's largest oil producer, but was not as strong in its overall power position as Britain (quadrant 1). Conversely, Germany was stronger politically, but, as a major oil consumer with no domestic supplies, was weaker in terms of oil and had few options in terms of oil policy and fewer means to influence other countries (quadrant 4). Mexico, Japan and Bangladesh were all weaker, both in overall power and in terms of oil than Britain and therefore were virtually unable to influence Britain's oil policy.

Turning to the international financial issue, due to severe balance of payments problems, Britain's finance position in 1976 was not as strong as its international oil position (see Figure 4.3). Britain's overall power position

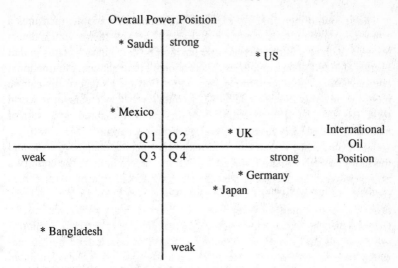

Figure 4.2   A Country's International Oil Position

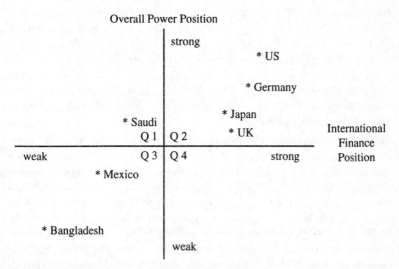

Figure 4.3   A Country's International Finance Position

remained the same, but its international finance position had deteriorated so that Britain barely remained in quadrant 2. In this case, I refer specifically to the government's reserves and revenues, not the size of the City of London's private financial industry. British policy makers were therefore more limited in their policy options in terms of finance than oil. This difference is obvious when the positions of the world's strongest financial countries are compared. Because of their strong position, Germany and the United States were the most able to influence British government policy decisions, with possibly some influence coming from Japan which was in a stronger financial situation but slightly weaker overall power position. Saudi Arabia, Mexico and Bangladesh were not influences due to their relatively much weaker positions (quadrants 1 and 3).

From the model, we would expect both the international financial situation and the structure of the oil industry to have affected British politicians' decision to sell the oil assets with the financial issue being more influential than the oil, but neither solely determining the outcome. The first two sections in Chapter 4 investigate these two areas in more detail. One of the major criticisms of realist (and neorealist) theory is that the importance of international organisations is not taken into account. Neoliberals argue that international organisations and regimes play a substantial role in shaping the international system and states' options (Krasner, 1985b). The third section in Chapter 4 examines whether international organisations were an important factor in Britain's decision to sell its oil assets.

INTERNATIONAL FINANCIAL PRESSURE ON BRITAIN

The importance of the world economy on domestic policy making is generally recognised. Andrew Gamble (1988) stresses its impact on Britain in the late 1970s and 1980s:

> Of overriding importance in shaping domestic policy in recent years have been events in the world economy. From this perspective there have been so far two crucial phases in the life of the Thatcher government, determined by the slump in the world economy between 1979 and 1982, and then by the recovery between 1982 and 1987 (p. 98).

Keith Middlemas (1991) confirms the importance of the world economic situation on British policy making in this period, as did the civil servants and politicians I interviewed. The world recession was such an all encompassing factor, though, that it is difficult to determine whether it was the primary cause of different outcomes such as privatisation. In general, it is agreed that the world recession was a contributing factor to national deficits by increasing demands for public spending, as well as decreasing government tax revenue. This background pressure was one of the reasons often cited why privatisation emerged on national agendas throughout the world

(Henig, Hamnett and Feigenbaum, 1988, pp. 445–7). Its specific effect was apparent before Thatcher though. As one Treasury civil servant stated: the impetus for the BP sales 'really started with the 1973–4 recession followed by the 1974–5 Labour spending' which caused the IMF crisis of 1976–7.

The civil servants and politicians that I interviewed agreed that the government would not have sold a 17 per cent shareholding in BP in 1977 if the IMF had not imposed strict conditions on its loan to Britain in 1976 (also see Gardner, 1987, p. 91). So it is important to understand why the IMF became involved, why the IMF focused on the Public Sector Borrowing Requirement (PSBR) and, critically, why an asset sale was accepted as negative spending. The details of the 1976 IMF crisis in Britain have been well documented elsewhere (Burk and Cairncross, 1992; Stiles, 1991; de Vries, 1985; Barnett, 1982; Benn, 1989 and 1990; Castle, 1989; Dell, 1991; Healey, 1989; Pliatsky, 1984; Donoughue, 1987). I draw on first-hand interviews only to supplement these analyses.

Britain was forced to go to the IMF after experiencing large and successive balance of payments deficits and failing to repay a six-month loan to the Bank for International Settlements (BIS, the central bank of Central Banks). Both the BIS and the IMF were heavily influenced by their largest donors, the United States and Germany, who felt that Britain's economic problems were deeper than a temporary insufficient cash flow. They therefore wanted the 'excesses and lack of scruples' corrected and structured the IMF agreements to achieve that end (Middlemas, 1991, pp. 151–4; and Stiles, 1991, pp. 140–1). While it is generally accepted that Britain had no alternative to the IMF loan, many, including Prime Minister James Callaghan, initially thought that the government could persuade the IMF through its leading members to lessen the severity of the conditions imposed. Callaghan was initially bolstered by gestures of support from Germany and the United States, but ultimately both gave their full backing to the strict IMF plan (Burk and Cairncross, 1992; Middlemas, 1991, p. 154; *Economist*, 4 December 1976).

The United States and the other industrialised countries had a self-interest in their concern for Britain's policies. There was a high degree of interdependence linking the welfare of Britain with the other industrialised countries. These links were embodied in institutions such as the North Atlantic Treaty Organisation (NATO) and the European Community (EC). The international role of sterling meant that a currency collapse would cause great financial instability which in turn could have been harmful to all the industrialised (and British Commonwealth) economies (Stiles, 1991, pp. 143–4). The importance to the international community of improving Britain's creditworthiness is therefore understandable, as is the pressure coming from those countries and organisations most able to influence Britain.

What is not as obvious, however, is why the level of the PSBR was seen as a crucial target in financial markets and the IMF boardroom when the actual problem was the balance of payments. The way that the PSBR dominated all other targets in discussions is illustrated by the letter of intent from Chancellor Denis Healey to the IMF, in which he refers to the PSBR in 11 out of 25 paragraphs. The next most discussed economic factor, mentioned in seven paragraphs, was public spending, a target closely related to the PSBR (Burk and Cairncross, 1992, p. 229). Moreover, civil servants in the Treasury asserted that the PSBR was not a dominant policy variable until the IMF intervened in 1976.

Why then did the IMF demand attention to the PSBR target? In part the answer lies in the practicalities of Britain's situation, and in part in the IMF's monetarist approach. The common financial market and international political view of Britain's economic problems was that they were the result of inflation and continued deficit spending. According to OECD statistics, Britain's public spending was growing faster than in any other European country, and the rate of inflation was the highest in Europe, except for Italy. Britain's creditors became reluctant to lend in sterling for fear that the value of their loans would depreciate due to inflation. The excessive spending of the British government was obvious to the IMF team in 1976. The accounts of the crisis convey direct approaches and solutions; no one mentioned formal theory or doctrinaire solutions (de Vries, 1985; Healey, 1989, p. 412; Callaghan, 1987, pp. 419, 436; Barnett, 1982, pp. 97–111; Dell, 1991, pp. 248–72; Donoughue, 1985, p. 66). Thus, the focus on the size of the PSBR can be justified as a visible indicator of the government's economic problems.

One problem with the interpretation that the IMF was seeing the PSBR as the cause of Britain's problems is that it does not explain why the IMF allowed countries to adopt 'easy' measures to decrease the PSBR. Jacques Polak (1991) of the IMF defines easy measures as those that are not durable or have widely varying effects on the growth of the economy and the fiscal situation in the medium term (p. 39). In addition to the sale of BP shares to offset spending, there are three other examples of the British government's choosing easy measures. First, the government altered the financing of the nationalised industries, for example by raising British Gas's prices and reducing the company's capital expenditure by £100 million. Second, the capital expenditure for BNOC was excluded from the public expenditure totals because they were a 'special case' according to the Secretary of State (Pliatsky, 1984,

p. 146). Third, the Treasury made three major changes in the definition of public expenditure in 1977 which reduced the ratio of public expenditure to Gross Domestic Product (GDP) in 1975–6 from 60 per cent to 46 per cent (Browning, 1986, pp. 232–3).

The IMF officials' emphasis on the PSBR target may be better explained by their belief in monetarism which emphasises the end target rather than the process of achieving the target. The IMF and most of the international financial community turned to monetary policy when the United States abandoned the gold standard in 1971 which caused the global system of fixed exchange rates to deteriorate, giving governments greater discretion over other country's monetary policy. Because monetary policy works primarily through exchange rates and current accounts, it tends to become the more powerful instrument for demand management in a free float system (Crafts and Woodward, 1991, p. 14; Burda and Wyplosz, 1993, pp. 219, 223–4; Burk and Cairncross, 1992, p. 143).

The IMF was particularly receptive to the use of monetary policy because it had found that in many countries monetary data had proved the most accurate and most readily available of all economic data (Polak, 1991, p. 34). The evidence from other cases of IMF intervention suggests that the IMF did indeed emphasise the visible PSBR indicator in general. In a survey of 105 IMF programmes from 1969 to 1978, nearly four-fifths included specific clauses in the agreements to limit the national government's borrowing, mostly by limiting their use of bank credit. Even the countries without specific clauses made policy statements citing their intentions, all of which included deficit levels and deficit financing targets, though few incorporated specific targets for the government's budget deficit or borrowing requirement (Beveridge and Kelly, 1980, pp. 220–1). The IMF has consistently focused on borrowing as a means of control across countries since 1969. In addition, in previous cases of IMF intervention in Britain (1967 and 1969), controlling public spending was emphasised (Strange, 1976, pp. 166–72).

Because monetary policy was accepted in the markets, there was an aspect of a self-fulfilling prophecy in reaching an agreement with the IMF using monetary targets. If world financial markets believed that the British economy was stronger by achieving certain targets, creditors would be more willing to lend to the government and the immediate balance of payments crisis would be solved. The IMF itself acknowledges the impact of its 'seal of approval' (Polak, 1991, p. 22). This is in fact what happened in Britain's case: once the IMF loan and conditions were put in place, there was a quick restoration of the pound's value. The ease with which Britain attracted foreign exchange in 1977 indicates that much of the original problem was one of perception (Stiles, 1991, p. 142; de Vries, 1985, pp. 463, 476).

It was IMF policy to let governments decide how specific targets should be met (Beveridge and Kelly, 1980, p. 205; Polak, 1991, p. 39; Pliatsky, 1984, p. 148). When the Cabinet decided to sell a portion of its BP shares, the Treasury elected to treat the sale receipts not as revenue, but as negative public expenditure. (For further description of the Cabinet's deliberations, see Chapter 3.) Treasury ministers confirmed that the IMF did not query this accounting practice. One Treasury civil servant pointed out that the IMF officials 'were the ones so concerned about the targets that they didn't have much room to argue'. The IMF has since changed its practice of non-interference in the detail, Jacques Polak (1991) explains, because governments tend to choose easy remedies, the outcomes can be 'ineffective and indeed counterproductive' (p. 39). As the IMF became more supportive of privatisation, it narrowed the range of acceptable accounting practices. Sale proceeds are now required to be considered as loan repayments, whereas previously asset sales could also be used to offset spending (IMF, 1977 and 1986; Mansoor, 1987, p. 2).

Taken in isolation, the 1977 sale of BP shares is neither complicated nor necessarily even very interesting. However, because the sale was successful in enabling the British government to meet its IMF agreed targets, it set an important precedent. The success was reinforced by the IMF as it became an advocate of privatisation. Although the privatisation concept was little used before 1983, a systematic survey of the *Financial Times* and the *Economist* from 1984 to 1990 reveals privatisation was a condition for an IMF loan in at least 15 countries. While Britain did not have to return to the IMF for loans in the 1980s, credibility in the world economy remained important. Thus, the acceptability of privatisation proceeds by the IMF made it an attractive option in the future.

Why the 1976 crisis was the first to lead to privatisation needs further examination. Britain experienced repeated sterling crises after the Second World War (1947, 1949, 1951, 1955, 1957, 1964, 1965, 1966, 1967, 1975 and 1976), most stemming from balance of payments deficits, and yet the only sterling crisis that produced an asset sale was in 1976. Why did the 1976 crisis result in an asset sale when the others did not? Britain had owned BP since 1914, and it could have sold shares on any of the previous occasions. In fact, the government had an offer to sell AIOC during the period 1953–7 (see Chapter 2), which coincided with the sterling crises of 1955 and 1957, and yet government ministers at that time decided not to sell any BP shares. Britain's financial position can therefore explain why an asset sale in general became an attractive policy option but cannot explain why ministers selected the option at one opportunity and not another or why they chose to sell *oil* rather than other assets.

BRITAIN'S CHANGING INTERNATIONAL OIL POSITION

Though oil has been an international currency since the 1950s, if not earlier, much of the reason why oil was an attractive asset to sell in the late 1970s and 1980s is explained by the changes in the structure of the international oil industry. These developments included the rise of OPEC, the discovery and development of new sources of oil, and the transition of the industry from control by an oligopoly to a market driven industry. Oil assets have in fact been a common choice for asset sales throughout the world, including France, Argentina, Malaysia and Portugal.

The Changing Structure of the International Oil Industry

In terms of ownership, the history of the oil industry consists of three distinct eras. The first, from 1900 into the 1960s, was the era of the oligopoly of private oil companies, the majors. The 'majors', or Seven Sisters as they were also known, included Jersey (Exxon), Socony-Vacuum (Mobil), Standard of California (Chevron), Texaco, Gulf, Royal Dutch/Shell and BP. There was also an eighth sister, the French national oil company, CFP. The second, during the 1960s and 1970s, was the era of the oligopoly of Middle East oil producing countries, via OPEC. Though brief, this second era was significant as the impetus for the transition from the first to the third era. And the third, the late 1970s to the present, is the era of the free market. To provide the necessary background, I review each period briefly before considering the implications for the British government's ownership of oil assets.

Following the break up of the Standard Oil trust in 1911, the resulting American companies, along with BP and Shell, sought to control the oil industry through formal agreements signed in 1928 and 1934 (Vernon, 1983, pp. 20–1; Yergin, 1991, pp. 204, 264; McBeth, 1985, pp. 76–7, 106–7). While the smaller oil companies looked upon the agreements as a conspiracy, the United States and British governments supported the arrangements (Yergin, 1991, p. 266; McBeth, 1985, pp. 76–7, 106–11). The dominance of the major international oil companies held through the 1950s and 1960s. In 1950 the majors owned 98.2 per cent of world crude oil production outside the United States and the communist countries.

Control of the industry by a few large companies ensured sufficient supply was produced and was distributed evenly during crises. This was especially important during the two World Wars (Lesser, 1989, pp. 43, 78–91; McBeth, 1985, p. 25; Eden, 1962, pp. 287–97; Yergin, 1991, pp. 319–23, 362–95; Turner, 1978, p. 39). International oil sharing measures were necessary to ensure supplies to Britain and all the members of the wartime alliances. The two largest companies, Standard Oil and Shell, however, were the mainstay of the system, and vast United States sources made it possible (Yergin, 1991, pp. 177–8; Ferrier, 1982, pp. 235–7).

The oil industry grew significantly after 1945 with the economic growth of the western economies and new oil discoveries in the Middle East. There was thus room to accommodate competition from the 300 private companies and 50 state-owned companies who either entered the international market or expanded their participation in it from 1953 to 1972 (Jacoby, 1974, p. 120; Stourharas, 1985, pp. 11–15; Levy, 1982, pp. 116–19). The sheer size of the industry can be seen from the investment required in the post-Second World War period. From 1955 to 1970, the industry spent $100 billion in exploration and development of oil, and a further $115 billion to produce and distribute it (Tugendhat and Hamilton, 1975, p. 301). The competition, including increased production from the Soviet Union, contributed to falling oil prices through the 1960s. But it also cut into the majors' control of world crude oil production which, by 1982, had fallen to less than 30 per cent of world crude production compared to 69 per cent in 1970 and 98 per cent in 1950 (Stevens, 1985, pp. 30–6; Levy, 1982, p. 117; Yergin, 1991, p. 515).

As a result of these factors, the majors' profits also began to fall, so that in the 1960s they were forced to renegotiate their tax rate with their Middle East host governments, marking the transition from the first to the second era. Resenting the cut in oil tax revenues, the Middle East countries reacted by organising politically in the form of OPEC to demand a larger share of the lucrative oil industry (Stevens, 1985, p. 30; Tugendhat and Hamilton, 1975, pp. 158–9; Bending and Eden, 1984, p. 14). OPEC's influence was at its peak during the 1973–4 oil embargo. The impact was greater than in previous crises because the United States was no longer able to serve as the provider of last resort by compensating for cutbacks by increasing its own production. And without domination by the majors, coordination of supplies was more difficult (Tetreault, 1985, p. 34; Turner, 1984, p. 206; Yergin, 1991, pp. 436, 504–8, 584–5; J. Robinson, 1988, pp. 102–11; Levy, 1982, p. 129; Maull, 1977, pp. 266–8).

BP suffered greatly because its business had been heavily dependent on its crude oil production in the Middle East. With this taken away by nationalisations and renegotiations, BP's other operations could not compensate for these losses (Shell Briefing Service, 1981, p. 8). Shell, on the other hand, had a greater downstream operation, and was not as badly affected by OPEC's assertion of control over oil production in the Middle East. As Group Treasurer Howard McDonald explained: 'We always could sell oil better than we could find it, so in a sense the OPEC changes were a good watershed for us' (R. Grant, 1991, pp. 104, 67–8). Nonetheless, all companies were forced to become more international and more diversified. The majors did so fearing that otherwise their oil cartel would shrink. Not only did the majors expand their oil operations downstream, acquiring marketing networks in Europe and elsewhere, they also enlarged their tanker fleets, built refineries in Europe and expanded into the field of petrochemicals (BP, 1970, p. 388).

The rise of OPEC set in motion the forces leading to the third era – that of the free market. In the wake of the 1973–4 oil crisis and increasing oil prices, sources of oil other than those in the Middle East which existed in more difficult places for exploration and production became not only desirable, but for the first time economically feasible. New sources were developed throughout the world, but the two largest finds were in Alaska and the North Sea. Thus, OPEC paved the way for its own demise, the price increases caused initially by the 1973–4 crisis led to significant changes in the industry, the diversification of sources of oil and the ever increasing number of companies made it virtually impossible for oligopoly control. Though OPEC remained a dominant player, by 1980, for the first time, the oil industry became market driven (Stourharas, 1985, p. 51). As a result of the majors' diversification away from oil and the growth in the number of players in the oil industry, there was no one who could control price or supply swings. At the same time, the international oil network as a free market became even more responsive to increased demand in the form of higher prices, thus marking the transition to the third era. The key element being, in a free market, that for a price oil can be supplied quickly anywhere in the world.

Consequences for the British Government's Oil Strategy

There were three major consequences for the British government's policy options resulting from the change in oil industry structure. The first implication was that Britain's oil security considerations changed from those of an importer to those of a producer. As a producer in an increasingly unstable oil market, the British government like many other governments created a national oil company. Thus, the British government's creation of

BNOC in 1976 can be seen as a response to this changing international situation. In addition to BNOC, the government could use access to the North Sea as a means of leverage to gain greater cooperation from the private oil companies. Department of Energy civil servants argued that the power of the British government in awarding exploration licences to operate in the North Sea was the reason that Britain suffered less than other European countries during the 1973–4 oil crisis (also see Stobaugh, 1975, pp. 192–3, 199).

Britain's economic security considerations also changed as Britain gained an enormous competitive advantage over most of its economic competitors who did not have domestic oil production and had to pay for oil imports. From 1980 to 1985, most advanced industrial economies decreased their total oil consumption and yet the cost of their oil imports increased. For example, France's cost for oil imports rose 23 per cent from £10.7 billion to £12.5 billion, while Germany's rose 32 per cent from £12.5 billion to £16.5 billion, and Japan's rose 36 per cent from £23.5 billion to £32 billion. In contrast, Britain went from paying £160 million in 1980 for oil imports to earning £7.7 billion as a net exporter in 1985 (IEA, 1992a and 1992b).

The second implication of the changing oil structure was a reduction in the value of ownership of BP in terms of national security. While the nature of a free market ensured that oil would be delivered for a price, it also precluded an international company from favouring one country over another for nationalistic reasons – the stakes were too high to risk retaliation. Therefore, while the government's ability to demand cooperation from the private oil companies operating in the North Sea increased, its means to control BP in general decreased. As a successful international company, BP had repeatedly shown that it would not function as a national oil company. As mentioned in Chapter 2, BP refused the Prime Minister, Edward Heath's, request to favour Britain during the 1973 oil crisis. This independence was further reinforced a few years later when newspaper reporters revealed that BP and Shell had subverted the government's sanctions against Rhodesia from their inception in December 1965 to the early 1970s. Though technically illegal, and politically infuriating, all the government could do was establish the Bingham Inquiry in April 1977 and publicise the actions. Because the government was also implicated, this publicity was, in the end, not encouraged by the government (M. Bailey, 1979, pp. 248–52). Thus, the national service BP would provide declined both in actual terms and in terms of political perception.

The third implication stems from the force that OPEC continued to exert. Although OPEC's domination of the oil market was broken by the end of the 1970s, the organisation's members still controlled a third of world production in 1980 and the majority of the world's oil reserves (Levy, 1982, p. 117; Turner, 1984; *Economist*, 12 June 1982, 25 December 1982 and 15 October 1983; *Financial Times*, 15 February 1988). OPEC's emergence as an international power had many implications, including drawing attention to the British government's own involvement in the oil industry. As a DEn civil servant and BNOC executives pointed out, this was domestically embarrassing because, as an oil producer, the government benefited from oil revenues which rose with the price of oil, but as an industrial country, Britain's many consumers suffered from high oil prices. Through BNOC, the government soon found it had the ability to influence prices, but as DEn civil servants explained the dilemma, as an oil consumer, Britain did not want to be seen as a price leader.

OPEC was at odds with Britain, especially as the price of oil began to fall in the mid-1980s. Continued British production and reduced prices, at least in appearance, undermined OPEC's effort to cut supply and raise prices, and drew hostile OPEC attention to the government's contradictory aims, regarding oil price and control and the free market. One BNOC executive recalled the political embarrassment caused when BNOC began to reduce its prices:

> The Saudis and the Nigerians were anxious and the government tried to stay out, but the Chancellor and Secretary of State had a few conversations with their counterparts.

According to Nigel Lawson (1992), Secretary of State for Energy from 1981 to 1983, OPEC officials were in constant contact with the government and applied pressure to get Britain to cooperate with them. In one extraordinary meeting, Ahmed Zaki Yamani, the Saudi Arabian oil minister, asked Lawson if Britain would like to join OPEC; Lawson declined. Yamani then got to the primary purpose of his visit and asked Lawson to cut Britain's oil production in order to keep OPEC oil prices from slipping further. Lawson explained that the government had no influence over the rate of production or prices, and claimed that it left the free market to decide (p. 193). In reality, as DEn civil servants revealed, BNOC was actively setting the price for contracts on half of North Sea oil production at the time (also see *Economist*, 2 April 1983).

The tension between OPEC and Britain continued. OPEC questioned the British government's denials of involvement in oil pricing, and threatened a price war. Because Middle East oil was (and still is) much cheaper to produce than offshore North Sea oil, OPEC producers could make profits at much lower prices than North Sea producers. Britain therefore could not win a price war (*Economist*, 6 March 1982, 19 February 1983, 14 July 1984, 19 January 1985 and 14 December 1985). The British government's difficult position was only finally resolved with the sale of Britoil and the abolition of BNOC. OPEC's pressure, however, was not a primary cause of the government's sales; it was one of several contributory factors.

Thus, the changing nature of the international oil industry had many implications for Britain: oil supplies could no longer be taken for granted, oil in the North Sea became financially feasible, and BP revealed its allegiance to the international marketplace was greater than to its home government. These factors forced Britain to re-evaluate its energy policy, but also changed the resources and the constraints policy makers faced in a macroeconomic sense in terms of value of the pound and balance of trade, and in terms of its specific energy policies – of regulating the North Sea and ensuring secure supplies of oil.

THE INFLUENCE OF INTERNATIONAL ORGANISATIONS

One of the main arguments by Keohane and Nye is that there are other international actors besides the state, and that international organisations specifically impact policy change (Keohane and Nye, 1989, pp. 54–8). Other scholars from the neoliberal institutionalism and neofunctionalism schools contend that international institutions and supranational organisations play a significant role in affecting the international environment in which policy makers choose options (Keohane, 1989, p. 3; Cornett and Caporaso, 1992, p. 238; Haas, 1964; Harrison, 1990). Such arguments make the European Community (EC) and the International Energy Agency (IEA) as large international organisations with specific energy interests difficult to ignore in this case. This section is therefore devoted to investigating their role. Surprisingly, I find that while economic interdependence in general between countries proved to be an influential factor, the EC and the IEA regulations were not.

Uncoordinated EC Energy Policy

The EC was founded on three distinct entities:

- The European Coal and Steel Community (ECSC) set up by the Treaty of Paris in 1951;

- The European Economic Community (EEC) created by the Treaty of Rome in 1957; and
- The European Atomic Energy Community (Euratom) initiated by a second Treaty of Rome in 1957.

The concern for energy within the EC has been evident from the beginning. The ECSC focused on making the price of coal more competitive (Prodi and Clo, 1975, p. 105; Collins, 1985, p. 14), while Euratom focused on the development of nuclear power (El-Agraa and Hu, 1985, p. 253).

Oil policy cooperation, however, consisted of only a few directives, and little action was ever actually taken. The first specific measure was a proposal by the EC Commission to create a common stockpile of petroleum in 1964. The original proposal (Directive 68/414/EEC) adopted in 1968 was to cover a 65-day period, which was extended to 90 days in 1972 (Directive 72/425/EEC). But the directive only took effect in January 1975, too late for the oil crisis of 1973–4 (Black, 1977, pp. 181–3). Britain did not join the EC until 1973, and was therefore only peripherally affected by these early developments.

Even the 1973–4 oil crisis did not mobilise more than minimal EC cooperation. The major obstacles to cooperation were the large discrepancies between members in terms of domestic resources and vulnerabilities. On the one hand, Germany and the Netherlands advocated coordinated responses, while on the other, Britain and France argued against any intervention. The EC countries were therefore left to scramble for oil supplies in competition with each other (Smith, 1988, p. 20). At the Energy Committee meeting prior to the November 1975 Energy Council, Henri Simonet, the Commissioner responsible for energy, castigated the nine members of the EC for their half-hearted efforts to adjust their national postures to facilitate a Community energy policy (Black, 1977, pp. 183–4).

Though the member states recognised in a June 1983 Commission Report that existing policies were insufficient, cooperation did not improve (El-Agraa and Hu, 1985, p. 258). Over the period 1973–85, the move towards a common EC energy strategy was hampered by the differences among member states in resources and energy priorities and by the reluctance of some member states to delegate part of their sovereignty to the Community (Bourgeois, 1988, p. 71; Lantzke, 1975, p. 217; Keohane, 1982, pp. 221, 225–6, 233; Ikenberry, 1988, pp. 81, 88, 90–4; *Petroleum Economist*, May 1982, p. 196). These differences prevented the EC from agreeing on internal energy questions or even presenting a united front in the International Energy Agency negotiations (El-Agraa and Hu, 1985, pp. 255–6; Prodi and Clo, 1975, pp. 107–8).

Britain was particularly obstructive of any coordinated action which meant sharing its oil, to the great frustration of other member states. The British government refused to sell North Sea oil to EC member countries at concessionary rates in normal times, and even refused to show a willingness to agree to policies concerning the size and stocking of reserves, or measures to ensure supplies to other EC countries (Deese and Miller, 1981, p. 200; El-Agraa and Hu, 1985, p. 255; R. Bailey, 1978, p. 331). Summing up the feelings of many of the member countries, a German official stated in 1979: 'Sooner or later Britain has to decide whether it is on the side of the Nine [EC member countries] or OPEC' (*Times*, 5 December 1979). Ironically, the demands by the Europeans made the British government realise the need to control the North Sea. According to a BNOC executive and a DEn civil servant, BNOC also provided a focal point for the EC and provided evidence that Britain could direct supply and prices despite the government's claims that they did not have the power to effect oil prices.

More progress was made on energy policy in the 1980s by combining energy issues with other objectives such as foreign policy, environment, technological advancement and regional development. By 1983, EC aid (subsidies and loans) represented 7.9 per cent of the gross investment in energy in Europe. The aid was distributed according to priorities determined by the EC's regional policy – not energy policy. This trend continued in October 1986 with the creation of the VALOREN programme, whose goals included making regions less sensitive to disturbances in the traditional energy markets, such as oil. Because Britain had more opportunities for large-scale projects and was better able to present them to the Commission than countries less well-off in energy terms, Britain received an exceptionally large amount of funds. This was particularly unusual given Britain's low priority status for regional assistance (Bourgeois, 1988, pp. 66–8, 85, footnote 1). At the same time, Britain did not have to share the security and economic benefits of oil ownership. Had EC policy been better coordinated, funds for energy development might have been tied to greater security cooperation. Even these measures would not have been sufficient to affect the government's oil ownership decisions, either to halt the creation of BNOC or spur its demise. In addition, as one DEn civil servant pointed out, once created, there were too many other state-owned companies within the member states for EC policy to apply pressure for its sale.

Although the institutions designed specifically to address energy policy were ineffective, EC countries gained important advantages through other broad measures. First, the general EC non-discrimination legislation meant that companies registered in EC member states could bypass the DEn's requirement that all oil must be landed in Britain before being exported, and had to be treated without discrimination on licences awards. Though, as DEn civil servants pointed out, the landing requirement was more theoretical because any request for a waiver was approved. Second, EC commitments meant that communication between foreign and economic ministers was frequent which proved to be very constructive during crises by minimising uncertainty and aiding cooperation (Prodi and Clo, 1975, pp. 106–7). While not directly affecting UK decisions to sell its oil assets, these factors may have helped to improve the oil market which in turn reduced the number and severity of oil crises.

The European Community and Economic Interdependence

Although Britain did not enter the EC until 1973, it steadily became more dependent on EC member states from the 1960s on so that by the 1980s approximately 60 per cent of legislation made in Britain at the national level involved European Community issues (Taylor, 1993, p. 93). The trend is also quantifiable in the trade statistics; Table 4.1 shows that both exports and imports have become more heavily concentrated on Britain's EC partners. In addition, Britain's trade with the US and Japan has declined markedly so that by 1988 only 11 per cent of British imports came from the United States and 6.1 per cent from Japan, while 12.9 per cent of British exports went to the United States and 2.2 per cent to Japan (Hitiris, 1988, p. 208; also see Winters, 1989, pp. 125–6).

The evidence from this case supports the contention made by Paul Taylor (1993) that the British government formulated its energy policies with consideration for its EC partners, but not because of specific legislation (pp. 94, 106). In other words, the forces of economic interdependence that provided the impetus for the EC have also led to the adoption of many

Table 4.1   British Exports to and Imports from EC Member Countries
(Per cent of Total UK Trade)

	1957	1974	1981	1986	1988
Exports to EC	14.6%	33.4%	41.2%	47.9%	62%
Imports from EC	12.1%	30.0%	39.4%	50.4%	64%

Source: El-Agraa, 1990, pp. 61–2.

common policies across Europe. This explains why, as Alan Walters (Mrs Thatcher's economic adviser from 1981 to 1983) has pointed out, all European countries reduced their adjusted borrowing and experienced fiscal contractions in recessionary conditions on a scale similar to Britain's (Walters, 1986, pp. 96–7). In addition, across Europe (France and Germany) and the industrialised world (Canada to New Zealand), there was interest in asset sales. According to a survey of privatisation as reported in the *Financial Times* and the *Economist* from 1983 to 1992, very few countries sold assets in the early 1980s most waited until the late 1980s or did not sell at all. Thus, since the EC remained constant throughout this time, change in other common economic factors must better account for the change in privatisation policy.

There is no evidence that EC laws restricted the British government's decision to sell its oil assets, yet the broader interdependent ties may have influenced the thinking of some civil servants and politicians in Britain. For example, during the 1973–4 oil crisis, Prime Minister Heath did not pass a law to require BP to favour Britain with oil supplies for, among other reasons, fear of antagonising Britain's EC partners. Similarly, a DEn civil servant explained that Britain's official position on oil prices was for lower prices because Britain could not overtly side with OPEC when higher prices would hurt its new European partners.

EC company legislation, however, had a peripheral effect on BNOC's evolution. The first time EC regulations were a factor was in 1976 when BNOC and the participation agreements were being created. There were concerns raised in parliamentary debates that BNOC's objective of supplying Britain in a crisis was inconsistent with international obligations, specifically free trade in the EC (*Hansard Parliamentary Debates (Lords)*, 9 November 1976 and 18 November 1975). Although the issue was raised by the Conservatives who opposed the creation of BNOC, it was not a major point of contention nor sufficient to delay the creation of the national oil company. BNOC was not in absolute control because there were other companies operating in the North Sea, there was oil from the Middle East and elsewhere, and the arrangements were only voluntary commercial agreements. Technically, BNOC could not be challenged but, as one DEn official observed, the government was always afraid it would be.

The EC's classification of public companies and takeover laws also affected the form British privatisation took. The government avoided retaining more than 50 per cent in companies in part because they would be classified as public companies in the EC, making the British government liable for debts of the enterprise (Gardner, 1987, p. 20). EC takeover laws affected the government's decisions with what they omitted. While member states could not forbid a takeover offer launched by an EC investor, there was no such rule prohibiting intervention in bids by non-EC corporate bodies (CBI, 1989, p. 43). This was a useful outlet in 1987 when ministers referred the case of Kuwait Investment Office's purchase of 21 per cent of BP shares to the Monopolies and Mergers Commission (MMC). Since Kuwait was not a member of the EC, it was not discriminatory for the MMC to rule against KIO and force it to reduce its shareholding in BP to below 10 per cent (*Financial Times*, 4 January 1989 and 24 October 1988). The effect of company legislation was limited, however, because there was little that was more restrictive than pre-existing British law. In fact, much of EC company law was based on British practice. EC legislation on takeovers, for example, was similar to Britain's City Code on Take-overs and Mergers (CBI, 1989, p. 42).

The International Energy Agency

In the wake of the 1973–4 oil crisis, Britain as an oil consumer was active in the creation of a new type of organisation, free from EC control. The IEA was formed by 16 industrialised countries including the United States, Japan and most EC countries, but not France who disagreed with the organisation's approach (Deese and Miller, 1981, p. 200). In addition to keeping records and providing a means for communication between countries, the main feature of the IEA was the oil sharing mechanism, called the Emergency Management System (EMS). Through the EMS all members were committed to reduce oil demand and to share available oil in the event of any significant disruption in the world oil supply, defined as a 7 per cent loss of normal supply by one or more member countries. The IEA also required every member country to maintain reserves enabling it to sustain consumption for 90 days without oil imports (Jones, 1988, pp. 232–8; IEA, 1983, p. 16; Smith, 1988, pp. 28–31). Britain had the advantage of the North Sea, which had enormous reserves. Stockpiles maintained onshore were costly, and most countries passed this responsibility and cost on to the oil companies. As a result the stocks were usually industry working stocks, such as oil waiting to be refined, and therefore not truly surplus (Krapels and Emerson, 1987, pp. 31–2; Blair, 1985, p. 117; *Petroleum Economist*, October 1982).

After North Sea oil came on line (in 1975) Britain was pressured to share its oil resources with fellow members, which in turn made the British government more possessive. This pressure by the IEA is illustrated by the way it calculated its statistics. The international organisation treated any energy resource within western Europe as indigenous to every country in the region. Thus, oil and gas produced by Britain and Norway were assumed to remain in western Europe and to be immediately available to all western European consumers, without entering into international trade – which was far from the actual case (Smart, 1985, p. 150). As a DEn civil servant explained, the government feared that their present comparative strength in oil supplies would commit them in advance to put substantial North Sea oil supplies at the disposal of other IEA countries.

BP and Shell were also very active participants in the development of the IEA mechanism. As both BP executives and DEn civil servants recognised, for the oil companies, an equitable distribution of oil, such as during the 1973–4 crisis, was in their best interests. The decline of the majors' control over oil supplies meant that they were no longer able to enforce such a system on their own. The IEA formal mechanism enabled the large number of companies entering the international industry to coordinate oil distribution where they might not have been able to otherwise. According to the IEA over 200 national and international companies and 21 countries participated in the 1978 Second Oil Allocation Systems Test. Real cooperation, however, was limited by US anti-trust legislation which prevented American companies from divulging information on oil pricing (Blair, 1985, pp. 116–17; IEA, 1983, p. 25). Given this fact, one British civil servant explained that the IEA had nothing better to do than prepare and practice, but that the efforts were only 'paper exercises'. The IEA's oil sharing mechanism has never been tested. Even during the 1979 oil crisis and Sweden's 17 per cent shortfall the formal sharing arrangements were never enacted. Because some members (such as Britain) would have refused to cooperate if the formal mechanisms had been enacted, the Agency instead resorted to attempts at informal coordination, consultation and advice (Blair, 1985, pp. 112–13; Smith, 1988, pp. 35–8, 68–84; Keohane, 1984a, pp. 229–36).

The 1979 crisis was alleviated and the drastic price rises avoided due to the willingness of Saudi Arabia to increase production, the high level of oil stocks and weakness in demand, and through IEA information-sharing and strong (but general) statements (Keohane, 1985, pp. 236–7). Within the DEn the IEA received no credit for smoothing the chaotic international oil turbulence, and a few civil servants even made jokes about the organisation. Only one civil servant suggested that the IEA mechanisms actually alleviated the need for BNOC, though several DEn civil servants recognised that some of their powers were being delegated to the IEA, such as the collection of statistics which occurred in the mid-1980s.

Britain's resistance to oil-sharing measures can be understood when the specific costs of sharing are recognised. Rodney Smith (1988) has calculated that per capita net losses from oil sharing for Britain in the early 1980s would have been \$4.02 with a 7 per cent supply disruption and \$5.56 with a 15 per cent supply disruption, while net gains would have accrued to Belgium, Denmark, Germany, Luxembourg, Sweden and Switzerland. Only Japan and the United States would have remained relatively unaffected (pp. 52–3). Despite minimal action by the IEA, the fact that it exists and that Britain is an active member illustrates that the member countries involved acknowledge their interdependence and the broader costs of not cooperating. As one DEn civil servant explained, Britain could see that even as an oil producer, not agreeing to share would hurt the world economy which would then hurt Britain.

Though academics have effectively made the case that international organisations are important players in the international arena, they have not been able to develop a model predicting how and when they are influential. Keohane and Nye (1979) admit the weakness of their international organisation model: 'it is more complicated ... it does not predict how international regimes will change ... it is much less deterministic ... [its variables] are also more temporary and reversible and its predictions could be rendered invalid by the actions of governments' (pp. 57–8). Finally, they admit that their two structural models dominate the international organisation model, and that above a certain level of conflict, the international organisation model becomes largely irrelevant (p. 58). The findings of this case study reinforce Keohane and Nye's conclusion. Though, interestingly, the more useful expenditure of effort is on the structural models, as information they require overlaps with the most critical aspects of the role of international organisations. This does not invalidate the claim that international organisations are players, but rather argues in terms of methodology, the more useful focus of analysis is on structures and issues rather than one player.

CONCLUSION

Although the structural model can explain why Britain was more susceptible to international pressures on financial issues and oil issues from 1975 to 1985, as Keohane and Nye warned, these types of models cannot explain the specifics, such as the 1976 IMF crisis, or change, such as the shift from an oil oligopoly to a free market for oil. The structural model does, however, highlight the fact that states work within constraints beyond their immediate control, and that a country's position in the international system sets the parameters for the policy options available to politicians. This proved to be true for Britain in the case of its oil assets, where the international financial situation and the structure of the international oil industry narrowed the range of what was possible, though only its financial position in 1977 had a direct impact. Though membership in international organisations was not specifically an influence, economic interdependence was, through a self-interest in the welfare of its trading partners. By focusing on an issue, the role of international organisations is already included; studying organisations separately is less revealing. As Susan Strange (1985) has argued: the study of regimes or international organisations is 'obfuscating and confusing instead of clarifying and illuminating, and distorting by concealing bias instead of revealing and removing it' (p. 337).

The effect of international factors on the British government's decision to sell its oil assets can be illustrated with a Venn diagram, in which the

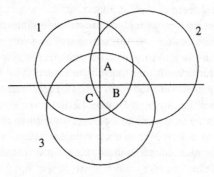

Figure 4.4   International Policy Parameters, 1974

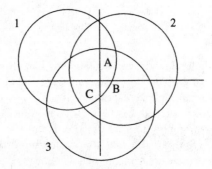

Figure 4.5   International Policy Parameters, 1977

intersection of circles represents the overlap of international parameters which sets the range of policy options (see Figures 4.4 and 4.5). The three international level variables examined in this case are represented by circle 1 for the policy options possible with the international financial position of Britain, circle 2 for policy options possible with Britain's position in the international oil industry, and circle 3 for the policy options consistent with Britain's membership in international organisations. In both figures, point A represents the policy to increase taxes, point B represents the policy to increase the budget deficit and point C represents the policy to sell oil assets. In 1974, just after the 1973 oil crisis, selling oil assets was not possible (as illustrated in Figure 4.4 by the exclusion of point C from circle 2). In 1977 the oil situation had changed so that a sale was possible as ownership was less effective in the free market (point C now included in circle 2 of Figure 4.5). As a result of severe balance of payments deficits and IMF intervention, however, Britain's international financial position had changed so that a budget increase was no longer possible (point B excluded from circle 1 in Figure 4.5).

Though the international level played an important role, it alone did not determine the government's options, contrary to many realists' claims. It is, therefore, necessary to look at other sets of intervening variables. The full force of international pressure has not been fully recognised as the intervening variables were also influenced by international factors. There are therefore both the direct and indirect effects of the international level. In the next chapters I examine sets of intervening variables and how these sets of parameters affected Britain's politicians' decision to sell the state's oil assets with brief attention to the impact of the international dimension on these variables.

5 Structure, Motivations and the Managers of the State-Owned Oil Companies

While recognised by scholars (and practitioners) as a factor in privatisation (Vickers and Yarrow, 1988, pp. 18–19), the role of public sector managers has not been fully understood. There has been little work on why many managers are opposed to privatisation and why some are not, nor has there been much consideration as to why some managers are more successful in achieving their preferences. One of the reasons the role of the managers has not been satisfactorily examined is that they do not fall into standard categories of analysis. Managers of state-owned companies are not private sector employees but rather state employees subject to ministerial directives, and partly supported by central government funds; however, they are not normally included in analyses of government bureaucracies (Aharoni, 1986, p. 5; Drewry and Butcher, 1991, pp. 16–17). Conventional public choice models of individuals as economic utility maximisers are not useful in this case as they predict that the managers of Britain's state-owned oil companies would welcome privatisation, because a move to the private sector would allow greater financial freedom for their company and higher salaries for them personally. Yet many managers actually impeded privatisation, in particular, the managers of BNOC and BGC worked against the government's plans. What the conventional public choice models do not take into account are the variations in the company structures and therefore constraints that managers face, which in turn affect their preferences. This chapter uses an institutional public choice approach but focuses more on the institution than the actors because in this case the 'rules of the game' have not yet been firmly established. This chapter makes an initial effort to do so.

Initial differences between the managers' reactions can be understood from the differences between types of companies. As Yair Aharoni (1986) has pointed out, not all state-owned industries are alike (p. 396). In the British case there were three distinct types of state-owned companies: the Morrisonian public corporation, the semi-detached corporation and the virtually private company. BGC was a traditional Morrisonian corporation created to serve the public interest while being run along commercial lines, breaking even one year with another. The company's charter was (re)created by Acts of Parliament in 1948, 1965 and 1972 which ensured government control over national assets, and its directors, appointed by ministers, were, as stated by Herbert Morrison (1933): to 'regard themselves as the high custodians of the public interest' (also see Veljanovski, 1987, p. 58; Heald, 1989, p. 34; Pearson, 1981, p. 98). BNOC, created much later than the traditional Morrisonian corporations and with closer attention to fiscal control and economic efficiency, represents the second type of company. Though still created by an Act of Parliament, BNOC's domain was more narrowly defined and more tightly controlled, both by legislation and by operating in the private-sector oil industry. BP represents the third type, a virtually private-sector enterprise. As a Companies Act company, the government acted only as a large shareholder and was not involved in the day-to-day running of the business.

Thus, even at a first glance, it is apparent how these fundamental structural differences start to explain why different strategies are rational for different managers and suggest why some managers in some companies are more likely to be more effective in achieving their objectives than others. By identifying the key structural factors, it is also possible to understand why managers of state-owned industries seem to act differently from civil servants or private-sector employees. Building on Aharoni's work on variables that explain the differences within the state-owned industries group, I identify three structural factors that influence how managers react to the possibility of privatisation, and help to predict how effective their support or opposition will be. These factors are organisational autonomy, financial control and success in achieving the company's missions. The consequences of these factors are summarised in Table 5.1.

The impact of the first variable, organisational autonomy, rests on the assumption that all companies desire to be autonomous. Managers will therefore resent any governmental interference in the organisation, and will employ tactics to maintain the company's autonomy. Similarly, managers of less autonomous companies will seek to become more self-sufficient through means which include: making commercial agreements with the private sector, expanding internationally and retaining profits by spending or reinvesting them, as well as urging the government to sell the company to the private sector. Managers will react positively to privatisation as it represents another means to increase their autonomy.

Table 5.1   Company Status and Objectives

Company Status	Management's General Objectives	Management Tactics in Response to Privatisation Proposals	Likelihood of Privatisation
Organisational Autonomy			
High	Maintain autonomy	Distance itself from the government Make private sector agreements	High
Low	Increase autonomy	Expand internationally Retain profits	Depends on mission
Financial Control			
High	Maintain independence	Same as high autonomy	High
Low	Obtain financial support	Seek government investment Seek private sector investment	Low
Success in Achieving Mission			
Profit	No government intervention	Same as high autonomy	High
National Interest	Retain government mandate for national interest mission	Achieve highest standards Publicise service provided Delay government efforts Lobby against privatisation	Low

Implications for privatisation are that the more self-sufficient the company, the easier it will be logistically to transfer it to the private sector, and the more likely the management is to see privatisation as a means to increase organisational autonomy. Conversely, the less autonomous the company, the harder it will be to transfer to the public sector, and the less likely the management is to see privatisation as a viable means to increase organisational autonomy.

The effect of the second variable, financial control, is based on the assumption that managers seek to command their company financially. Therefore, managers of companies which are financially independent seek to remain that way, and will employ the same tactics as autonomous companies to do so. Managers of companies which depend on government finance may, however, resist a move to the private sector as it could mean selling off their assets, closing down the company and ultimately unemployment. In terms of privatisation, they will most likely resist by using delaying tactics and lobby government ministers in order not to lose their financial backing.

Finally, the impact of the third variable, success of mission, rests on the assumption that managers seek to fulfil, as fully as possible, the company's purpose or objectives, or in other words, the company's mission. These objectives can be defined by law, the company's articles of association and/or corporate culture. Managers of companies that have successfully fulfilled their mission will seek to keep the company on-going as a whole. Success breeds loyalty and pride.

Predictions about managers' behaviour in terms of privatisation depend on the type of mission, whether it is profit or national interest. National interest is defined here as: 'the concept of the security and well-being of the state' (Plano and Greenberg, 1989, p. 498). The management of companies with a profit motive have limited allegiance to their government owners, and may in fact resent limitations the government may place in terms of capital expansion or international growth. This will be true especially of companies who have successfully fulfilled a profit mission. Those who have not been successful may be forced to depend on the government for financial support, as the private sector may be unwilling to back an unpromising company. In contrast, the managers of a company with a national interest mission depend on government ownership for a justification of their non-profit mission, and therefore will seek ways to maintain that mandate, including highlighting the usefulness of the service they are providing and continuing to improve their role. The impact of mission is less clear for managers of companies who have been less successful in fulfilling their objectives. Depending on their financial control and organisational autonomy, they may be frustrated and therefore may be more willing to consider alternatives, including privatisation, or they may be fearful for their future, and thus resist change (see Figure 5.1).

The impact of company structure is two-directional, it impacts managers' motivations and therefore their strategies, but it also impacts what they are capable of doing – irrespective of their preferences – in two ways: ability to lobby government and the degree of difficulty in transferring the

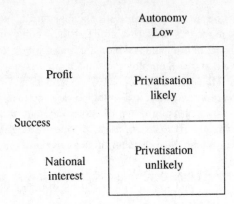

Figure 5.1   Low Organisational Autonomy versus Mission

company to the private sector. Managers in companies with high levels of financial or organisational independence have a greater ability to persuade the government to implement their preferences using financial and other resources, high level contacts and credibility. In contrast, managers of a company that is financially dependent with little success in achieving its mission will be less able to influence the government as they have fewer resources and less credibility. Though they have one advantage, frequent contact with the government, this may only serve to reinforce their negative image (see the third column in Table 5.1).

In summary, the companies where the feasibility of a sale is highest are those which are financially and organisationally independent and operate with a profit mission because the management has no significant ties to the government and sees gains from the sale (see Table 5.1). The most difficult to sell are those with a national interest mission and either low organisational autonomy or low financial control because they rely on the government to function and would suffer costs from a sale.

BRITISH PETROLEUM UNDER THREAT

By the 1970s, BP was financially independent from the government, successfully established internationally and struggling to redirect itself into more profitable areas. The company's independence was threatened in two ways: by an increase in the government's share ownership and by the need for new capital. These precipitating conditions led the management to reconsider the costs and benefits of government ownership.

Fear of Government Reasserting Control

The government's holding in BP decreased steadily over time (see Figure 5.2). In fact, from the 1950s, BP had a strategy of increasing the total capital of the company in order to dilute the government's shareholding. As BP expanded, according to annual reports, it issued new shares to pay for purchases, such as the Trinidad Petroleum Company in 1955, Apex (Trinidad) Oilfields in 1960, Kern Oil Company in 1961, an asset purchase from the Distillers Company in 1967, and a merger with Super Test Petroleum Corporation in 1971. As one BP executive recalled:

> If you look at when Morris Bridgeman was chairman, he was always keen to hit the 49 per cent spot … There were various attempts, at various times, to use shares to purchase companies with the thought that the small change might bring HMG [Her Majesty's Government]'s holding below 51 per cent. It was all part of eroding the government's shareholding.

In fact, according to annual reports, under Bridgeman in 1967 the government's shareholding dropped to 48.9 per cent due to the issue of new shares to purchase the chemical and plastics interests of the Distillers Company. Government ministers assisted in these efforts by not subscribing to two of BP's new share issues, in 1957 and 1981.

Why BP followed this strategy of reducing the government's stake is not clear. The views of senior BP executives were mixed. Some argued

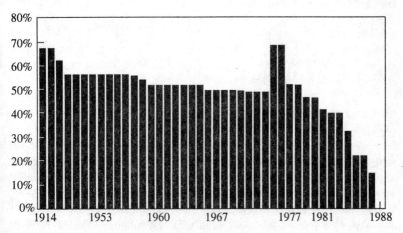

Figure 5.2   British Government's Holding in BP, 1914–88

that the 50 per cent mark was not necessarily important because it had no legal significance. The company's articles of association, not the size of the government shareholding, gave the British government the veto and put two ministerial nominees on the board of directors. Others pointed out that government ownership did make a difference to BP's operations abroad. Some countries such as Venezuela and Guatemala refused to allow foreign government-owned oil companies to operate in their territory. This impact was evident by the fact that as soon as the British government sold 5 per cent of its BP shares in 1979, bringing the total down to 46 per cent, BP became eligible to operate in Venezuela and immediately set up facilities there.

The best explanation of the management's attitude that an executive offered, however, was that an ideological or psychological barrier existed to government ownership over 50 per cent. The management valued its independence, and government ownership over 50 per cent threatened its image of itself as a sovereign company. The managers perceived that government ownership handicapped them, limiting their decisions unnecessarily. These feeling came through as late as Sir Peter Walters' speech to BP shareholders after buying back KIO's holding in BP in 1989. The emphasis was on independence – from any government (*Financial Times*, 1 February 1989).

When the government reversed this trend by purchasing Burmah Oil's holding in BP, thereby raising its holding to 68 per cent – more than two-thirds of the company's equity – BP's managers were shocked and dismayed. BP, in fact, had always disliked having Burmah as a major shareholder. One BP executive explained:

> [We] had to have a couple of Burmah chaps on the board who never contributed anything ... I'd always been wondering how we could shake Burmah off our backs who had no particular oil expertise but had this say ... [they] just got a dividend and passed it on to their own shareholders.

When Burmah ran into financial difficulty in 1974, company executives approached BP managers to determine whether BP would be prepared to take over Burmah. According to those involved, BP could not have bought back its shares from Burmah because there were laws against it at the time (these have since changed). Instead, BP was offered some of Burmah's properties. But after examining Burmah's accounts, BP executives realised that the situation was far worse than had been conveyed, so disappointedly, they were forced to decline the offer. One BP executive counselled Burmah to go 'very quickly to the Governor of the Bank of England'.

Burmah did go to the Bank of England and, as part of the rescue plan, the Bank purchased Burmah's holding in BP. Though the BP managers knew of Burmah's troubles and even recommended that they go to the Bank, they did not suspect the result would be an increase in the government's holding in BP. As one BP executive complained:

> It's one thing to have your 51% but to have a majority as big as that for the government would have made it too much of a temptation for the government to break the Bradbury letter agreement. I wasn't very keen on that. Not that I was consulted as I remember.

The chairman of BP, Eric Drake, was furious, and demanded on several occasions in writing and in person to the Prime Minister that the shares be sold. One such occasion, documented in the annual report, was on 15 July 1975 when Drake told Benn that the government's holding must be kept below 50 per cent, otherwise it would destroy BP's credibility in the US, New Zealand and elsewhere (BP operated in over 80 countries).

Exacerbating BP's fear of increased government ownership was the fact that the share increase occurred under a Labour government, which included Tony Benn as the Secretary of State for Energy, who advocated socialist measures such as nationalisation. Benn, conveyed one executive, increased BP's fears of government intervention by questioning the structure of the relationship between BP and the Treasury and proposing policies such as participation that sounded all too similar to the measures that had abolished their oil concessions in the Middle East. As another BP executive explained: 'Obviously we wanted the government around less, especially because Benn had made us aware of the threat the government's stake could present.' The fear was reinforced by the impression that BP executives gleaned when visiting Benn's office. One BP executive described the horror of finding BP included on a wall chart of government owned energy industries, and commented: 'But Benn didn't own BP, the Treasury did.' BP was thus on alert for the possibility that partial government ownership could evolve into a complete takeover, or nationalisation, of the company.

All of the BP executives whom I interviewed pointed to the Bradbury letter as the guiding principle of the relationship between BP and the government. To BP, this letter meant that the government would not intervene in the running of the company, and that autonomy was valued highly at BP. Whenever the party in power changed, BP made a point of getting a question asked in Parliament about the government's policy towards BP. In 1975, a BP company memo stated: 'As we all know, what we want is ... an unequivocal statement in the House of Commons that the practice of non-intervention, non-interference is to continue' (BP memo, December 1975. See also statements in *Hansard Parliamentary Debates (Commons)*, 29 April 1965, 26 February 1969 and 18 March 1974).

In fact, the Bradbury letter and the subsequent Bridges letter (1951) are vague agreements that in reality would not have prevented direct intervention into BP's affairs. For example, the government agreed not to use its right of veto unless the activities of the company affected the government's foreign, naval or military policy; or the company's status changed; or BP planned new activities with control implications; or where fuel oil was sold to foreigners in a situation which might endanger the fulfilment of current Admiralty contracts. (See copies of the Bradbury and Bridges letters in Appendix II.) The letter does not elaborate on these exceptions; they are, therefore, open to interpretation.

Thus, it was not the Bradbury letter per se, but the Treasury's interpretation of that letter that has been the foundation of the non-intervention relationship between BP and the government. According to executives, BP saw the Treasury as being a defender of their independence because they profited from the investment in BP and had developed a satisfactory working relationship over decades. As one BP executive explained: 'The Treasury was the department responsible for our shareholding; and they couldn't have cared less what we did as long as we went on being a profitable and successful and efficient company.' When Benn came into office, he questioned not only the Treasury's relationship with BP, but the interpretation of the Bradbury letter itself. A review of the House of Commons debates shows that while the government's ownership had been controversial over time, Benn was the first to question the structure of BP's relationship with the government. Benn argued, according to civil servants, that the government should use its now dominant shareholding to control the company and the shareholding should be transferred from the Treasury to the Department of Energy as part of a move to make BP into a national oil company (also see Blackstone and Plowden, 1990, p. 81; Fry, 1985, pp. 15–17).

BP executives saw their independence being threatened by this challenge to the Bradbury letter, and thus lobbied hard against the Department of Energy controlling the BP shares and against becoming a national oil company. In addition to the problems of increased government ownership, outright nationalisation could mean retaliation against their downstream operations in Europe and production interests in Alaska (Turner, 1978, p. 120; Turner, 1975, p. 97). Aiding BP's efforts was the fact that the company had the specific goal of getting the government to sell its shareholding, and several means to achieve it (Grant, 1980, p. 157). In addition to contacts with the top level civil servants, BP also had political connections. As one BP executive explained: '[We] had access to the Prime Minister, the Chancellor, the Foreign Secretary or any other minister ... at the drop of a hat.' Though not contributing directly to the Conservative Party, as part of a complex relationship with the government, BP was a large public contributor remaining one of the top five contributors to charity in Britain, with contributions rising from £500 000 in 1979 to £14.5 million in 1992. For example, in 1979 BP was the fifth largest public contributor, in 1986 and 1987 the largest, and in 1992 second only to BT (*Independent*, 3 February 1993 and 17 January 1989; *Economist*, 26 December 1981). Most significantly, as one of the 10 largest companies in Britain, in terms of revenue and profit and therefore overall impact on the economy, BP has been a company that no government can afford to ignore (Grant, 1984, pp. 2–3).

In lobbying the government, BP took advantage of a perceived split between Benn and the rest of the Cabinet. BP managers understood that several Labour ministers were moderates who could see the benefits of keeping BP as an independent company and maintaining the government's tradition of non-intervention. According to BP executives, these moderates included Prime Minister James Callaghan, Chancellor Denis Healey, Paymaster General Edmund Dell and the Chancellor of the Duchy of Lancaster Harold Lever. All were regarded as much more reasonable and balanced in their views than Benn. One minister claimed:

I saved BP from Kearton [the chairman of BNOC] though I was for a British owned oil company, I was not in favour of harming BP. It was a big successful company; it was nonsense to harm it. Therefore, I opposed it, and fortunately successfully.

In 1976, the chairman of BP changed, and the new man David Steel saw that in order not to jeopardise the Cabinet's support, it was essential for BP to be seen to be cooperating with the government. According to Steel's colleagues, even though BP was strongly opposed to the government's proposed participation policy for North Sea oil production, the company continued to put forward their best people in negotiations and worked hard preparing papers for discussion. The government's desire to get an agreement from BP on participation was very strong, as it would set an important precedent for the rest of the companies operating in the North Sea. On this one issue the Cabinet did appear united, and BP executives perceived that it had become politically important for the Labour government to show progress on its energy policy.

BP thus set its priorities and offered its cooperation on participation in exchange for the reduction of the government's shareholding. The link was made only at the highest level, between the Secretary of State for Energy, the Prime Minister, and the chairman and deputy chairman of BP; lower level managers did not know of these discussions. Tony Benn (1989) records an evening at Chequers where the subject was discussed:

> Then we sat round the log fire with coffee, brandy and cigars and Harold Wilson said, 'We take no decisions at Chequers. This meeting didn't take place. Tony has explained your position but I didn't understand a word; will you tell me.' David Steel then launched into BP's objectives: independence, cash flow from the Forties Field, North Sea operations and international operations to be preserved. He said, 'The BP shares owned by the Bank of England are a problem. We can offer you help but no more' (p. 566).

Callaghan and Benn formally insisted, however, that the issues were not connected. Whether they were secretly linked or not, BP agreed to a final participation agreement in July 1976 (*Times*, 26 February 1976 and 2 July 1976, p. 21); five months later in December 1976 the government announced that it would reduce its holding from 68 per cent to 51 per cent, and the company's independence was thus maintained.

Government Could not Come up with the Cash

Changes in the structure of the international oil industry had caused BP to expand in new and costly ways, which forced the company by 1981 to raise cash from its shareholders. The company's independence was threatened if its major shareholder was unable to meet the new demands placed on it, and the government, in fact, had always been a reluctant investor (Ferrier, 1982, pp. 242, 212–14). As one BP executive explained:

> There had always been a problem over the years. Whenever we wanted capital, it was always the wrong time to get it. The government would respond that they couldn't find the money this year, or could we do it some other way than affecting the government's shareholding, like convertible debentures?

BP's cash needs arose after the flush period of the mid-1970s. Though BP's sources of crude oil were declining, profits increased through the 1970s with the price rises beginning in 1973–4. These profits provided the funding for BP's exploration in the North Sea and Alaska, as well as diversification through acquisition into new geographical areas for oil exploration, and new industries including chemicals and nutrition. The problem many BP managers argued was that BP paid too much for many of those acquisitions. When the oil price dropped, the cost of exploration and production in the North Sea and Alaska remained high and the non-oil businesses were still not making a profit. Therefore, BP found itself in a position where its turnover continued to rise through 1985, but its profits declined steadily, see Figure 5.3. Beginning in the late 1970s, BP managers became concerned that although their resources exceeded their immediate requirements, the company had insufficient retained earnings to replace its diminishing reserves of crude oil (*Petroleum Economist*, September 1983, p. 327 and May 1984, p. 169).

Traditionally, BP's only other source of finance was from its shareholders. Because the government was reluctant to invest further, BP was forced into an uncomfortable position of turning to debt markets, selling subsidiaries or reducing growth (*Petroleum Economist*, September 1983, p. 333, October 1983, p. 383 and May 1984, p. 166). The sheer size of the financial commitment to invest in further share offerings can in part explain the government's reluctance. The sums involved were vast. For example, BP's investment costs in 1983 worldwide were £2.8 billion and in the North Sea alone, from BP's first investment in the late 1960s to 1984, BP spent £4.5 billion in the North Sea, paid £11 billion in taxes to the British government and realised £7 billion in profits (*Economist*, 12

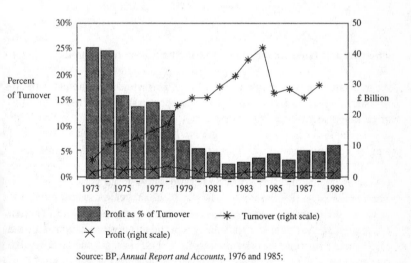

Source: BP, *Annual Report and Accounts*, 1976 and 1985;
BP Financial and Operating Information, 1985–89.

Figure 5.3   BP Profit and Turnover, 1973–89

May 1984). The cost to the government would have increased if they had enlarged their shareholding, unless the government chose not to subscribe in which case their percentage was diluted. The government's potential liabilities for BP's actual share issues in 1972 and 1981 for different percentage holdings were enormous, ranging from £36 million to maintain 48 per cent in 1972 to £624 million to maintain 100 per cent in 1981. The cost of nationalising BP was not a one time expense of the acquisition of outstanding shares, but a continuous cost because the company required capital inputs to grow, as estimated in Table 5.2.

Table 5.2   Cost for Retaining BP by Shareholding: Actual and Hypothetical by percentages, £ million (nominal prices)

	1972	1981
Actual		
48%	36	–
46%	–	288
Hypothetical		
68%	51	424
100%	75	624

Source: BP, *Annual Report and Accounts*, 1972, p. 29 and 1981, p. 44.

The Costs of Government Ownership Overcame the Benefits

As assistance in the Middle East had proved beyond government capability (see Chapters 2 and 4), from BP's perspective the remaining benefit to government ownership was preferential treatment in the North Sea. This was particularly important to BP as the North Sea was a major source of supply, revenues and profit, more so than to the other major international oil companies. A BP executive estimated that by 1980, 60 per cent of its UK sales came from the North Sea compared with 20 per cent for Gulf, Shell and Exxon. By the mid-1970s the BP management realised that the costs of government ownership were clearly greater than the benefits, especially as they realised that the government chose to favour BP and Shell based on their British ownership (Shell was 40 per cent British owned) and size of company, and therefore ability to invest in the North Sea, but not British government ownership per se. The costs as previously mentioned were financial constraints and liabilities abroad.

BP's relationship with the government had changed over time and become more complicated. When BP was operating abroad and repatriating profits back to Britain, the government benefited from the inflow. In the North Sea, however, if BP diverted profits from the North Sea abroad, the government would realise an outflow of funds from Britain. BP did in fact need to invest North Sea profits abroad. Annual reports reveal that revenues were needed to meet their growing international business, especially in Europe. The British government's interest had also shifted. Though they were still concerned with the companies' revenues, making sure that the oil was available for Britain re-emerged as the priority.

The determining factor for the BP management, however, was the discovery of oil in Alaska and the growth of BP's markets abroad. British government ownership was a liability in the United States where there was a long history of protected markets and favouritism for American producers. It was, therefore, difficult for BP, a British company, to enter the market and gain concessions to fields in Alaska. According to British civil servants, politicians and BP executives, the United States government did not want BP exporting Alaskan oil to Britain (or anywhere) if a crisis should occur and there were oil shortages in the United States. Even today, BP oil produced in Alaska cannot be exported.

The shifting centre of BP's activities is evident from the statistics presented in annual reports. By 1980, over 20 per cent of BP's crude oil production came from Britain and over 30 per cent came from the United States; by 1985, these proportions had reached 33 per cent and 59 per cent respectively. Britain had always been the largest source of crude oil sales, representing 57 per cent in 1980 and 52 per cent in 1985, but the importance of the United States grew rapidly during the late 1970s and early 1980s. The United States represented 25 per cent of sales in 1980 and 36 per cent by 1985. While not determining factors, BP executives also recalled that a government share sale was seen as a way to increase the number and geographical distribution of its shareholders, something they thought necessary for an international oil company.

THE BRITISH NATIONAL OIL COMPANY AND THE NATIONAL INTEREST

By the early 1980s, BNOC was financially independent from the government and was grudgingly recognised as a success both in terms of profit and achieving national objectives. The management of BNOC was proud of both successes and by the early .1980s were exceptionally loyal to the entity they had created. Though BNOC's credibility remained linked to government ownership, there was tension with ministers which heightened the management's desire for greater autonomy from government intervention. When the government proposed to split and sell only half of the company, however, the BNOC management was opposed, placing greater importance on the company being whole than on the form of ownership. Because of BNOC's relatively small size and influence, they were limited in their ability to prevent the move.

Profit and Grudging Respect

Because BNOC's objectives for serving the national interest were not stated explicitly, it is hard to measure the company's success in those terms. In market terms, however, there is more concrete evidence. The management was able to raise funds from the private market beginning in 1977 with a loan of $825 million from a consortium of 12 United Kingdom and United States banks, and expanded internationally (as discussed in Chapter 2). Most importantly, the company's finances were strong. The company's turnover increased from only £24 million in 1976 to over £9 billion in 1984, and was making a healthy profit of over £21 million by 1979 and £88 million in 1980. In 1981, however, Britoil was separated from BNOC, and the profits of the company were drastically reduced (see Table 5.3).

Table 5.3   BNOC Accounts

	Turnover £ mil	Net Profit (Loss) £ mil
1976	24	(2)
1977	28	(2)
1978	432	(3)
1979	3245	22
1980	4323	88
1981	5752	77
1982	6465	58
1983	7910	0
1984	9562	(12)

Source: BNOC, *Annual Report and Accounts*, 1976–84.

In 1979, the new Conservative government eliminated BNOC's special privileges including access to the National Oil Account, the ability to sit on all operating committees of North Sea oil fields, exemption from paying Petroleum Revenue Tax, the right of first refusal on all leases changing hands, and 51 per cent of all new licences. The private oil companies operating in the North Sea had treated BNOC with contempt and suspicion because of these privileges (*Times*, 3 March 1976; *Economist*, 2 June 1982). Their elimination was a boost to BNOC's commercial image, because the privileges were seen as politically imposed liabilities rather than privileges. One BNOC executive explained: 'We were heartily thankful. I was delighted because we didn't want all of those political duties.' Those in the DEn though saw it as a reduction of BNOC's power. One Department of Energy civil servant stated: 'It was a "body blow" to BNOC; they saw that their special position would be eroded.'

Serving the National Interest

The managers of BNOC were committed to their company and excited by BNOC's potential ability to serve the country which they felt they could do better than any other organisation. There were many references to BNOC's expertise versus the government's lack of understanding. A BNOC executive argued:

BNOC could have developed the whole North Sea, and cost was not the problem. BNOC had no problem raising the funds in 1977, and could have done this on a much bigger scale, five to ten times larger. At the time $820 million could be paid back by one BNOC well [offshore oil field] in four to five years. $820 million is now equal to $4 billion. What was missing from government, and always is, was vision or purpose.

In many cases, the BNOC management argued that they could serve the national interest better than the government. For example, in terms of the minimum percentage of North Sea oil required to be refined in Britain, one BNOC executive explained:

The percentage that could go through the UK was larger than the [oil] industry had persuaded the Department of Energy it could be. BNOC's conviction was stronger than the department's. BNOC regularly surpassed the percentage requirements.

Two of BNOC's objectives were often in conflict – supplying oil to Britain in a crisis was not always compatible with maintaining a stable oil price. In order to set the price of oil, or at least strongly to influence the price in the short term, BNOC used contracts agreed quarterly or longer (R. Bailey, 1978, pp. 2, 4; Mikdashi, 1986, pp. 35, 71; *Petroleum Economist*, June 1982, p. 253 and April 1984, p. 123; *Hansard Parliamentary Debates (Commons)*, 13 March 1985). The use of long-term contracts compromised BNOC's ability to supply oil to Britain quickly. The 1979 oil crisis was BNOC's only real test, and (as described in Chapter 2) the business contracts that it had made, meant that BNOC could not shift the oil immediately. In addition, by honouring a preset price, even when short-term oil prices were falling, BNOC was forced into a loss-making situation. The management fought to end long-term contracts in favour of the current business practice of short-term or spot market purchases but, despite their arguments and substantial losses, the government required the continuation of long-term contracts (*Hansard Parliamentary Debates (Commons)*, 14 May 1985). The primary explanation for the government's resistance was financial. Because the price set by BNOC was the price the government used as a tax reference point, a BNOC executive pointed out, the higher BNOC's price in a declining market, the less the government lost in terms of taxes. And the more stable BNOC's prices, the better the government could predict its oil revenues (also see *Hansard Parliamentary Debates (Commons)*, 18 December 1984).

BNOC executives envisioned a larger role for themselves, but one that depended on governmental support. As part of their justification for remaining a whole company in government ownership, the management tried to convince the government of the importance of its potential role. As one BNOC executive explained:

> There could develop the situation where the North Sea was not attractive and [the private oil companies] would move elsewhere. At that time, the government would need a competent British company whose first priority was to develop North Sea oil in the interest of Britain as distinct from any commercial interest. Commercial and national interests may diverge.

Because the government had explicitly ensured that daily revenues were deposited in the National Oil Account, BNOC had no way of retaining funds to develop the company infrastructure necessary for such non-commercial growth. To institute this new objective, BNOC was dependent on government backing. From the beginning, finance was an important aspect of the company, and Treasury funds were made available only to meet BNOC's most basic development needs. In fact, as one

Department of Energy civil servant remarked: '[The] Treasury's real concern, once BNOC was established, was that it would not represent an additional burden to the PSBR.' For example, there were no funds available for BNOC to expand to the refinery stage as intended from their original business plan.

The management of BNOC was quick to point out the power BNOC had, in the words on one executive:

> BNOC decided who got the oil and for how long. The price was set by the world market, but the power was in who received the oil and for how long. This was a great bargaining advantage for BNOC and the UK.

He gave several examples of how BNOC used this advantage to serve Britain. These included how he negotiated a favourable contract with Germany to calm threats about going to the EC to settle the question of sovereignty over the North Sea, developed plans to convince all companies to explore west of the Shetland Islands, and aided British Airways during the 1979–80 oil crisis.

Other BNOC executives also mentioned services BNOC provided. In the late 1970s, ministers requested three times that BNOC place orders for drilling rigs on Clydeside yards, but BNOC was not sure they could buy the rigs and sell them at a profit. BNOC therefore requested an official direction from the Secretary of State for Energy before fulfilling the order (also see Department of Energy, 1978, p. 10). In another case, BNOC served the government's development needs by moving BNOC's headquarters, in a controversial decision, to Glasgow instead of Aberdeen (McCall, 1979, p. 146). Possibly the most important event for the functioning of the business though was when BNOC's needs were deferred to the government's financial needs and the development of the Clyde oil field was delayed for three years in the mid-1980s (*Petroleum Economist*, June 1981, pp. 249–50).

In terms of protecting the environment, Andrew Berkeley, Secretary of BNOC from 1981–3, contends that BNOC had 'an insight into the complex technical realities of oil operations far exceeding that which, with the greatest respect, government departments could ever have'. With this expertise, as well as serving as a 'conduit' between government and operators, had BNOC not been abolished, Berkeley argued, environmental and political problems such as Shell's reversal of its Brent Spar dumping decision could have been avoided (*Times*, 24 June 1995).

BNOC also arranged forward oil sales in 1980 and 1981 which enabled the government to record the revenues one year in advance, to meet the government's short-term financial objectives. A BNOC executive explained how these sales came about:

> In the summer of 1979 the government came to BNOC and told us that they were £500 million short, could we sell something, were any fields worth £450–£500 million? We responded by asking, if we can raise the money another way, can we avoid breaking up BNOC? We knew that once the government started [selling off BNOC] they wouldn't stop. The concept of a forward sale of oil confounded them, but to us, it was old hat, we had raised $820 million in 1977 in that way. The government thought it would take us six months (the sale of an oil field would have taken that long) but it only took us 17 days to raise £620 million.

BNOC was able to raise £620 million in this way to credit the 1979–80 PSBR. The following year, BNOC again sold oil forward, this time raising £550 million to credit to the 1980–1 PSBR (*Hansard Parliamentary Debates (Lords)*, 9 October 1980; Redwood, 1984, p. 109; *Economist*, 4 October 1980). A BNOC executive went on to add his disdain for the government's lack of understanding about the power of oil: 'Oil was valuable, but the government did not recognise it. The whole thing bedazzled them.'

The Management's Dilemma

With the prospect of privatisation, the BNOC management was forced to decide and defend its ownership preference. While government ownership was not obviously important, keeping the company whole and retaining the right to fulfil their original mission was (see discussion in Chapter 3). All of the executives and board members whom I interviewed expressed a sense of accomplishment and pride. They were attached to the business they had helped create and were determined to defend its future. The reasons why they joined BNOC and why they wanted it to continue varied, however, from nationalist to commercial arguments. BNOC was described as 'a great opportunity' and a chance 'to get in on the ground floor of something interesting and new'. One former civil servant joined because he was worried about his finances and could earn more at BNOC than in the civil service. Others had enjoyed working with Kearton previously and were persuaded by him to join BNOC.

The one thing they did have in common, a BNOC executive explained, was that 'most employees had a belief in the need for BNOC; they identified with it, and they had strong motivations'. The new chairman, Frank Kearton, believed that the state should participate in the advantages of North Sea oil, but also believed these assets should be controlled by a commercially run entity. A few of the early board members, however, were committed to the ideology of state-owned industries. By the time Kearton retired in 1979, the remaining members were predominately business oriented, with some degree of regard for the national interest. One BNOC executive claimed: 'I actually got more kick from believing that I was doing something which was in the community's interest ... than I got from the salary.' A BNOC executive summarised the position of most managers: 'BNOC was capitalist, but not Thatcherite. We all strongly believed that the UK should have a state oil company, and BNOC proved this in many ways.'

The management's strategy to prevent a change was to delay the government's moves towards a sale. As one BNOC explained:

> We made sure that they [the Conservatives] were aware of all the complications, legal implications with the joint ventures, international markets etc. ... by the time we finished with them, they were really confused. We thought that the Conservative's desire [to sell BNOC] would pass, so delaying tactics were best.

As a result, BNOC cooperated with the new Conservative government in terms of selling exploration acreage and licensing new developments in existing fields to other operators in order to avert moves to split the company or sell more valuable assets. Executives saw this as necessary, with BNOC a relatively young company, three years old at the time, the creation of a Labour government and not well-connected in the Conservative Party. The management was tentative over its future and, therefore, thought this might be a means to appease the Conservatives.

The commitment of the management to the company was an important factor in all of the asset sales but the government's ability to appoint a new chairman negated the power of this factor in the case of BNOC. Executives explained that the Conservatives' choice, Philip Shelbourne, was committed to privatisation, but even he was not enthusiastic about the idea of splitting BNOC. Since his loyalty was to the government, however, he took on the task of convincing the board to accept the government's decision even though they were strongly opposed (*Times*, 17 June 1980; Cameron, 1983, p. 168).

For the personnel of BNOC in 1981, the split and the sale meant that all operations stayed intact, but separately. Britoil became a private sector company, with Shelbourne as its chairman, and BNOC remained an oil-trading operation headed by the deputy chairman Lord Croham. Those who went with Britoil were reluctant, as one BNOC executive said: 'I would have liked to stay with BNOC, but didn't think it was viable.' They were persuaded that they might still be able to serve the national interest by further developing the North Sea; only one executive resigned when Shelbourne was appointed, which by all accounts was for personal reasons (*Times*, 31 May 1980). In fact, the management of Britoil continued many of BNOC's practices which were oriented towards serving Britain's interest, such as focusing on exploration in the North Sea. Some argued that this was to the detriment of Britoil's future and one of the reasons why the company was such an easy takeover target.

For those in the trading operation, prospects were not as good. Though Ian Goskirk, a dynamic oil executive, remained to head the trading operations, it was clear that BNOC's days of controlling the majority of North Sea oil were over. Once the government's plans of splitting the company were confirmed, two senior officials in the trading operation resigned to return to the private sector (*Financial Times*, 25 February 1982). One executive who stayed with BNOC confessed:

> I would have preferred to go to Britoil, I was more interested in physical operations than trading operation. I had only planned to work for 5 years after retirement from civil service anyway.

Another recognised the limitations the split imposed for the career opportunities for younger employees as previously there had been much back and forth between the production and trading operation that would no longer be possible. Ultimately the remaining trading operations of BNOC were wound down in 1985 and Britoil was taken over by BP in 1988, thus confirming the management's initial fears in 1980.

BRITISH GAS CORPORATION: DEFENDING ITS EMPIRE

By the early 1980s, BGC had proved not only that it was financially successful, but that it was a strong and independent company finding and providing gas efficiently to British customers. As such, the management was proud of what it had achieved, but as a large, long-established and successful company also had important resources to defend its interests, which it chose to use in the face of the government's plans to disassemble and sell its oil assets.

Independence and Success

BGC became financially independent by 1980: it was greatly aided by the discovery of gas in the North Sea, and also by the structure of the company as defined in the Gas Act 1972 and its monopoly power. One of the crucial clauses in the Act prevented the government from taking British Gas's profits directly (as it could do with BNOC). When the Gas Act was written in 1972, the corporation was small and only limited quantities of gas had been brought ashore from the North Sea. The financial legislation, therefore, focused on borrowing requirements and assistance, not on profits and profit retention. While the Secretary of State was given the authority to withdraw excess revenues (should there be any in the future), there was a caveat that became important later. As stated in the Gas Act 1972, the Secretary of State could have excess revenues paid to him, *provided*:

> that no such direction shall be given as respects any financial year unless the total of the sums standing to the credit of the Corporation's reserves at the beginning of that year exceeds 10 per cent of the value at the beginning of that year of their net assets as for the time being defined for the purposes of this section by the Secretary of State.

In practice, according to an internal BGC memo, this meant that the government could only extract profits after British Gas had made provisions to build adequate reserves (also see Jewers, 1979, p. 2). The finance managers of British Gas acknowledged that the amounts necessary to replace existing assets were not easy to determine, especially during periods of high inflation. The problem was that existing reserves had to be replaced at current prices rather than historic costs. Officially, the rates of depreciation, as well as BGC's financial targets, were set by the Ministry of Trade and Industry and later the Department of Energy, in consultation with BGC. As the main provider of information, the management, however, was very influential. They convincingly argued that savings based on historic cost alone would oblige British Gas to borrow money to meet current costs just to maintain the business in its existing state, potentially creating an interest charge burden that BGC could not support (Jewers, 1983, pp. 330–1; Pearson, 1981, p. 100). One BGC finance executive argued that it was his responsibility to ensure that the replacement of existing assets at current cost was met from current revenues (Jewers, 1979, p. 8). BGC, according to an internal BGC memo, also had (or created) room to manipulate the accounts to protect its own interests. For example, two measures which were introduced in the mid-1970s to increase the amount of revenues set aside for building reserves also had the effect of keeping profits down. In the 1976–7 fiscal year, BGC introduced a supplementary depreciation charge into the revenue account to provide for the current replacement cost of assets, and from the 1975–6 fiscal year BGC charged certain day-to-day items of replacement expenditure to revenue (Jewers, 1983, p. 332).

By the early 1980s BGC began to assert its independence more and its management became adamant that they and not ministers should run the business. Even though the government officially had the power to set the financial targets, BGC even challenged this role. In 1980 the chairman Denis Rooke argued to David Howell, the Secretary of State for Energy, that the BGC management did not agree with the government's financial targets. According to a BGC executive, Rooke said that the gas industry was his industry, not the government's, and BGC should, therefore, be setting the financial targets. The government ultimately had the final say. For example, in 1984 BGC wanted to expand internationally by purchasing gas from Norway's Sleipner field. In the company's view this step was consistent with serving its customers and preserving the future of the business. Access to the enormous Sleipner field would have ensured adequate long-term supplies. Christopher Brierley, Head of Economic Planning, explained: 'British Gas cannot gamble with its customers' supplies' (*Petroleum Economist*, December 1984, p. 445). In February 1985, ministers rejected the proposal because they wanted to ensure that gas resources in Britain were developed. BGC managers were deeply disappointed and resentful of the government's interference (*Petroleum Economist*, December 1984, p. 445 and March 1985, p. 84).

BGC also gained some independence by increasing its private sector operations. In 1976–7, BGC was granted permission to operate in the commercial market (Pearson, 1981, p. 100). Given the valuable assets the company had developed, a BGC executive pointed out that the private sector was willing to finance most of its needs. BGC worked to increase its production as well as the number of supply contracts with private companies. As a consequence, it was necessary for BGC to follow current business practices so that private companies could better evaluate the corporation, which forced BGC to act more like a private company. This strong business attitude was welcomed by the Treasury, which BGC saw as an ally. As was the case for BP and BNOC, the management of BGC perceived that the Treasury supported their business success. As one executive explained, 'what was good for BGC was good for Treasury. BGC profits meant a better PSBR for the Treasury'.

Being a monopoly in the gas industry, the corporation took advantage of the power, but being government-owned it was also subjected to political intervention. For example, in 1976 the government imposed an increase in the price of gas, not because the industry required it but for political reasons, a BGC executive explained, to help offset the rising PSBR (also see *Petroleum Economist*, 19 February 1980, p. 80). Though oil was not the corporation's core business, the management feared that the oil asset sales were another means for the government to interfere, they were especially worried because the measures could set a precedent for the rest of their business.

BGC's position was also weakened because its financial success (linked to the Gas Act 1972 structure) became too conspicuous. By 1981, not only had BGC repaid its loans to the government, it started lending money (£200 million in 1979 and another £100 million in 1980 according to BGC annual reports) to the government under a 'reverse' National Loans Fund arrangement with an interest rate agreed between the Treasury and BGC, approximately two points below the going rate (Jewers, 1983, pp. 330–1). The government also developed means to extract extra revenue from BGC through taxes and levies. According to annual reports, BGC went from paying £184.8 million to the government in taxes (excluding VAT and PAYE) and royalties in the 1979–80 fiscal year and £87.6 million in 1980–1 (in addition to the loans in both years) to £1 billion in 1982–3 (when no further loans were made). The tax bills declined slightly in the following years but only to £704.9 million in 1984–5. At the same time, however, the government received the £392.2 million proceeds from the sale of BGC's offshore oil assets (also see Enterprise Oil, 1984, p. iii).

Illustrating the corporation's political power, instead of accepting the tax increase quietly, the company passed it on to customers and enclosed a leaflet with every household gas bill which effectively blamed the government for the rise in prices. Conservative Members of Parliament were inundated with complaints from constituents who held the government responsible (Lawson, 1992, p. 172; *Daily Telegraph*, 31 July 1981; *Petroleum Economist*, 19 February 1980, p. 80). BGC's strong public campaign demonstrated its corporate emphasis upon autonomy and its readiness to exploit available resources actively to contain adverse policy shifts by ministers.

The Management's Commitment to its Corporation

The BGC management was loyal, proud of the corporation, and resented government interference. Many of the executives explained that they had the choice of working for either a private sector company or BGC and chose BGC despite the lower pay. They were rewarded with a sense of accomplishment in building up an organisation they saw as a national asset. As a whole, one BGC executive explained, BGC was a valuable British resource:

Britain is fighting an economic war against the rest of the world. BGC is a little bit of it with international obligations. Rather than try and carve everything up in Britain and make every man at every level compete with his brother, what you [the government] should be doing is try to build up a number of significant lead industries in Britain which are important to the core industry and strong enough to be independent and fly world wide. What you should be doing is to reinforce success where you find it, because there is too little of it in Britain. What you are doing is carving up companies whether they are successful or not, just on some theoretical model.

Like BNOC, the management opposed any division of their corporation. The BGC management argued that selling discrete pieces such as its oil assets would undermine their ability to serve the national interest. The 1980–1 annual report stated: 'The corporation believes that disposal [of the oil fields] would impede or prevent the proper discharge of its statutory duties' (p. 10). The pride managers felt in their achievement made them adamant that none of BGC's operations should be destroyed or diminished. Managers also had less noble reasons, such as benefits that stemmed from being employed in a lucrative monopoly. Treasury civil servants pointed out that BGC's offices were plush and there were non-salary benefits such as daily chauffeur transportation to and from work for top level executives. As one DEn civil servant surmised: 'Profits were part passed on to customers in cheap prices, part to government and part BGC spent on extravagances.'

The management's commitment to preserving the whole company intact, for national service or personal perks reasons, is evident from the corporation's flat refusal to sell any of its assets unless ordered to do so. The issue of selling its oil assets first arose on 28 February 1975 when John Smith, as Parliamentary Secretary in the Department of Energy, announced that the assets of the National Coal Board (NCB) and British Gas would form the basis of BNOC (Corti and Frazer, 1983, p. 104). A BGC executive explained that they fought the sequestration by arguing that it was difficult to distinguish between oil and gas fields before they were developed. When BNOC was created in 1976, very few of BGC's fields had been developed. By the early 1980s, however, these arguments no longer held as most of BGC's fields had been explored and were producing, making it obvious which were gas and which were oil fields. At the same time, the general relationship between BGC and the government had changed too. In the mid-1970s, BGC was still repaying loans to the government; by the early 1980s, BGC was highly profitable and was loaning money to the government.

Using its corporate expertise and well-established government contacts, the BGC management was able to resist implementation of the government's plans. One DEn civil servant stated: 'I thought Rooke was as obstructive as he could decently be. Other people thought he was inde-cent.' The management used all available means to block the sale includ-ing lobbying Members of Parliament, giving information to opposition parties who then called for hearings and investigations, and arguing over the value of the field itself. The management argued that the bids were not high enough and delayed the negotiations. They even tried to retain a small shareholding, without success.

The implications for delaying the sale were significant as illustrated with the Enterprise Oil sale. The timing of the 1983 election meant that the Secretary of State for Energy Nigel Lawson almost failed to implement the sale of Enterprise Oil. As Lawson (1992) explained,

> I was just about to sign the instruction to [Rooke] … when the 1983 election was called. Constitutional propriety required that any further action be delayed until the outcome of the election was known (p. 215).

Had Labour won, or even a more sympathetic Conservative minister replaced Lawson after the election, BGC might not have been forced to sell its oil assets. In fact, the new Secretary of State was Peter Walker who later proved to be more sympathetic towards BGC. Lawson, however, was determined that only a (highly improbable) Labour victory should thwart the sale. He signed a letter to enact the disposal before leaving for the campaign trail, and gave it to his private secretary for safekeeping with instructions to destroy it if the Conservatives lost the election, but to send it on upon receipt of a telephone call if they won. Lawson telephoned the day after the election, and the letter was sent. It turned out to be Lawson's last act as Energy Secretary before becoming Chancellor of the Exchequer. It seems that the Cabinet Secretary, Robert Armstrong, looked the other way at this breach of previous convention.

In BGC's case, ministers did not take advantage of the end of the chair-man's term to replace Denis Rooke, a very vocal opponent of privatisa-tion. When his first term ended in 1980, David Howell reappointed Rooke. Some Department of Energy civil servants thought that Howell was intim-idated by Rooke and was too frightened of making waves not to reappoint him. Lord Lawson explained in an interview that there was no reason to replace him:

> Howell was not yet thinking about the privatization. The only thing that was being discussed for sale at the time was the BGC showrooms which

were introduced by the Department of Trade and Industry (DTI) in response to a poor report on competition policy.

When Lawson became Secretary of State for Energy, he could not fire Rooke. But (as described in Chapter 2) he could and did appoint new board members to minimise Rooke's power and increase Lawson's information about BGC.

Ultimately, BGC's management could not prevent the sale of their assets, and thus the sale proceeded. One final point of clarification: the matter of retaining the proceeds was not the key point of conflict. In fact, BGC management had demonstrated its preference was to keep the assets. When the government announced its intention to separate and sell the oil assets of BGC in 1980, but before any concrete plans had been made, Rooke was approached by the chairman of RTZ Alistair Frame who wanted to buy BGC's offshore oil assets. According to those involved, even though BGC could have received the proceeds from a sale to RTZ, Rooke refused and the board backed his decision. Shortly thereafter, the government passed the Oil and Gas (Enterprise) Act 1982 which gave the Secretary of State for Energy the authority to direct BGC to separate and sell its oil fields and directed the proceeds to the Treasury instead of BGC.

CONCLUSION

The variations in the management of the three companies' reactions to privatisation do seem to reflect the different structures in terms of the three variables outlined above: organisational autonomy, control and success in achieving the company's mission. In terms of their effect on managers' strategies towards privatisation, we can track the relationship between government control – of either finance or organisation – and financial independence, earned through either government regulations or success in mission, and predict in which situations and combinations privatisation is most likely (see Figure 5.4). BNOC started in 1976 as a company with a large amount of government control and little financial independence (quadrant 1). After obtaining finance in the private sector and increasing the size of its production and trading operations by 1980, BNOC became financially independent, but because of the government's narrow legislation remained under government control (quadrant 2).

BGC was a financially unsuccessful company controlled by the government (quadrant 2) until 1972 when its governmental control mechanisms were re-written with the Gas Act 1972; it then became more autonomous

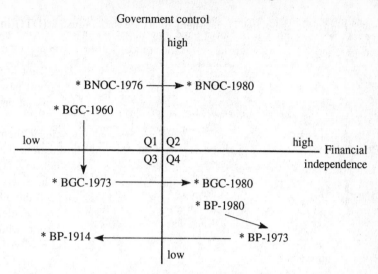

Figure 5.4   Company Status: BNOC, BGC and BP

(quadrant 3). After its North Sea fields began to produce, BGC's position shifted again to one that was more financially independent (quadrant 4). As government ministers sought new means to assert control over the company and capture the company's increased profits, BGC managers sought to preserve their autonomy and independence (in other words they feared a return to quadrant 2).

When the government first invested in BP in 1914, it was because BP was in need of financial assistance. But the financial dependence did not mean a loss of organisational autonomy as the government agreed to a non-intervention arrangement (quadrant 3). With its exploration and production success in the Middle East, BP became financially independent and became increasingly so with the oil price rises in the mid-1970s (quadrant 4). When BP faced cash shortages and turned to its shareholders, managers feared a return to financial dependence on the government (quadrant 3) and thus sought alternative means to maintain its independence.

Generalising these findings, companies in quadrant 4 are the most receptive to privatisation and are the best able to influence the outcome. Companies in quadrants 2 and 3 have mixed preferences towards privatisation and are less effective in demanding their preferences. Finally, managers of companies in quadrant 1 are resistant to privatisation and such companies are the most difficult to transfer to the private sector.

A company's mission becomes important for privatisation implications when a company has low autonomy and a profit motive in which case the managers will be more enthusiastic for the company to be privatised than they would if the company had a national interest mission. The one exception is a company that has successfully achieved its mission, either high profits or good national service, and needs to be split in order to be sold. In such cases, the management will desire government ownership of the whole company over greater autonomy or independence. Because the companies in this case were all successful in achieving their missions, the managers were attached, loyal and protective of their respective companies. For the managers of BP, this was not an important factor as the company was already autonomous and independent and had a profit motive – and the government did not consider splitting BP. Privatisation of BNOC and BGC's oil assets, however, entailed splitting the companies and therefore the managers resisted the privatisation measures, making privatisation more difficult.

The ability of the managers of each company to resist was a product of the organisational autonomy, financial control and their success in achieving their mission. Because BP was the most autonomous, had most financial control and was successful in achieving its profit mission, its managers were the most effective in keeping their company whole and maintaining their autonomy. Because BGC was autonomous and in financial control yet still susceptible to government interference, its managers were only able to delay the sale of the company's oil assets. Finally, because BNOC was not autonomous despite having financial control, its managers were the least successful in maintaining the company as a whole. BNOC managers' efforts to delay or prevent the split of the company and privatisation were thwarted by the government's appointment of a chairman favourable to privatisation.

6 Public Choice and the Government Bureaucracy

While civil servants have been the object of many more studies than the managers of state-owned enterprises, much of the conventional wisdom regarding civil servants' attitudes towards privatisation is not accurate, at least not in this case. Civil servants are commonly perceived as the obstacle to the reduction of any government agency or programme, and especially to privatisation. This view is reinforced by the public choice arguments set forth in the budget-maximising model. Budget-maximising theories assume (mostly from American experience) that bureaucrats not only want the power and status that comes with bigger governmental departments, but the pecuniary benefits that come through bigger budgets. The theory predicts that bureaucrats always demand bigger budgets and search for new means to create bigger departments (Niskanen, 1971; Goodin, 1982; Mueller, 1989; Peltzman, 1980; Melzer and Richard, 1978). In the post-war period, departmental budgets have mostly grown, providing some prima facie evidence that these assumptions could be correct. The specific evidence, however, is thin.

Several recent empirical studies have shown that the link between budget growth and pecuniary benefits is weak if it exists at all. Studies such as Ronald Johnson and Gary Libecap's show: 'At best, agency size would have to double for salaries to increase by 4.4 percent over a five-year period' (p. 448). Further contradicting the budget-maximising model, Andrew Dunsire calculates that staff cuts in the British civil service from 1980 to 1984 of 8 per cent actually produced a 5 per cent salary increase (1991, pp. 192–4). Similarly, contrary to expectations that civil servants will resist any reduction of their department's size, I found that the civil servants in the Department of Energy provided no opposition to the government's oil asset sales and in several cases aided the process.

Again, the problem stems back to a lack of recognition of the institutional structures or 'the rules of the game'. This neglect is highlighted from the different results obtained in cross-country studies. Such cases suggest that the basic assumptions of the budget-maximising model need to be reconsidered and new explanations developed. If bureaucrats are not always motivated by pecuniary budgets, how can we explain their actions? One explanation is that bureaucrats' actions cannot be explained by their motivations and public choice theory is not a useful path of study. If so, bureaucrats' behaviour must be explained alternatively, such as via class background, bureaucratic culture, institutional hierarchy or other more traditional explanations (Allison, 1971; Halperin, 1974; Wilson, 1989). In this chapter I look again at British civil servants and suggest that public choice theory can be adapted further to consider the impact of different countries' bureaucracies and the possibility of non-pecuniary motivations, and then investigate the impact of civil servants' motivations and actions. These alternative explanations are supported by evidence from DEn and Treasury civil servants.

THEORETICAL APPROACH

In this first section, I briefly challenge the budget-maximising model in terms of motivations and constraints and collective versus individual strategies. Then I set out a new typology. Finally, I consider the interactive nature of structure, perceptions and capabilities.

Motivations and Constraints

A new genre of public choice theory suggests a wider array of motivations do exist among civil servants which better explain the actions we observe. In his bureau-shaping model, Dunleavy (1991) argues that:

> higher-ranking bureaucrats place more emphasis upon non-pecuniary utilities: such as status, prestige, patronage and influence, and most especially the interest and importance of their work tasks (pp. 200–1).

Accepting the importance of non-pecuniary motivations makes it possible to understand instances where it is in the interest of civil servants to reduce the size of their departments or of the government apparatus in general. Dunleavy argues that bureaucrats collectively pursue such strategies when greater power or job satisfaction can be achieved as a result (pp. 204–5, 239–48). These goals and motivations of bureaucrats have been confirmed by other studies as well (Lynn, 1991; Campbell and Naulls, 1991).

What is still missing, however, is why bureaucrats in some cases are motivated by pecuniary benefits and in others are not. Because most case studies on budget-maximisers were done in the United States, there was little reason to consider institutional variation. Recent cross-country comparisons, however, have highlighted the importance of institutional structure as a determinant of bureaucrats' behaviour and outcomes (Lynx, 1991; Campbell and Naulls, 1991; Hood and Dunsire, 1989; Peters, 1991). Such studies have also raised the question whether or not institutional arrangements vary within the United States government, between departments for example, as well as between countries.

Three institutional factors help explain British civil servants lack of resistance to budget or bureau shrinking policies such as privatisation. The first institutional factor is the generalist civil service. This structure provides flexibility with security for civil servants. Because the civil service terms of employment provide greater job security than do contracts in the private sector, civil servants do not need to fear the reduction of one part of the bureaucracy, they can always move to another. Thus, while a company selling off assets might find strong resistance from its employees, civil servants do not need to interpret policies in terms of the effect on their own future employment. Change is an accepted part of being a civil servant (Ham, 1981; Fry, 1985).

Second, the British bureaucracy is a career civil service where officials advance in many cases by moving between departments or at least undertaking 'tours of duty' in central departments. Consequently, the very strong organisational loyalties which exist in the United States government departments or in the British nationalised industries, for example, do not develop to the same degree (Hood and Dunsire, 1989; Campbell and Naulls, 1991; Peters, 1991). From the point of view of a minister wanting to advance policy, this can be very frustrating, as described by Cecil Parkinson (1992), a former Secretary of State for Energy.

No Civil Service job ever seems to be an end in itself. It is all part of the process of training for the next job. I lost track of the number of times over the years that I discussed personnel changes with senior civil servants and heard the expression: 'This move will be very good for his or her career development.' Career development seems to be the number one priority, ranking way above actually doing any particular job. This means that however good the person is at the job he or she had, they will only be there for a matter of time before they are moved on to the next, and probably unrelated, job (p. 153).

The third structural factor explaining civil servants' motivations is that promotions at the higher levels of the service are centralised. Rather than being reliant on the discretion of a bureau chief, civil servants depend for their advancement on their abilities as perceived by their professional peers, by ministers and (in very prominent cases) by the Prime Minister (Hogwood and Peters, 1983; Lawson, 1992; G.W. Jones, 1989; Drewry and Butcher, 1991; Ridley, 1983; H. Young, 1991). Thus, a civil servant needs to be regarded as reasonable and competent within his or her department, but also across departments.

Collective versus Individual Action

The remaining factor that needs to be addressed is why most scholars of bureaucratic behaviour have focused on the *collective* action of bureaucrats, and why very few examine individual strategies. Though Dunleavy correctly notes that a civil servant 'can most directly and strongly improve her personal position using an individual strategy' (p. 175), he does not elaborate on what those individual strategies might be or when they will be used. In fact his bureau-shaping model itself only analyses collective strategies. This omission is especially surprising for public choice theory where the individual is the basic unit of analysis and the problem of collective action has been well recognised (Olsen, 1971). But this convention can be traced back to some of the first applications of the theory: Downs (1957), for example, discusses parties as entrepreneurs, when in fact individual politicians are much more likely to be entrepreneurs and to gain advantage, that is standing within the party, than for the party as a whole to work together in such an enterprising fashion. In fact, parties may be more interested in their own continuation than election, the Labour Party in the 1980s provides a recent example. By focusing on collective strategies, we have been missing much of what is happening in government today.

Some aspects of bureaucracies may facilitate collective action, such as access to information, more time to devote to the issue than ministers, and common bureaucratic culture. It is, however, much more likely that the competition for promotion and the segmentation of work will mitigate against collective action. In a bureaucracy, jobs are hierarchical and clearly defined. Full information is only known to those at the top. Civil servants I interviewed pointed out that their work was so focused that they did not have the time or the reason to know what their colleagues in other divisions, even in their own department, were pursuing. One said simply: 'I only know the people on this floor working in this area.' More importantly, civil servants have few means of effecting policy outcomes. They have no legislative authority, cannot ask for parliamentary time, submit a bill to Parliament or even participate, unless requested, in a parliamentary debate (Rose, 1984; Campbell and Naulls, 1991). Thus, they are confined to affecting the policy-making process by providing information and analysis. Civil servants do have a network of personal contacts in other departments gained by moving between ministries or by interacting on committees with officials holding related positions in other departments which, not significant in terms of collective action, may facilitate finding new positions when changes occur.

A New Typology

Recognising the impact of different government structures and the differentiation of form of action, it is possible to identify a more accurate set of civil servant schematics where budget-maximising is only one of four possible strategies for bureaucrats (see Figure 6.1). The most significant structural feature is whether the bureaucrat is tied to one bureau or department or whether there is movement between divisions and departments. The individual then has the choice of using individual or collective means to achieve his or her desired goals. As illustrated in Figure 6.1, in bureaucracies where there is little movement between departments, or such movement is only for demotion, bureaucrats will pursue strategies to enhance their immediate situation. As many studies have shown, this can be done in a collective manner by padding budgets, proposing large, inefficient projects and increasing the size of the department's staff, known as *budget-maximising* (quadrant 4). But this can also be done on an individ-

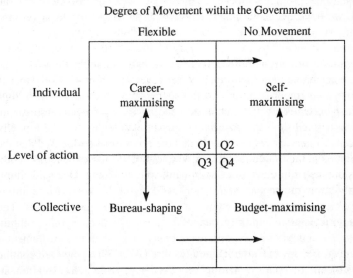

Figure 6.1 Strategies and Structures

ual level where civil servants will try to enhance their situation using numerous techniques ranging from delegating work to others to seeking additional job titles to hoarding departmental stationery; in other words, *self-maximising* (quadrant 2). While the individual may choose between individual and collective strategies and many employ more than one strategy at a time (illustrated by the double arrows between quadrants 2 and 4), his or her situation is restricted by the bureaucratic structure.

Bureaucrats in a more flexible bureaucracy have less allegiance to one department and are therefore more concerned with their own personal advancement than with the growth or even continuation of their present department. This is done in a collective manner by contracting-out non-core functions and eliminating menial tasks, and is known as *bureau-shaping* (quadrant 3). It can also be done on an individual level. Techniques include working on high profile projects, efficiently implementing politically popular policies and protecting one's superiors (on whom promotion depends) or, in other words, *career-maximising* (quadrant 1). Bureaucrats in more flexible bureaucracies can choose between individual career-maximising and collective bureau-shaping strategies (as illustrated by the double arrows between quadrants 1 and 3). They also have more choices than their counterparts in restrictive bureaucracies because, in some cases, they can choose not to move between departments, depending on their own personal capabilities including limited managerial abilities. In these cases they can select self-maximising strategies or if others have decided likewise, budget-maximising strategies (illustrated by the one-way arrows from quadrants 1 to 2 and quadrants 3 to 4).

Movement within bureaucracies can occur at three levels; between departments, between divisions within departments and within divisions. The greater the movement possible, the more individuals will employ career-maximising and bureau-shaping strategies. When movement is within divisions only, bureau and self-maximising strategies are most likely. Movement between divisions but within a department presents an interesting intermediate case in which strategies are more likely to be mixed between career and self-maximising, and between bureau-shaping and budget-maximising.

Perceptions and Capabilities

The two dimensions affecting a civil servant's response to policy are perception of the change, whether negative or positive, and their ability to respond as determined by the power of their position, in other words the strength of their department (see Figure 6.2). Assuming that bureaucrats are rational utility maximisers, they will react to a policy change based on how they perceive the personal effect of the policy. What a civil servant perceives as a threatening situation is in part determined by his or her situation, in general, his or her ability to move away or retaliate. When there is a high degree of movement, very few policies are actually perceived as personally negative because the civil servant can move to avoid such effects. Thus, most civil servants in flexible bureaucracies will not be threatened personally by change (box 3 or 4). Bureaucrats' abilities to respond are also determined by the strength of their department. A department's strength is a factor of its visibility, importance to the public, size and political 'clout' (Dunleavy, 1991, p. 181; and also Hood and Dunsire, 1989, p. 49). Collective action will not be effective in weak departments and therefore is perceived as not worth pursuing. An individual in a weak department who perceives change to be negative will resist that change individually by employing a range of techniques from voicing concern to selectively revealing information to threatening to resign (box 2). An individual in a weak department who perceives change to be positive need not employ any strategy, just accept the proposal and work to implement it (box 4).

An individual in a strong department who perceives change to be positive may do the same as their counterpart in a weak department and accept it, or because of their greater resources may encourage the policy further by

	Strong department	Weak department
Personally negative change	**Retaliate** collectively	**Resist** individually
	1	2
	3	4
Personally positive change	**Initiate** primarily individually but collectively possible	**Accept** individually

Figure 6.2   Bureaucrats' Strategies: Individual and Collective Responses to Policy Change

suggesting efficient ways to implement the policy or additional arguments in favour or even block alternatives (box 3). Should others perceive the same, these actions can be done collectively as well, though it will be less advantageous because credit for the success will be more difficult to attribute. A civil servant in a strong department who perceives change to be negative will fight back with all the resources available, including fellow colleagues and the department's assets (box 1). This might entail devising alternative strategies or embarrassing the ministers proposing the changes. Fighting back is of course a high risk strategy because failure may prevent further career advancement or reduce departmental functions, but because personal negative change may threaten one's job altogether, it may be worth the risk.

The evidence of this case supports these general assertions and provides additional examples of career-maximising strategies. In this study, I focus on the top level civil servants (G1–7) in the Department of Energy and the Treasury. Higher level civil servants are the ones with the greatest ability to affect government policy. And while the Admiralty and later the Ministry of Defence, the Foreign Office, and the Department of Trade and Industry also had interests in the oil asset sales, they were less affected by them and therefore are only considered tangentially in this analysis.

CIVIL SERVANTS AS CAREER MAXIMISERS

Contrary to conventional public choice models, privatisation was not seen as a threat by DEn or Treasury employees, in part because it did not infringe on civil servants' jobs or the core function of the department. In fact, because privatisation provided interesting work and a chance for some civil servants to be in the policy-making limelight, it was generally well received by high-level civil servants in the DEn and Treasury.

Interesting Work and Career Advancement

The primary motivation for the civil servants I interviewed (see Appendix III for list) was interesting work. Drawing from their statements, but also their actions, career advancement was their primary objective. While interest in perks and lax work schedules would not be revealed to an outside interviewer, the frequency and variety of ways in which interest in their work was expressed suggests that it was a genuine factor, particularly since these opinions were often volunteered in the context of other questions. For example, one civil servant described the thrill of working on policies at the 'heart of affairs'. Another civil servant explained: The civil service is 'not badly paid, provides interesting work, is at the centre of power, and stimulating – especially times when working with ministers, but we're not power crazy.' Civil servants' desire to be involved and even to influence policy in most cases, though, could not be construed as wanting to initiate or independently make policy (also see Wass, 1983, p. 11; G.W. Jones, 1989, p. 245).

Many of the civil servants recalled that their favourite periods in the civil service were when they were part of policy changes (confirmed for civil service in general by Watson, 1992; H. Young, 1991). The two periods most frequently cited by Department of Energy civil servants were the mid-1970s, when the participation arrangements were being negotiated with the oil companies operating in the North Sea, and in the early 1980s, when privatisation was being implemented. Initially, DEn officials were unsure about oil privatisation. As one civil servant described it, 'every conceivable shade of opinion was represented in the department'. Over time the civil servants supported the sales because they provided interesting work, eliminated problematic responsibilities for the DEn and emphasised the importance of the Oil Division. One civil servant described being surprised at the time and stated: 'Privatisation, in fact, proved to be very interesting work.' Another said working on a privatisation bill was one of his 'happiest times' in the civil service.

Summarising the interviewees' responses, the reasons why privatisation was interesting work can be grouped into four categories which also highlight the career-maximising connection.

(1) It was a newsworthy governmental policy. To be involved meant that the civil servants had the prestige of having their work discussed in the newspaper as well as among their clientele, the oil companies, and among friends and colleagues. Some of this status, though, may have come after the fact, which explains why the interviewees' memories were so positive.

(2) It was a new policy; the specifics were not predetermined. Civil servants therefore had room to offer suggestions and influence final outcomes. The DEn was the first government department to undertake large-scale privatisation, and hence was navigating uncharted waters. Civil servants described writing proposals and considering many different methods of sales, since the process was new and had not yet been worked out (also see Lawson, 1992, p. 218). As one official explained, by 1980, there were:

> several proposals under consideration for selling off, as well as other options and ways and means. We were writing one Cabinet

paper a week. It was like the Labour Party in '46 who came in to nationalise the coal industry; they got in and then didn't have a plan of how to do it. DEn began meeting with merchant bankers trying to work out how to do it.

In these initial privatisations, the DEn took the lead, though many civil servants perceived privatisation to be driven by the Treasury. DEn civil servants found it stimulating to be involved in high profile policy projects, though it was more rewarding when proposals were accepted and they began to implement them under Lawson.

(3) It was an achievable task with a clear end. So much of governmental work is on-going administration without clear goals or targets. Privatisation provided a more satisfying sense of achievement. There was a clear end to a sale with large proceeds to show and work was created in the form of regulation of the North Sea. In the case of BGC's oil assets, civil servants had another result to show: Enterprise Oil. As one civil servant described it: '[We] made use of the situation and made another independent British company.' Civil servants' attitudes toward the Wytch Farm sale emphasise how important the immediate result was. Because BGC was able to delay the sale for two years, instead of being exciting work and a specific achievement, they saw the sale of Wytch Farm as a long, drawn-out and frustrating process. On the more humorous side, a civil servant pointed out the future tasks which the sales would create. He described civil servants before one privatisation joking that they would be back in five years nationalising what they were today privatising.

(4) It was a high government profile policy. As such, work on privatisation increased the civil servants' contact with higher level ministers in their own department but also the Treasury. It also increased their contacts with outside experts, mostly from the City. For example, one civil servant noted the excitement of working with Nigel Lawson on the privatisation legislation:

> When I was working on the privatisation bill in 1982, Lawson would call me at home, rather than using his personal assistant to make the call. It was hard work, but these were some of my happiest times in the department. Lawson was stimulating to work for.

The underlying importance of 'interesting work' was its connection to ministers and career advancement. Because a minister's recommendation could be crucial to a civil servant's promotion, officials were extremely sensitive to their ministers' goals and views. This is evident from the way DEn civil servants protected their ministers in Select Committee testimony, and also from the way they accepted their ministers' attitudes toward policies (House of Commons Energy Select Committee, Second Report, 1981–2; House of Commons Energy Select Committee, Third Report, 1981–2; House of Commons Energy Select Committee, 1989–90; and House of Commons Energy Select Committee First Report, 1981–2). Civil servants under Lawson were very careful with the handling of the policy. In fact, one civil servant who voiced some objections to policy change was told by other civil servants 'not to rock the boat'. In theory, the development of privatisation expertise would enhance a civil servant's future job prospects in the civil service as well as outside, though there is no evidence that any DEn civil servants were moved to oversee privatisation in other departments nor any evidence of officials leaving to join merchant banks.

Further support for these four DEn civil servants' priorities is the way they were reflected in the civil servants' views of their different DEn ministers. One civil servant observed the general differences between the three ministers:

> Under Benn the department was in the wilderness. Under Howell, whose [political] stock was not very high, not much got done. Lawson was great; he would take decisions, and win.

Benn lost his fight with the Cabinet over the retention of BP shares, as well as transferring ownership of the shares from the Treasury to the DEn. He was perceived by the civil servants to be outside the political mainstream both in British politics as a whole and within the Labour Cabinet where he consequently had little power. Civil servants complained that much of their time was spent implementing damage limitation measures. Benn was also notorious for being suspicious of civil servants, although this was not felt directly in the oil and gas divisions, and his stance caused a general tension in the department, which many civil servants saw as a reason for low morale within the DEn at that time (also see Blackstone and Plowden, 1990, p. 81; and Fry, 1985, pp. 15–17). One BP executive even commented: 'I suspect that many of the civil servants were embarrassed by the things they were asked to do by Benn.'

By contrast, David Howell was a much more middle of the road politician. Yet because of his personality and weak political links to the Prime Minister, many officials felt that things were no better under him. He did not accumulate much influence around Whitehall and rarely won his argument in Cabinet meetings. A few bitter civil servants complained that after losing in Cabinet, Howell would turn and blame them for his defeat. In general, while Howell was respected for his intellect, the consensus was that under him morale in the DEn was very low.

Nigel Lawson was the DEn civil servants' preferred minister, but not because of his ideas (many admitted concern or alarm over some of his beliefs). Rather they were unanimous in praise of his leadership. Lawson was 'a breath of fresh air'. He was complimented for getting his way in Cabinet, for being decisive, and for being a team player. One civil servant described him as 'being demanding on those who worked for him, but that was okay when the department was winning', and by another as 'the best Secretary of State I ever worked for'.

Not a Threat

At first glance, privatisation appears to have caused, or at least coincided with, job losses in the DEn, as the number of jobs dropped from over 1300 in 1976 to under 1000 in 1991 (see Figure 6.3). While figures for the overall DEn are readily available, the breakdown by division is not as accessible. By combining the statistics published in a Select Committee on Energy report in 1981–2 with those published in the 1983–4 and 1986–7 Supply Estimates, it is clear that the number of civil servants working on oil matters decreased before privatisation, but actually increased over the

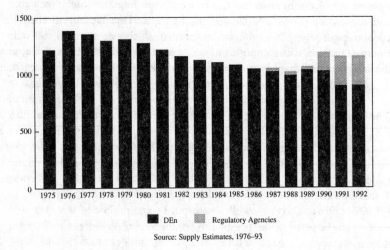

Source: Supply Estimates, 1976–93

Figure 6.3   Number of Staff in the Department of Energy, 1975–92

period in which the privatisation occurred, 1982–7 (see Table 6.1). This is confirmed by informal estimates from DEn civil servants.

Contrary to current concerns over the privatisation of internal functions (*Times*, 6 May 1993), DEn civil servants were not concerned about job security. Because no independent regulatory agency was set up for the oil industry (as there had been for gas), the DEn itself was the only means left to regulate the oil industry. The DEn civil servants whom I interviewed also pointed out that there were plenty of job options with the new regulatory agencies that were created in the wake of privatisation, and other departments (also see Hogwood and Peters, 1983, p. 145; and Hood and Dunsire, 1989, pp. 123–4). Beginning with the Office of Gas Supply in 1987 and then the Office of Electricity Supply starting in 1989, DEn civil servants had a new source of employment opportunities (see the second portion of the bar in Figure 6.3). Also minimising the harmful effects of the sales was the fact that though the DEn's overall staff numbers were decreasing during the early 1980s, overall salaries were increasing. Andrew Dunsire has calculated that while the number of total British civil servants declined by 14 per cent, salaries for those remaining increased by 21 per cent, though this did not compensate for the 52 per cent decrease in salary which occurred during the 1976–80 period (Dunsire, 1991, pp. 192–4).

DEn jobs were linked more strongly to North Sea oil development than to privatisation. The real threat to DEn jobs came when the department was amalgamated with the DTI in April 1993. Instead of being privatisation, many of the department's functions, such as economic forecasting and accounting services, were usurped by the DTI in an effort to achieve economies of scale. One civil servant estimated that by the end of 1993 the Energy Division was composed of only about 550 civil servants. Thus, in the long run, all divisions of the DEn suffered job losses, and once the

Table 6.1   Department of Energy Staff in Oil and Total

	1979	1981	1983	1986
Employees in oil	390	337	334	359
Total DEn staff	1267	1182	1135	1075
Per cent of total	31%	29%	29%	33%

Source: Supply Estimates, 1983–4 and 1986–7; and Select Committee on Energy, 1981–2, HC 231.

last shares of Britoil were sold, there were no more assets to sell nor the interesting work such sales provided. To civil servants, however, the long run could represent several departments and promotions away.

DEn Civil Servant Mobility

To assess the extent of career mobility of civil servants in the DEn, I traced what happened to the 73 senior DEn civil servants listed in the *Civil Service Yearbook* in 1982 and found considerable movement. By 1985, only 36 per cent of the 1982 DEn civil servants remained in the same DEn division, a figure which was more than halved again to 13 per cent in 1988 and then fell to just 4 per cent by 1992. Over the time period of the major privatisations, 1982–8, less than one-sixth of the higher level civil servants were in the same division in which they started while 40 per cent had left the department entirely (see Table 6.2).

These statistics show that movement was in fact high within and out of the Department of Energy in the 1980s, supporting the connection between career-maximising type strategies and a flexible bureaucratic structure. This connection is called into question by the fact that a quarter of officials who were in the DEn in 1982 subsequently left the civil service between 1982 and 1988. If they were forced to leave, this would suggest a severe personal negative threat to civil servants from privatisation, and would then negate the motivation for career-maximising strategies. While reasons are not available for the DEn specifically, according to the *Civil Service Statistics*, during the 1980s at most 4 per cent of all leavers were

Table 6.2   Percentage of Senior Department of Energy Civil Servants Remaining in Post or Changing Division or Department, 1982–8

	Total, N=73	
	1982–5	*1982–8*
Same division	36	13
New division	32	45
New department	10	15
Left civil service	22	26
Total:	100	100

Source: *Civil Service Yearbook*, 1982, 1985, 1988 and 1992.

made redundant or were retired prematurely 'in the public interest'. All others were voluntary resignations, retirements, deaths or illnesses (HM Treasury, 1980–90, p. 37). If the DEn is consistent with the rest of the civil service (and there is no obvious reason to suspect otherwise), we can assume that few if any of the civil servants who left were forced to do so.

This movement is also supported by descriptive evidence, as a DEn civil servant related in terms of his department:

> In the Department of Energy there were mostly career civil servants in the administrative jobs. It was exceptional to be entirely in one department. Typically, civil servants moved to other departments. The brighter ones went to the Treasury for two or three years or stayed permanently, and a few came to the Department of Energy from the Treasury. Civil servants move more at the senior level, Permanent Secretary and Deputy Secretary, and at one stage there was an organised swapping programme ... Experience rather than expertise is the requirement. Civil servants are to know whom to ask, not necessarily know it themselves, like a barrister does. A few went to work for industry and one came back. When oil was found in North Sea, all engineers and geologists which made up the Petroleum Production Division came from private companies. Traditionally, civil servants have an Oxbridge background, more than half, but some have made their way up from the bottom.

THE DEPARTMENT OF ENERGY: A WEAK DEPARTMENT?

This section attempts to identify what determines the strength of a department or, in other words, the ability of a department to make its own objectives and implement them. First I look at the strength of the DEn, overall and compared to other departments. Then I examine the strength of the DEn compared to the nationalised industries.

The Strength of the DEn in Whitehall

Drawing from the history of the Department of Energy (see discussion in Chapter 2) and accounts of civil servants, I estimate the relative strength of the Department of Energy over time using the four criteria mentioned above: size, visibility, importance and clout (see Figure 6.4). Size is merely the measure of a department's staff and budget. Visibility is how much the public is aware of the department or the department's functions,

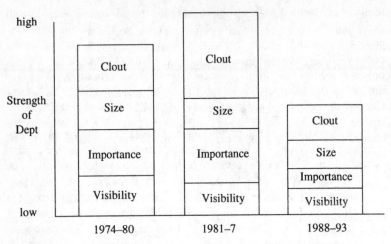

Figure 6.4   Strength of the Department of Energy, 1974–93; A Hypothesis

which can be raised quickly though through specific events or crises. Importance measures the department's contribution to the country, either in terms of revenues or service. Clout is a measure of the department's connections and stature in Whitehall. This can be established over a long history or through the strong leadership of a minister.

During the initial period 1974–80, energy issues were very visible with the 1973–4 and 1979–80 energy crises; the department's role was therefore very public. Similarly, the department's importance in terms of influencing prices, ensuring supply and providing large revenues for the Treasury became very important to Britain, and contributed to the department's strength. The department's size grew very quickly; having been formed in 1974 it reached its peak in terms of staff in 1976. The department's clout during this phase, however, was not high in Whitehall, with the exception of Lord Carrington's (1974) and Harold Lever's (1975) brief tenure as the Conservative and Labour Secretaries of State respectively. Under Tony Benn and David Howell, for different reasons, the department suffered Cabinet defeats and endured poor leadership.

From 1981 to 1987, the department's strength reached its peak. While the department's visibility declined as energy supply issues subsided, this decline was partially compensated for by the visibility of the department's privatisation programme and its new Secretary of State, Nigel Lawson. Similarly, compensating for the department's declining importance in terms of controlling energy supplies was the increasing importance of the department's privatisation proceeds on top of its already large oil revenues. Oil revenues reached a peak in 1984 of £13 billion, enormous compared to the department's budget of £50 million. In addition, privatisation proceeds added £549 million to the Treasury's revenues in 1982, £617 million in 1984 and £450 million in 1985 (Supply Estimates 1983–4; and Central Statistics Office, 1983 and 1987). The department's size had started to decline, though only slightly during this period. The factor that changed the most from the previous period, however, was that of the department's clout. As the leader in privatisation and under the direction of Nigel Lawson, the department's clout in Whitehall was greatly expanded. Even when Lawson left in 1983 to become Chancellor, the privatisation proceeds remained important and thus as Chancellor, Lawson retained high contact with the new Secretary of State and Cabinet veteran Peter Walker.

After 1988, when the department's oil and gas assets had been sold, the more difficult sales of electricity and coal remained. In addition, with the drop in the price of oil, revenues from the North Sea also declined. As a result, the department's strength declined in terms of importance and size. In terms of visibility, DEn civil servants lamented, 'the lack of crises has lulled people into accepting the free market and thinking that controls aren't necessary'. In terms of size, the department's staff numbers and budget continued to fall. In fact, according to a DEn civil servant, the department had so little activity, one of its Secretaries of State, Lord Wakeham, had his job divided between Energy and special assignments for Thatcher.

The strength of a department is relative to other departments. Building on work by Dunleavy (1989b) and Hood and Dunsire (1981), I estimate the overall strength of the DEn compared with the Treasury and the Department of Industry (and later the DTI). As illustrated in Figure 6.5, the DEn was a relatively weak department in terms of budget and staff throughout, even at its peak in the 1981–7 period (see Figure 6.5). The relative weakness helps explain why budget-maximising strategies were not observed in the DEn: the department was too weak for them to be effective.

The one example where the department's core functions, and as such civil servants' immediate work tasks, were threatened was in 1983 when the Treasury sought to end the department's discretionary licensing system in favour of auctions for licences. Though this had been tried in 1971, the issue did not resurface until 1983 when ironically the DEn was at the zenith of its power. Being at its strongest, we could expect collective

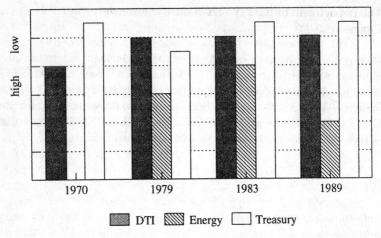

Figure 6.5   British Government Departments' Relative Strengths, 1970–89

action with a chance of success. Though the department was not strong enough to prevent the auctions from actually taking place in the 1983 licensing round, they were only for seven blocks while the other eight blocks were awarded according to the department's discretionary criteria. The department, however, was able to prevent the auctions from being repeated subsequently. The strategies employed to secure that the auctions were not repeated included emphasising the importance of the discretionary nature of the licences. The DEn pointed out that the discretionary system ensured: (1) acceptance of the terms of royalties; (2) current information about the North Sea, including potential tax revenue; (3) profits of foreign companies were not repatriated; (4) the oil companies purchased British supplies; (5) British companies were awarded a reasonable share of the North Sea. Thus, explained DEn civil servants, the department also had important political allies in the British oil companies. These arguments were made, individually or collectively, by DEn officials and the British oil companies because the discretionary system saved them money up-front. Unfortunately, the specific strategies were not revealed through my interviews. The fact that the DEn's primary means of control in the North Sea was challenged at the height of the department's power accentuates the DEn's relatively weak position versus the Treasury. It also suggests that the DEn had another dimension of strength, not included in this chart or anticipated by the Treasury, the ability to coalesce with the private-sector oil companies.

The Department of Energy versus the Government-owned Oil Companies

Due to the semi-autonomous nature of the nationalised industries, DEn ministers were often embarrassed in the House of Commons because they could be questioned about all energy matters, explained those in the DEn, including the activities of the nationalised industries over which the DEn had little control (also see G.W. Jones, 1989, p. 257). This proved to be a problem with BP, but more so with BNOC and BGC.

BP

In connection with BP, one DEn minister explained that 'the DEn has little say in the relationship'. BP used its traditional links to the Treasury to secure influence with the government. Officials in the DEn found BP particularly difficult to deal with because the company was constantly trying to assert its independence. Many civil servants agreed that Shell was a more effective company in terms of supplying oil for Britain, and one civil servant argued: 'BP had not actually been a useful tool for energy policy matters.' Even so, the sale of the government's BP holding in 1977 and later sales were Treasury decisions. Civil servants in the DEn were not consulted before the 1977 sale, although Tony Benn, as Secretary of State for Energy, was very vocal in his opposition. In 1979 the Treasury did ask the DEn whether the government's control of BP would be affected if their stake fell below the 51 per cent mark. Thus, the DEn's only contribution to the sales was the judgement that the government would maintain the same level of control even with a smaller shareholding.

Though BP and the DEn worked closely together, and some argued that the department often favoured BP, both BP executives (see Chapter 5) and DEn civil servants, recognised that this relationship could continue whether BP was publicly or privately owned. Because the closeness was often perceived negatively, some civil servants thought that private owner-ship would make it easier for the DEn to work with BP. A BP executive emphasised the point:

> In the early days, BP did get an extra good cut. Civil servant Angus Beckett was fired for being too close to BP. That must be symptomatic of the fact that BP was too close. I rather doubted that he did favour BP too much. However, without his benevolence, the North Sea wouldn't have been produced as fast as it was.

BNOC

Relations between the DEn and BNOC were more intertwined: from the DEn's perspective as a whole, or the Oil Division in particular, there were no strong reasons to keep BNOC or Britoil. A civil servant explained that DEn relied more on licensing awards than it did on BNOC to influence events in the North Sea. On the one hand, the sale of BNOC imposed no negative effects because it did not reduce the DEn's capabilities. On the other hand it provided two positive effects: it reduced the tension between the companies and the DEn, and the creation of Britoil fulfilled a DEn objective of encouraging regular British commercial involvement in developing the North Sea.

The 'friendly tension' between the DEn and BNOC, according to DEn civil servants, began when the company was created. The department's officials were jealous of BNOC in the 1970s because the BNOC staff got better terms and working conditions. The two were thrust together immediately to negotiate the North Sea oil participation agreements, which is how some of the animosity began. As one DEn civil servant admitted, BNOC executives had a brasher but a more effective style. The DEn was concerned that in carrying out a role for itself, BNOC was destroying the government's long-term relationships with the private oil companies. On a professional level, BNOC had better technical skills and more direct access to information. In addition, BNOC was given the statutory duty to offer advice to the government, and DEn civil servants were irritated by the fact that the company took full advantage of this formal power. However, there were also some strong ties between the DEn and BNOC. The DEn appointed two civil servants to the board of BNOC, and a few civil servants were also seconded to the company. Both steps eased communication problems and helped relations. The civil servants who worked with BNOC relayed how proud they were of the company's accomplishments. Most civil servants, however, recognised that a constant level of tension was sustained merely by BNOC doing things differently from the way DEn wanted them done. Rather than being antagonistic or offensive, one civil servant explained, BNOC was merely 'inconvenient'.

One of the most striking features of my interviews with BNOC executives was their enthusiasm for ensuring British development and control of North Sea oil. This was markedly different from the more politically pragmatic view of DEn civil servants. The result was that some DEn officials felt that BNOC was at times 'unnecessarily extreme'. The DEn civil servants saw BNOC's enthusiasm for getting more than the required percentage of oil refined in the UK – surpassing the DEn's requirement – as naiveté (see Chapter 5). As one civil servant explained: 'The more you know about refining in the UK, the less feasible [the policy] was.' Another civil servant pointed out that the DEn had other constraints which BNOC did not have, including the EC, the Treasury's budget pressures and the interests of the private sector. The DEn saw the policy as a politically necessary target that need not be adhered to in practice, so that whenever a waiver was requested by an oil company, it was granted. Some DEn civil servants also feared that BNOC was or would become too powerful. This was felt even more strongly by the ministers as one claimed: 'BNOC was becoming so damn powerful', and there was already the precedent that 'Statoil was practically dictating to the Norwegian government, and that BGC and the NCB were already enormously more powerful than the government'.

Some of the differences between the DEn and BNOC can be explained by their different goals and constituencies. The DEn's main client in terms of oil and gas policy were the private oil companies and their pro-motion depended on ministers. BNOC, in contrast, *competed* with the private oil companies and their jobs were relatively secure from ministerial intervention. As one civil servant saw it, BNOC wanted to determine North Sea developments and emphatically did not want the private sector oil companies to be making such decisions. The big oil companies, however, wanted freedom to operate, and applied pressure on the DEn to achieve this goal. One civil servant described the DEn as playing 'the role of honest broker between the companies and BNOC'. However, a BNOC executive found that if 'the industry was lobbying the department on a particular point, it would take a very strong argu-ment for the department to back BNOC'.

BGC

Turning to the relation between BGC and the DEn, the department often found that the corporation did things differently from the DEn's preferred course of action. While DEn civil servants were proud of the corporation and, as a large company, it was one of their biggest clients, they were also frustrated that the department could not stand up to the major nationalised companies it oversaw. Specifically, the DEn was unable to make BGC do anything it did not wish to do. One DEn civil servant described the nation-alised industries boards as 'law unto themselves', and complained that board members and the chairmen were virtually impossible to unseat. From the other side of the table, BGC executives argued that in the 1980s the 'Department of Energy understood what was going on, but it didn't account to a row of beans'. The real aggravation was between BGC and DEn ministers because they were seen as impotent compared to Denis

Rooke, the chairman of BGC. In the early 1980s, according to a Treasury civil servant, Rooke refused even to talk with ministers from the DEn. In reply, DEn ministers made the argument that Rooke was getting too powerful and stood up to the government too much. Opinions regarding BGC among DEn civil servants, however, were mixed. For those working on the sale, the priorities were interesting work and high profile activities, not the long-term viability of BGC. A civil servant not working on the sale, however, argued in favour of BGC, pointing out the competitive advantages for BGC to be in the oil industry.

DEn officials' stances were more harsh regarding the Wytch Farm sale because of the embarrassing delays created by BGC managers' opposition. Because BGC administered the sale, the lengthy and frustrating progress emphasised the DEn's impotence which was publicly highlighted and keenly felt by DEn ministers and civil servants alike. Many wished the government had waited until the Oil and Gas (Enterprise) Act 1982 as this gave the government clearer authority which would have strengthened their position *vis-à-vis* BGC and facilitated the sale. The sale of Enterprise Oil provided some spiteful pleasure for DEn ministers, but was viewed merely as a more successful implementation of policy by civil servants, who this time had complete control of the transaction. As one BGC executive explained, they 'just told us what to do'.

THE TREASURY'S THREAT

As the department in charge of all spending, the Treasury was an interested player in the activities of the nationalised industries, including BP, BNOC and BGC. In addition, as a 'super-control' agency which oversaw the central government organisation as a whole, the Treasury had the means to influence the future of the companies (Pliatsky, 1989, p. 3; Blackstone and Plowden, 1990, p. 83; Rose, 1980, p. 39; Dunleavy, 1989b, p. 400). Its encouragement of the DEn's privatisations can be seen, unlike DEn civil servants' individual reaction strategies, as a collective-action strategy to ward off threats to its own core functions from the Conservative Prime Minister and Cabinet, as well as from the energy nationalised industries themselves.

While the Treasury had the reputation of being the most powerful department staffed with the best and brightest civil servants, it attracted some criticism early on in the Thatcher government. Most notably, Thatcher and her Cabinet colleagues questioned the Treasury's capabilities, especially with regard to the PSBR, an innovation of the Treasury in the 1960s. As the residual between two very large numbers, the government's income and expenditure, the average error in the PSBR over the decade of the 1970s was in fact about £3 billion – 1.5 per cent of GDP; these errors continued into the 1980s (Pliatsky, 1989, p. 13; King, 1985, pp. 48–9; Prior, 1986, p. 122; Lawson, 1992, p. 26; Walters, 1986, p. 80; Morris, 1982, p. 94). Not trusting the Treasury civil servants, Prime Minister Thatcher and Chancellor Howe both appointed outside advisers to brief them and proceeded with policy formulation assuming that the Treasury alone could not be trusted to deal with public spending (H. Young, 1991, pp. 152–3; Thatcher, 1993, p. 134; Hillman and Clarke, 1988, pp. 143–4; Keegan, 1984, p. 167). The Treasury's defence was that the PSBR was the difference between two huge numbers which were not easy to predict. Beginning with the IMF crisis in 1976, a Treasury civil servant recalled they were against policy being strongly focused on the PSBR because it was so variable. Nonetheless, Treasury officials thoroughly agreed with the Conservatives on the desirability of controlling public expenditure (H. Young, 1991, p. 155).

The Treasury had means to alter the PSBR figures in the short term. A former Chief Secretary of the Treasury, Joel Barnett, recalled that 'finding ways of cutting the PSBR without having any real effect, especially on employment, occupied our most fertile minds' – an activity which he refers to as 'fiddling the figures' (Gardner, 1987, p. 120). One former Treasury adviser recalled that during his time at the Treasury, he could change the PSBR by £1 billion in the course of a morning's work (Prior, 1986, p. 131). However, these illusions could not be sustained indefinitely.

Privatisation as a negative contribution to spending was useful to the Treasury. According to a former official, privatisation:

> has gone farther and faster than was ever planned at the outset, and the receipts from these special sales of assets have helped significantly in reducing the need for public borrowing (Riddell, 1989, p. 91; also see Pliatsky, 1989, pp. 24, 112).

Under pressure to get the numbers right, the Treasury became more vigilant against arrangements that would delegate spending power. They also became more interested in short-term cost control measures, even at the expense of longer-term benefits (G.W. Jones, 1989, p. 257). Privatisation became one of those short-term measures (Garner, 1980; *Times*, 21 October 1981). The fact that proceeds from privatisation were counted as negative spending was one of the most important factors in the decision to sell BP shares in 1977. As one politician explained, in terms of its effect on the balance sheet, 'selling shares had the same effect [on the PSBR] as cutting old age pensions ... the government always cut where it was easiest'. Had share sales been counted as revenue, the government's spending totals would have been higher, revealing how difficult it was for the Treasury actually to decrease spending (Pliatsky, 1989, p. 36).

The costs of this strategy were minimal in the short term and provided the Treasury with the means to counteract the government's oil companies which threatened the Treasury's strength. The Treasury and BP were on fairly good terms with each other; they shared the common goal of increased profits, and met on an annual basis to discuss BP's dividends. While BP saw the Treasury as an ally, not everyone in the Treasury was an enthusiast of BP. In fact one civil servant involved with BP, like some officials in the DEn, thought that the company provided no advantage to Britain, and that Shell did more to serve the country. Most civil servants in the Treasury were in accord with BP in wanting the complete sale of the government's shareholding.

The Treasury had the most difficulty with controlling BGC's finances. As BGC's financial arrangements were made in the Gas Act 1972, when the company was loss making, they focused primarily on loan arrangements and did not specify how profits would be allocated (see discussion in Chapter 5). Because of this, a BGC executive explained that once profitable the company was able to retain most of its earnings. The Treasury thus sought the means to break BGC's control, first by creating a new gas tax in 1981, and later by forcing the sale of BGC's oil assets, Enterprise Oil and Wytch Farm. As one Treasury official explained: 'The Treasury felt that the sale could help the PSBR. But the issue really was one of rationalising the interests of BGC.' In general, the government argued that a national gas company should not be involved in oil.

Turning to BNOC, the Treasury was sceptical about the enterprise from the beginning. As one Treasury civil servant explained, BNOC was:

> an unnecessary brass plate company. The government already had the power it needed to control the North Sea. BNOC just oversaw paper transactions of the sale of oil; they had no relevance. They had little or no management, with their equity stakes they were just sleeping partners ... the government had the power it needed to control the North Sea, such as taxes and regulations.

The Treasury also had problems controlling BNOC's expenditure, despite the control measures written into the company's charter. The Treasury's orientation towards saving money often put Treasury officials at odds with BNOC, whose goal was the expansion of its oil business. Particularly when BNOC was being created in the mid-1970s, an executive explained, these spending constraints limited what the company could do. However, as BNOC grew with the acquisition of Burmah Oil's assets and was able to raise funds in the private market, the Treasury mattered less to the company's development.

Eventually, BNOC was able to thwart the Treasury's controls. Working in the private sector, BNOC had to abide by private sector business practices. The North Sea oil fields were operated through consortia of companies and run by the partner with the majority holding, all other partners were bound by law to contribute according to the schedule agreed with the majority partner. Therefore, when BNOC had a minority holding, investment schedules were determined by the stronger partners and the Treasury's hands were tied. As a BNOC executive pointed out: 'if BNOC was seen to be constrained by the government, then BNOC would find it very hard to join consortiums for licensing rounds'. He concluded that 'while the Treasury had control in theory, in practice it didn't really'.

There is one exception where the Treasury was able to defer development of BNOC's interests. Because BNOC was the majority partner in the Clyde field, BNOC, and de facto the Treasury, could control the development schedule. In the name of a graduated depletion policy, the government decided to delay the development of the field for five years. According to the civil servants and ministers involved, it was well known that the Treasury was opposed to any restrictions on production and the ensuing taxes, so many assumed that the reason for the delay was the lack of funds due to pressure on the PSBR. BNOC executives argued fiercely with the Treasury that their reputation as an operator of profit-making fields would be ruined. Eventually the two sides reached a compromise with a three-year deferment of the development of the field, which was long enough for Britoil to be privatised and the investment burden to be transferred to the private sector.

Even though BNOC's expenses were reported outside the PSBR, the Treasury was reluctantly tied to ventures in an inherently risky business. To stem BNOC's expansion, the Treasury supported the move to sell BNOC's exploration acreage. They were also placated, according to DEn officials, against any more intrusive moves in the first round of spending cuts by the forward sale of oil. The Treasury was aided by the Conservatives' support and BNOC's cooperation with measures that avoided privatisation. One of the proposals made by BNOC in 1980 to prevent the privatisation of its production operations, conveyed a DEn civil servant, was to sell bonds to the public. The Treasury opposed this proposal because they feared all future profits would accrue to the bondholders rather than to the Treasury, while the proceeds from the bond offerings would yield less than a straightforward sale of the production assets.

The reason for the Treasury's reserve over BNOC, a company executive complained, was because they did not understand the oil business:

> In February 1980, civil servants came to me to ask how much the company was going to borrow or retain by the end of March because the PSBR was really tight. I asked them how much they wanted the amount to be. They said that this was a serious meeting so I asked again how much money do you want, and explained I had 10 or so tankers at sea for which I could pay or get paid before or after March. When I told them I had £50 to £70 million to swing either side of March, the civil servants were amazed, as they were only looking for £1 million or so. They just didn't understand the magnitude and power of oil.

One final point of contention was resolved when BNOC was abolished. BNOC set the price for oil and the Treasury's revenues were dependent upon that price. A higher price meant higher Treasury revenue yet, according to those involved, this was often in conflict with BNOC's own goals, such as increasing the amount of oil refined in the United Kingdom, and profits, especially when the price of oil was falling. The conflict was resolved once BNOC was abolished because the Treasury took over the role of deciding the tax reference price (*Economist*, 16 March 1985).

From 1983 onwards, with the level of the PSBR improving, the Treasury's policy-making role expanded again. In part, this was due to the proceeds from the oil asset sales. One sign of the Treasury's rehabilitation was that Prime Minister Thatcher appointed the Treasury the lead department in charge of coordinating the whole privatisation programme. Because it increased their control over spending and receipts, the Treasury was one of the few departments in Whitehall actively to be committed to the new strategy, and the only department in the central position necessary to make the concept into a coherent policy and the central theme of the Conservatives' second term in government (Lawson, 1992, p. 7; Abromeit, 1988, pp. 74–5; Riddell, 1989, p. 92). Symbolising the Treasury's strength compared to the DEn, no DEn civil servants were moved to the Treasury, even though one DEn civil servant lamented that the DEn was the department with the most experience of privatisation.

In terms of department strength and collective action, unlike other measures, encouragement of the privatisation programme could not be done at the individual level. The coordination, planning and perseverance by Treasury officials demanded collective action for success. Ironically, the strategy was to shape another department rather than their own, which emphasises the point that different options are available to departments with different levels of strength. As possibly the strongest department in Whitehall, 'government-shaping' may have been a strategy uniquely available to the Treasury.

CONCLUSION

The traditional public choice view is that bureaucrats are budget-maximisers, but based on a structure and means typology, I argue it is only one of four possibilities. As such, bureaucrats can also be bureau-shapers, self-maximisers and career-maximisers. Because British civil servants have a high degree of mobility within the government bureaucracy, their loyalty is to the central government apparatus as a whole rather than a particular department or division. As such, few policies are perceived as personally negative, so that rather than fearing for their own survival, their primary interest is in work tasks. An important element of that definition is its use as a vehicle for promotion, apparent from officials' emphasis on contact with ministers and top level civil servants, and definable projects where success can be easily determined. Part of this analysis is drawn from civil servants' direct statements, which contradict broader surveys on the subject of civil servants' priorities; this is not surprising as career advancement is not necessarily the kind of goal a civil servant wants to reveal. Support for this analysis is also drawn indirectly from the civil servants' descriptions of their ministers which fit well with previous research on ministers (James, 1992, pp. 36–7; Hogwood and Peters, 1983, p. 139; *Times*, 27 June 1987).

Though the strength of the DEn rose and then declined again, it was relatively weak compared to the Treasury, DTI and energy nationalised industries throughout, and it is therefore not surprising that no collective strategies were detected in the DEn. The individual strategies observed, adding to our definition of career-maximisation, included: providing feasible means of implementation, preventing other civil servants from objecting, working the long hours necessary and facilitating ministers' wishes. In contrast, the Treasury as a strong department with its core functions under threat did employ collective strategies to regain its pre-eminence over PSBR planning. One of the strategies included encouraging privatisation in another weaker department, the DEn. Because the Treasury was a super-strong department, it may have had unique options available to it including actions beyond its own department, that is, government shaping.

Turning to a larger debate on the subject, there is some fear that the generalist structure which provides room for political influence on civil servants' careers has politicised the British civil service unduly. This generalist structure, however, is the key factor in this study that enabled officials to be cooperative with privatisation policy. Rather than party loyalty, British civil servants are committed to the existing government. As such, when officials are presented with new policies by new political masters, they will implement the policies cooperatively as they did their antipodes. The real problem, this case suggests, is not politicisation, but rather short-termism. Civil servants implement policies and then move to another department. They therefore have little responsibility for their work in the long run. The elimination of the flexible structure would increase long-term accountability, which combined with politicians' notorious short-term horizons might provide a useful balance. A non-flexible structure, however, also encourages self and budget-maximisation, and would increase the civil servants' reputation as the source of government growth and being the politicians' nemesis.

7 Politics, Careers and Elections

At the final level of analysis, or the narrow end of the funnel, are the political process and the politicians. Though the previous levels have set the parameters to what was possible, they by no means determined the outcome of privatisation of oil assets. Politicians had a choice in whether or not to sell the oil assets. This chapter explores the process by which they made that decision. While that process begins to look clearer in the latter stages of privatisation, in the beginning, when the oil asset sales took place, the situation was not as clear. Not surprisingly, most explanations of privatisation have focused on the latter stages of the Conservative programme (Marsh, 1991). Most of these theories, as discussed in Chapter 1, do not hold for the oil asset sales.

Taking into account low public demand, I offer a supply-side explanation as to why both the Labour and Conservative governments chose to sell oil assets to existing shareholders with minimal publicity over a ten-year period. Based on evidence from this case, I identify the institutional factors that play into politicians' decisions and preferences. Policy decisions are not made in a vacuum. They often occur incrementally, or are based on a number of preceding event. A general description of this process can be illustrated with a multi-step decision tree (see Figure 7.1). The first branch stems from the demand for the policy. If there is large demand, politicians have very little room for choice and, therefore, adopt the policy where the demand and intensity are highest as most traditional public choice theories predict. When there is low demand (that is, apathy, but not to be confused with opposition), the process is very different because politicians have greater discretion in whether to select a policy and how to implement it. Politicians then calculate according to two different sets of criteria, personal and electoral.

(1) The personal calculation is whether the policy will provide individual political advantages to politicians, such as a promotion into the Cabinet or an increase in their public profile.

(2) The party political factors are a complex calculation comprising two additional sets of variables: the concentration of costs and benefits to supporters and opponents over time, and the position and intensity party members. Depending on the combination of these factors, the policy is rejected or it is adopted and the most advantageous position selected.

139

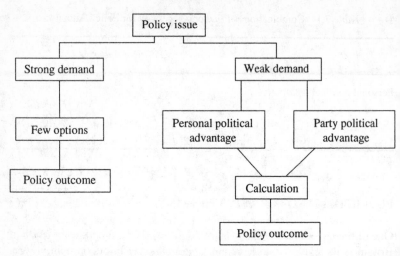

Figure 7.1   Demand and Supply Policy Considerations

Both personal and party supply factors are necessary for the adoption of a policy. To be adopted, a policy must have an entrepreneur willing to bear the initial costs of developing the policy. To entice a politician to take on such costs, there must be clear personal advantage to be gained. In addition, there must be clear electoral advantage for the party to adopt the policy and risk tainting all their candidates with an unpopular or infeasible policy. To be selected, either personal or party political advantage must be strong (+) to provide the impetus. Selection will be facilitated if both are strong; however, as long as neither is opposed (–), that is, their stance is positive or neutral (0), policy selection is possible. Opposition from either side is normally too large an obstacle to overcome, especially as other policies may offer easier alternatives. The necessary combination of these personal and party political factors is represented in Table 7.1.

In the next section I survey the evidence on the demand for privatisation and apply existing explanations, first using the median voter model and then an alternative, the directional theory of voting. Though the directional theory offers some important insights, neither theory is sufficient to explain how privatisation appeared on the electoral agenda or why the Conservatives chose the position they did. To explain these two decisions, I turn to supply-side factors, and argue that from personal political advantage and then party political advantage factors a much fuller explanation of the oil asset privatisations can be achieved.

Table 7.1   Combinations of Factors Necessary for Policy Adoption

		Party Political Factors		
Personal political factors		(+)	(0)	(−)
	(+)	Yes	Yes	X
	(0)	Yes	X	X
	(−)	X	X	X

PUBLIC DEMAND FOR PRIVATISATION

One of the most misunderstood aspects of the privatisation phenomenon in Britain is its level of public support. The majority of public opinion was unfavourable to the specific sale of government industries throughout (see Table 7.2). A closer look at public opinion polls provides some additional insight.

Table 7.2   Attitudes towards Change in Ownership of Specific Industries

	Bad Idea	*Good Idea*
Nationalisation		
Banks (1976)	76	14
Insurance companies (1976)	76	15
Privatisation		
Water (1989)	75	15
Electricity (1988)	66	24
Electricity (1989)	60	26
Coal Board (1988)	54	34
Steel (1988)	50	38
British Rail (1988)	49	40
British Gas (1985)	47	36
British Telecom (1983)	46	39

Source: MORI poll, May 1976; Gallup polls, November 1983, November 1985, March, August and October 1988 and February 1989.

Public Opinion and Privatisation

Information from various opinion polls reveals that privatisation was not a popular policy nor an intensely held policy position by the majority of the British electorate, either for or against. The status quo, in fact, was the preferred position over time as the public was opposed to both Labour plans to nationalise banks and insurance companies in 1976, and Tory plans to denationalise (or privatise) specific companies in the 1980s (see Table 7.2).

On the issue of government ownership in general, the status quo has been the most favoured policy since the 1960s (see Figure 7.2). The terminology used, however, was altered adding some complication to comparison over time. From 1966 to 1979 the question the pollsters used was whether there should be 'more nationalisation' or 'some denationalisation'. Since 1983, the pollsters asked whether 'more should be nationalised/ in public ownership' or 'more should be privatised/sold off'. In all cases, respondents were also given the choice of 'status quo' or 'don't know'. Some differences can be attributed to this change in phrasing from 'some' to 'more' privatisation and including public ownership with nationalisation. The *Economist* noted the effect of wording in 1976:

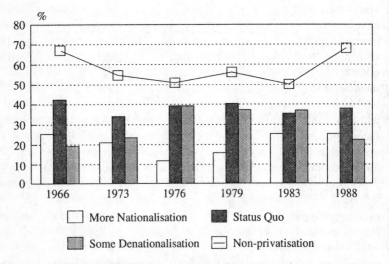

Source: MORI and Gallup Polls

Figure 7.2   Public Opinion towards Government Ownership

The bad image surrounding the concept of nationalisation is partly semantic: when questions were asked about public ownership the position improved. For example, only 19% of voters agreed with the statement that 'More nationalisation would be good for the country', whereas 35% expressed agreement when the words 'public ownership' were substituted (*Economist*, 11 September 1976).

According to Figure 7.2, the status quo was the preferred position over time, except when 'more should be privatised' slightly surpassed the status quo in 1983. Though there were shifts between 'some nationalisation' and 'more denationalisation' those for 'more denationalisation' were never greater than those who favoured 'some nationalisation' and the status quo combined, as represented by the line above the bars. When the status quo was not an option and the issue was presented as two-sided, the status quo position split so that opinion was almost perfectly divided with 44 per cent for more privatisation and 43 per cent against with 13 per cent having no opinion (MORI, November/December 1984, p. 7).

Though there have not been specific measures of intensity of opinion on privatisation, its low salience is evident from its poor showing in the only four polls of important issues in which it was mentioned. Public ownership as an issue was only mentioned twice between 1978 and 1987 in Gallup's monthly poll of most important issues, in 1978 and 1979. Both times voters were asked: 'Here is a list of topics that might be discussed at the next General Election. Which, if any, of them do you think should be concentrated on by the politicians?' In both years, nationalisation was 11th with only 10 per cent of those polled mentioning it, compared to the number one issue, the cost of living, which 68 per cent of those polled mentioned (Gallup Poll, 14–23 December 1979 and December 1978). Its low salience is also evident from the BBC Election Surveys in May 1979 and May 1983, when voters were asked: 'Think of all the urgent problems facing the country at the present time. When you decided which way to vote, which TWO issues did you personally consider most important?' In 1979, nationalisation/public ownership was number 13 on the list and only 3 per cent of those polled considered it one of the two most important issues; in 1983 it was again last and this time only 1 per cent of those polled mentioned it (MORI, May 1983 and May 1979). Other polls focusing on the salience of issues and why people voted for one party over another do not even mention privatisation/nationalisation. Specifically in terms of the sale of oil assets, there were not even any opinion polls asking about the privatisation of oil companies, suggesting that the issue was not salient enough to warrant conducting a poll.

Building from these pieces of evidence, I hypothesise that the distribution of positions regarding privatisation during the late 1970s and early 1980s was fairly symmetrical (see Figure 7.3). The Labour and Liberal Democrats' positions were close to the centre with Labour slightly further to the left, point A, than the Liberal Democrats, point B, and the Conservatives on the other side of the status quo to the far right, point C. From this distribution, the median voter model, using only the spatial proximity of position, predicts that voters will choose the candidate with the stance closest to their own, which in this case would be the Liberal Democrats followed by Labour, with the Conservatives receiving the least number of votes. Because the Conservatives won both the 1979 and 1983 elections, these predictions hardly seem accurate.

An alternative explanation is the directional theory of voting advocated by George Rabinowitz and Stuart MacDonald (1989). The theory argues that voters react to politicians' direction and intensity on an issue. The direction of the policy is more important than proximity and, therefore, those even slightly favouring privatisation will vote for politicians advocating vast privatisation rather than a status quo position that is closer but in the opposite direction (p. 114). While the theory argues candidates are punished for positions outside a 'region of acceptability', any position within that region is competitive (p. 108). The second dimension of the theory is the intensity of opinion. The theory argues that 'if a voter is

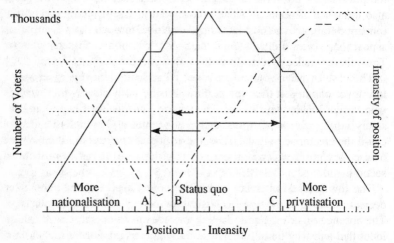

Figure 7.3   Hypothesis of the Distribution of Public Opinion towardsPrivatisation

directionally compatible with a candidate, increasing candidate intensity makes the voter like the candidate more' (p. 101). Thus, the theory suggests that the Conservatives advocated a more extreme position to heighten the importance of the issue.

When the electorate is evenly divided on an issue, as we estimate they were for privatisation, the theory predicts that if the candidates are on opposite sides, each gets half of the vote because voters choose according to direction not proximity (p. 109). In this case (and directly contradicting the median voter model), the Conservatives would receive half the votes because they were the only party on the right, no matter what their position. Labour and the Liberals, both being on the left would share their half of the votes. The Conservatives' position according to the theory was constrained only by the 'region of acceptability' and the need to raise the level of intensity. According to Rabinowitz and MacDonald, elections of specific positions in these situations, however, 'are virtual lotteries' (p. 115) and chosen according to 'factors such as the state of the times or candidate personality' (p. 109) or the preferences of the elites (p. 111).

To understand better the position that politicians do choose, we need to relax two of Rabinowitz and MacDonald's assumptions. First, intensity of opinion is not necessarily correlated with the extremity of the position. Voters can feel strongly about a moderate policy position or their opinion may be weak for an extreme position. The implication is that voters will not vote according to an issue if they feel weakly about it – no matter what the politician's position. Second, while voters react to candidates, they also influence candidates. Therefore, instead of the one-way direction of influence Rabinowitz and MacDonald describe, through their intensity on a position, voters can influence the policy position candidates choose. Thus, there is actually a two-way flow of influence.

The case of privatisation can better be understood as an issue with a low level of intensity for the majority of the population who therefore voted according to other issues. Though the Conservatives chose progressively more extreme positions, the level of intensity on the issue did not cause the electorate to react. Thus, the politicians were able to select their own policy positions according to other criteria, as discussed in the next section.

The low level of intensity was in fact a key aspect of the politicians' decision making at the time, as Nigel Lawson explained in our interview. The absence of strong public feeling was the most important condition he identified and why he felt he was initially able to implement the oil asset privatisations.

There was no organised lobby. There *was* a general uneasiness, a fear of what could happen. But also it was nothing that directly touched the man or woman in the street ... If a North Sea oil company is going to be privatised it is not something that the man or woman in the street is going to feel strongly about.

His focus was fear of electoral punishment, not pleasing public demand or gaining votes – at least not in these early privatisations. This lends support to the view that voters do not always respond to stimuli from politicians and that politicians can have other reasons for selecting a policy position.

POLITICIANS AS POLICY SUPPLIERS

The development of most policies demands a policy entrepreneur to initiate and promote the ideas, not necessarily the same as a political entrepreneur who organises political interest groups (Dunleavy, 1991, pp. 34–5), though a policy entrepreneur may choose that strategy. A policy entrepreneur risks the costs and the possibility of policy rejection or the unsuccessful implementation of the policy for the rewards of influence, patronage and social prestige for the successful adoption of his or her policy. There are three sets of costs to initiating a policy: development, information and promotion. The start-up costs are the development costs which include defining and articulating the policy. Then there are the information costs associated with identifying potential supporters and opponents and devising a feasible plan for implementation. Finally there are the promotion costs with include publicising the policy, either within the party or more broadly, as well as addressing grievances and opposition.

Policy entrepreneurs do not necessarily have to be politicians, though many of the rewards for success are most easily bestowed upon politicians, as was the case with the privatisation entrepreneurs in the Conservative Party. In the case of the 1977 sale under the Labour Party, however, the policy entrepreneurs were BP executives and IMF officials. They took on the cost of promoting the idea, building support and overcoming technical obstacles, such as promoting the sale and arranging the underwriting. Though the final decision was made by Labour politicians, the initial impetus came from outside. But notably, there were no politicians willing to take a personal stand of opposition. To do so they risked their Cabinet seats, one of the prize personal political benefits. The BP sale was a singular case, possibly even a one-off because the sales might not have been sustained if there had not later been Conservative Party policy entrepreneurs.

The Prime Minister and her Strategy

In Britain, many of the personal political benefits are bestowed by the Prime Minister. And because he or she has the power to make ministerial appointments, many MPs initiate policies that are favourable to the Prime Minister's own strategies in an effort to gain his or her favour and advance their own careers (Gamble, 1988, p. 110). In addition, because the Prime Minister has considerable control over the policy-making apparatus, including top level bureaucrats' promotions, the legislative timetable and Cabinet committees, support from the Prime Minister is important for the success of the policy. For the case of the oil asset sales, it is therefore necessary to understand the Prime Minister's own personal and electoral strategies and how they were affected by privatisation. I then examine the role of four politicians in the development of the oil sales and the subsequent effect on their careers.

Though the extent to which Prime Ministers utilise the resources of office varies, the Conservative Prime Minister Margaret Thatcher did so rather fully. She sought to control the agenda and further her own ambitions by appointing her close supporters to key Cabinet committee positions (Middlemas, 1991, p. 259; Gamble, 1988, p. 131; H. Young, 1991, pp. 142–3, 149; James, 1992, p. 169), shrouding the budget in secrecy until the morning of the budget speech (House of Commons Treasury and Civil Service Select Committee, 1981–2; Gamble, 1988, p. 109; Pliatsky, 1989, pp. 81–5; H. Young, 1991, p. 149; Holmes, 1985, p. 76; Prior, 1986, p. 119), and removing or side-lining her most prominent critics (Thatcher, 1993, pp. 130–1, 152–3; Prior, 1986, p. 132; Gamble, 1988, p. 110; St John-Stevas, 1984, p. 19; King, 1988, p. 59). Thus, more so than other Prime Ministers, her own personal and electoral strategies were important influences on the development of other policies. Thatcher's position was strengthened by the Conservatives' disciplined party organisation and the British first-past-the-post electoral system which allowed the Conservatives a larger majority than represented by the population (H. Young, 1991, p. 324). For example, the Conservatives' victory in 1983 was secured with fewer votes than in 1979, yet their parliamentary majority increased by 100 constituency seats to 144.

Thatcher was also well known for consistently rewarding those MPs loyal to her and her strategy. Norman Tebbit (1988) recalled that towards the end of 1980, Thatcher:

made it plain that she wanted to begin the reconstruction of the government to bring forward more of those who believed in the policies on which we had been elected, [or in other words] who believed that the policy of government was right and that it could be carried through (pp. 9–10).

In retrospect, many Conservative politicians have been criticised for allowing Thatcher to proceed unopposed. One of Thatcher's leading adversaries, Jim Prior (1986), defends himself against these criticisms, explaining that though he would have been prepared for the personal setback, he had been elected to represent his constituency and could not let them down (pp. 140–1). He later pointed out that resignation of the whole opposing faction within the Conservative Party:

might have brought down the government. Certainly if all those who had strong disagreement with the policy had resigned, it would have brought down the government. And we were not elected, as it were, to resign and bring down the government. So we stuck in there (BBC1, 20 November 1993).

The strategies that Thatcher chose and, therefore, that policy entrepreneurs needed to accommodate, stemmed from her concern with her leadership image (Bulpitt, 1986, p. 21). A decade of U-turns had made British voters sceptical of their politicians' ability to stay the course. Thatcher saw this as the cause of Edward Heath's demise: 'It was also irritating that it was because we had done a U-turn with the previous Conservative government that we had lost, because people had lost respect for the government' (BBC1, 20 November 1993). She therefore chose to differentiate herself from both the Labour Party and the previous Conservative leadership. She portrayed an image of determination and strength which emphasised credibility over popularity (Lord Home interviewed in Murray, 1980, p. 140; Grant, 1980, pp. 151–2; Keegan, 1984, p. 134; Budge, *et al.*, 1988, p. 14). Thatcher, in fact, staked her career on providing strong leadership. This came to mean a clear direction for the party without any policy U-turns. While there were benefits to such a strategy, there were also serious consequences; Thatcher set expectations and was then compelled to adhere to her pronouncements at the risk of losing credibility (Thatcher, 1993, pp. 15, 148–53; Keegan, 1984, pp. 160, 183; Pym, 1984, pp. 5, 10; H. Young, 1991, pp. 212, 319).

Thatcher's overall success is evident from her high favourable ratings as a leader, while the policies she used to establish that profile were not as highly rated by the public (see Figure 7.4). Because the Conservatives

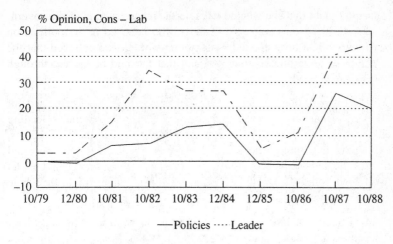

% Opinion, Cons – Lab

—Policies ···· Leader

Source: Gallup Polls, 1979–88

Figure 7.4   Public Opinion, 1979–88; Conservatives Favoured over Labour

won elections in 1979, 1983 and 1987 with Thatcher as their leader, the policies may have only been of secondary importance, but there are no polls which measure the relative salience of leadership and issues to confirm this point.

One of the primary means Thatcher, and thus the Conservative Party, used to demonstrate her steadfastness was monetary policy. The changing international situation had made monetary policy an effective policy tool that no party could ignore (see Chapter 4). There was, however, a marked shift in emphasis under Thatcher who used it as a policy weapon capable of producing powerful results (Wright, 1981, p. 9; Browning, 1986, pp. 264–87; Riddell, 1989, pp. 16–17; Ranelagh, 1991, p. 226). The way monetarism was used to ensure financial confidence was by enhancing stability and forcing the government to act predictably, rather than engineering carefully timed changes through policy actions (Meltzer, 1993, p. 131; Keegan, 1984, pp. 65–6; Lawson, 1992, pp. 90, 414). In other words, its success depended on the government's unflagging commitment to the policy over time (Gardner, 1987, p. 90). One of the means the government devised to build the financial market's confidence was the Medium Term Financial Strategy (MTFS), a statement of intermediate range targets including the PSBR (Holmes, 1985, p. 105; Hillman and Clarke, 1988, p. 146). Given the difficulty in forecasting the PSBR, many economists have noted that it is surprising that it remained a central plank of the government's strategy (Morris, 1982, p. 99; Devereux and Morris, 1984, pp. 39, 42; and Devereux *et al.*, 1984, p. 38). It did, however, continue to be of great importance and public attention therefore focused upon it.

The problem with this strategy was that the government failed to meet the targets, yet could not afford the credibility repercussions by admitting it (C. Johnson, 1991, p. 68). Privatisation as a means to help meet the PSBR target was, therefore, a welcome policy initiative, and those who developed it were well rewarded by Thatcher. Although the Treasury did 'fiddle the figures' (see Chapter 6) and the Bank of England overfunded the debt (selling more government securities to the investing public than is necessary to meet the government's own requirements), these measures were primarily cosmetic and could not be sustained in the long run (Pliatsky, 1989, p. 126; Lawson, 1992, pp. 448–9; Browning, 1986, p. 294; Likierman, 1988, pp. 9–10). The real contributions were politically difficult – such as cutting spending or raising taxes. Privatisation provided another method of reducing the PSBR which had the same effect as cutting spending, and was therefore very appealing both to the politicians who had staked their credibility on monetary policy and to the Treasury whose reputation was under question (as described in Chapter 6).

The way privatisation worked was that an asset sale simply allowed expenditure (or cuts in taxation) in the current period, beyond the extent feasible without it, by raising current income at the expense of future income streams (Mansoor, 1987, p. 4; Gamble, 1988, pp. 124, 250). If the marginal increase in spending was less than was actually raised from the sale, the PSBR would be lower, all other things being equal. With an asset sale, however, the PSBR would be larger in future years *unless* the sale price reflected the loss of revenue to the government in the form of current and future profit *and* if the government used the sale proceeds to purchase other financial assets providing a similar yield or to retire an equivalent amount of outstanding debt (Hemming and Mansoor, 1988, p. 16; Mansoor, 1987, p. 5). According to *The Government's Expenditure Plans*, the British government, however, often used the proceeds from asset sales to offset spending which continued to increase from 1977 to 1989.

Both the Labour Party in 1977 and the Conservatives after 1979 used privatisation as a means to achieve PSBR targets. The Cabinet discussions of the Labour government in 1976 during the IMF crisis illustrate why cutting the PSBR was important but spending cuts were difficult for political reasons (see Chapter 3). Similarly, the Conservatives entered office in 1979 having made too many promises to cut the PSBR on the one hand, and too many promises to increase spending on the other. As Lawson (1992) acknowledges, the sale of BP shares was particularly important in 1979 and 1983 to help the Conservative government achieve its rigorous spending reductions in the least harmful way (pp. 34, 284). Asset sales soon became a regular part of the Conservatives' budget planning. In fact, asset proceeds were posted in the preceding year's budget, creating risks if the government failed to deliver. Failing to reach privatisation receipt targets would have negative budgetary as well as political credibility consequences, which explains why some privatisations proceeded in the face of difficulties and complications (Letwin, 1988, p. 41; Gamble, 1988, p. 131).

Privatisation proceeds were the first major contributions to reducing the PSBR while at the same time maintaining the spirit of the MTFS (Keegan, 1989, p. 94). Leo Pliatsky (1989), a former Treasury civil servant, explained the electoral advantages of this:

> The government's supporters found some consolation for this setback [inability to cut public spending] in the better than expected success of the programme of privatisation of publicly owned industries and companies and disposals of publicly owned assets; this form of cutting the public sector became to some extent a kind of psychological substitute for cutting public expenditure. The receipts from these sales also brought some material help to the government's accounts (p. 210).

The specific impact of oil on the PSBR was enormous. Oil, in fact, may have been the largest contributor to the government's revenues as sales of oil assets were the largest individual contributor to privatisation and oil revenues from the North Sea began to dwarf the PSBR by 1984. The effect of total privatisation and oil revenues from the North Sea from 1977 to 1989 is illustrated in Figure 7.5 as compared to the PSBR;

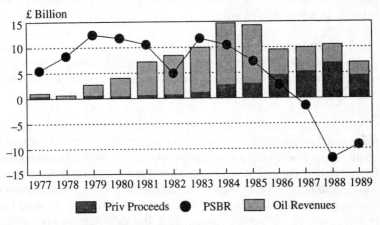

Source: CSO and Department of Energy

Figure 7.5   Government Revenue versus PSBR, 1977–89

it should also be noted that expenditure was increasing throughout the period. Privatisation proceeds rose steadily through 1988, while oil revenues peaked in 1984 and began to fall as the price of oil collapsed in 1986.

Policy Entrepreneurs – Successes and Failures

With these political and logistical advantages, privatisation, especially of oil assets, was useful to Thatcher and thus the Conservatives' overall political strategy. Thatcher, contrary to the conventional wisdom, was not an entrepreneur of privatisation or even an initial supporter (Lawson, 1992, p. 199). Once she was shown the political virtues of the policy, she supported it wholeheartedly and rewarded those who had taken the initial risks (Thatcher, 1993, pp. 677–8). I review the case of four Conservative politicians, Nigel Lawson, John Moore, David Howell and Hamish Gray, and examine their entrepreneurship and corresponding rewards.

Nigel Lawson was one of Thatcher's most important lieutenants. As Chief Financial Secretary to the Treasury in 1979, Nigel Lawson's career advancement and personal credibility were bound together with the government's commitment to the MTFS (Keegan, 1989, pp. 60, 70–2; Holmes, 1985, p. 62). He approached privatisation from the political perspective, seeking revenues to meet the government's targets, and thus advocated the sale of Amersham International in 1980. When the sale was 24 times oversubscribed, it appeared he had gambled to ensure it was a political success and lost some personal credibility. Lawson (1992) acknowledged the implications:

> at the time I felt deeply humiliated, and resolved that the next privatisation for which I was responsible, namely Britoil, would have to be a tender. Whatever happened, I could not afford a second Amersham (p. 210).

As Secretary of Energy from 1981 to 1983, Lawson was the driving force behind the DEn's privatisations. He wrote the Oil and Gas (Enterprise) Bill 1981, got it passed, privatised Britoil and prepared Enterprise Oil for sale. One civil servant thought that Lawson was self-serving and only trying to improve his ministerial image: because Howell had been so indecisive, Lawson saw that 'the easy way to look good was to make a move'. It was also perceived at this time that his advocacy of privatisation might also be seen as a means of raising revenue to cut the

PSBR to ensure that his MTFS targets were met (Keegan, 1989, pp. 94–5). The oil privatisations were especially important to Lawson. As a policy entrepreneur and a young member of Thatcher's Cabinet moving to the Department of Energy, which was not one of the most sought after posts, he had to work with what was available to make his mark. Oil was especially critical to Lawson's success because other types of energy – coal, electricity, nuclear, even gas – contained too many obstacles for privatisation to proceed quickly, so much so that none was even targeted for privatisation in the Conservatives' 1983 manifesto. The importance of oil, however, is revealed by the space it occupies in his memoirs (1992): oil asset privatisations receive three chapters and oil prices a further chapter in the 11 chapters devoted to his experience as Secretary of State for Energy; the first one was even titled: 'Jewel in the Crown'; the 1987 BP share sale received a further two chapters in the section on being Chancellor.

For taking an entrepreneurial risk, Lawson achieved policy success, and his abilities and loyalty were much appreciated – and rewarded – by Thatcher. She promoted him from Energy to Chancellor of the Exchequer after the Conservatives won the 1983 election, recording her regard for him in her memoirs (1993):

> Whatever quarrels we were to have later, if it comes to drawing up a list of conservative – even Thatcherite – revolutionaries I would never deny Nigel a leading place on it. He has many qualities which I admire and some which I do not. He is imaginative, fearless and – on paper at least – eloquently persuasive. His mind is quick and, unlike Geoffrey Howe who he succeeded as Chancellor, he makes decisions easily ... I doubt whether any other Financial Secretary to the Treasury could have come up with the inspired clarity of the Medium Term Financial Strategy which guided our economic policy (pp. 308–9).

Another Conservative minister who made political capital out of privatisation was *John Moore*. As Parliamentary Under Secretary in the DEn, he was in charge of the sale of Amersham in 1980, and involved in the Britoil and Wytch Farm sales. In 1983, Moore was chosen to head the new Treasury unit overseeing the privatisation programme as a whole as the policy became a central part of the Conservative programme (Riddell, 1989, p. 92; Pliatsky, 1989, p. 110; Abromeit, 1988, p. 72). Moore was cast as a trailblazer and Thatcher rewarded him with successive appointments to the posts of Secretary of State for Transport in 1986, Social Services in 1987, and Social Security in 1988.

David Howell's handling of privatisation provides an example of an unsuccessful policy entrepreneur. As an author of *The Right Approach* (1977) and the 1979 and 1983 manifestos, David Howell also initially gained recognition for his work developing Thatcherite ideas. Appointed to the Cabinet in 1979 as Secretary of State for Energy, he was unsuccessful in turning the idea of privatisation into a concrete policy. Howell drew up the original studies on privatisation and wrote a draft bill to privatise BNOC. He instructed the British Gas Corporation (BGC) to sell Wytch Farm (under the Gas Act 1972), but he never got the BNOC bill passed or completed a privatisation. In fact, many of the civil servants I interviewed had to think for a few minutes before recalling that Howell did start the privatisation process. They all pointed to the fact that it was actually Lawson who got them going and, therefore, Howell's contribution paled in comparison. The reason, according to a fellow minister, was that he 'could come up with 440 ways to answer a question but could not make a decision. The thinking was initiated under Howell, but things didn't get done'. According to a DEn civil servant the delay in privatising BNOC from 1979 to 1982 could specifically be attributed to Howell's indecisive personality.

As well as stepping back from privatisation, he did not perform well in crises, particularly the threatened coal strike in 1980. He also muddled the DEn's oil depletion policy and created additional problems over gas and electricity prices. One civil servant stated simply, 'it was embarrassing'. Howell was moved to head the Department of Transport in the September 1981 Cabinet reshuffle, and was dropped from the Cabinet after the 1983 election. The case of Howell demonstrates that competence as well as ideas were necessary to create a successful policy in Thatcher's Cabinet.

Hamish Gray is an example of a Conservative minister failing to support Thatcher's policies or propose more successful alternatives. As a Scottish MP and Minister of State for the Department of Energy Gray sought to direct benefits to Scotland in general and his constituency in particular, through government involvement in the oil industry. He advocated keeping BNOC. He also supported the DEn's gas pipeline proposal as well as the department's plans for depletion policy, all of which would have aided the future of the Scottish oil and gas industry. These issues, however, according to a DEn civil servant, found little favour with Lawson and Thatcher, and all were eventually defeated, except for the retention of BNOC's trading operation (also see Lawson, 1992, p. 184). Gray was not a policy entrepreneur, but a policy realist with limited aims. After gaining the concession that it would remain in Scotland, he withdrew his opposition to the sale of Britoil. As one civil servant explained:

Gray was an old school Tory. He was pragmatic; he didn't argue for change. But he did not die in a last ditch effort to prevent change, and didn't have the power to do so anyway.

He was described by a Conservative minister as 'a pair of safe hands. He saw that privatisation was right, but that it was difficult. He would never have ventured out on it on his own.' Gray lost his seat in the 1983 election, but because of his Scottish base, he was made a Lord and appointed to the Scottish Office for two years. Ministers pointed out, however, that the Scottish Office was not nearly as interesting or as prestigious as the DEn.

PARTY POLITICAL ADVANTAGE FOR THE CONSERVATIVES

There are two dimensions to party political advantage. The first is a cost-benefit analysis which computes the costs and benefits for supporters and opponents over the short and long term. A positive outcome influences party leaders to place the issue on the political agenda. The second dimension is the distribution and intensity of Conservative voters on the issue. By calculating the demand within the party, leaders can determine the position of greatest advantage.

The Cost-Benefit Analysis

The supply-side calculation of electoral advantage, for policies without strong demand factors, includes the distribution of costs and benefits and the time horizon of their impact (Wilson, 1973, Chapter 16), see Figure 7.6. Politicians and parties seek policies that will target benefits towards their supporters. While benefits ideally go to supporters, costs ideally go to opponents. The time horizon of costs and benefits are especially important to politicians as the electoral cycle means they may not be in office for the long term. Therefore, benefits which can be achieved in the short term are the most attractive, so that the politicians in power can receive credit for the benefits. Conversely, costs which can be delayed beyond the next election are the most desirable.

The possible variations of the concentration of costs and the time horizon are the key factors that determine how easy and how worthwhile a policy is to pursue. The more concentrated the costs, the less likely there will be a free-rider problem and the more likely opposition will be co-ordinated and effective. The possibilities are depicted in Figure 7.6.

	Benefits Target Supporters (all cases)	
	Short-term	Long-term
Costs Target Supporters – Concentrated or Dispersed		
Short-term	**Do Nothing** 1	**Do Nothing** 2
Long-term	**Be Very Careful** 3	**Do Nothing** 4
Costs Target Opponents – Concentrated		
Short-term	**Be Very Careful** 5	**Do Nothing** 6
Long-term	**Be Careful** 7	**Be Careful** 8
Costs Target Opponents – Dispersed		
Short-term	**Be Careful** 9	**Be Careful** 10
Long-term	**Act Fast** 11	**Act Fast** 12

Figure 7.6   Electoral Analysis of Cost-Benefit Concentration and Time Horizon

Should costs go to supporters, for example in a situation where costs are dispersed and the impact is subtle (boxes 1–4), it is only worthwhile to proceed if they are felt in the long term, and even then it is a risky strategy (box 3). If costs are targeted to opponents and concentrated, politicians need to proceed very carefully with the policy, especially if costs are concentrated in the short term (box 5). If the benefits in this case accrue to supporters in the long term, the policy is not worth the risk (box 6). However, if the effect of the costs are felt by opponents in the long term, the policy may be worth pursuing carefully (boxes 7 and 8).

When costs target opponents and are dispersed, collective action problems come into play reducing risk of opposition, and therefore the appeal of the policy increases. When the costs are felt in the short term, there is still need for caution (boxes 9 and 10) but worth the risk because benefits go to supporters. When the costs are dispersed among opponents in the longer term, this is the ideal situation for a party and the politicians should therefore act fast and implement the policy (boxes 11 and 12).

The change in the Conservatives' stance on privatisation from one of caution to one of action can be understood as the movement between the boxes in Figure 7.6. The Conservatives' initial delay in privatising the oil assets can be explained by the perception that there would be a high cost to the sales in the short term. The government feared they would be caught in an oil crisis and suffer from oil shortages and high prices because they would not have control of their own resources. At this point ministers feared that the costs of privatisation would be large in the short term *and* that they would be dispersed among both opponents and supporters (box 1 of Figure 7.6). DEn civil servants pointed to the weight ministers gave to public concern over control of the North Sea; as one stated: 'Ministers saw that it would be politically indefensible to have North Sea oil and still suffer from an oil shortage.'

Despite Thatcher, Moore and Lawson's retrospective claims to the contrary, privatisation was not part of the Conservatives' original plan nor was it spelled out in the 1979 manifesto. There are several pieces of evidence that illustrate the government's hesitation and lack of commitment to the policy. The accounts of the decision-making process for the sale of BNOC and other early privatisation by ministers and civil servants clearly reveal hesitation over the policy and an ad hoc beginning (Thatcher, 1993, p. 688; S. Young, 1986). Thus, even though David Howell began developing the policy, there was initially no action. In 1980 Prime Minister Thatcher was concerned about retaining national control of the North Sea and, according to DEn ministers, rejected a number of BNOC privatisation options on these grounds at an important meeting of the Cabinet's Economic Committee (also see Lawson, 1992, p. 217). A Conservative minister described the slow process in 1979 and 1980 of finding a workable policy for oil privatisation:

> In 1980, no one was in favour of selling oil assets. There was little support from other ministers or from Number 10. I could not even persuade Thatcher that it was a good idea. At that time no one had begun to see wider share ownership or privatisation as the effective political weapon that it was.

In 1981 Thatcher again hesitated, according to DEn civil servants and ministers, either for political reasons or because of the complications raised by BNOC executives, and through her control of the legislative timetable was able to prevent the proposed Bill from getting a slot to debate in Parliament that year (Steel and Heald, 1982, p. 333; Veljanovski, 1987, p. 65; *Times*, 26 March 1981).

In addition, BNOC chairman Frank Kearton was replaced by an interim chairman in 1980 instead of a pro-privatisation chairman. According to other BNOC executives, the government had not yet decided what its policy was going to be. Similarly, Denis Rooke was reappointed as chairman of BGC in 1980 by David Howell in part because privatisation was not yet on the agenda. Civil servants reinforced the initial uncertainty and lack of action. They thought that the denationalisation of BNOC was a fait accompli when the Conservatives arrived in office. Instead, civil servants conveyed how they were surprised by the numerous alternative options that were considered, including the sale of exploration acreage and forward sales of oil.

Most importantly, there was no structural evidence within the government of a privatisation programme until 1982–3, and thus, until then, it was only a piecemeal response to other problems. For example, the CPRS was not commissioned until 1982 to review the 'state monopolies' and consider the case for returning them to private ownership. And the privatisation unit in the Treasury was not set up until 1983 (Blackstone and Plowden, 1990, p. 83; Riddell, 1989, p. 92; Pliatsky, 1989, p. 110). Thus, most civil servants recognised that the privatisation policy grew in importance over time, while the more cynical thought that the Conservatives had 'stumbled' upon it.

By the early 1980s, the Conservatives realised that instead of potential immediate costs they were in a situation where the costs would occur in the long run and the benefits would accrue immediately (they were therefore no longer in boxes 1–4). The primary change was in the structure of the international oil industry. As discussed in Chapter 4, the industry had become a free market by the end of the 1980s making state-ownership less necessary and less effective. This was clearly recognised by politicians and Nigel Lawson recalled discussing the reduction in BP's effectiveness:

> She [Thatcher] recalled, or I reminded her, that during the original problems in the Middle East, it was easier to persuade Shell than it was BP, even though we had a majority shareholding in BP at the time.

With potential costs to supporters minimised, the other important factors in the calculation became the short-term benefits of privatisation to supporters and short-term costs to opponents. The short-term benefits to supporters included its contribution to MTFS targets and the promised economic revival (Middlemas, 1991, p. 249), its visibility as a successfully implemented policy and one that received international attention (Keegan, 1989, pp. 174–7; McAlister and Studlar, 1989, p. 174; Wolfe, 1991, p. 248), and its elimination of the need for the party to achieve its electoral promise of disciplining the nationalised industries, which they had been unable to achieve thus far (Pliatsky, 1984, pp. 199–200; Hillman and Clarke, 1988, p. 82; and C. Johnson, 1991, p. 154). As such, privatisation provided a morale boost to the party which had few policy successes and was unable to agree on many aspects of economic policy.

The main attraction of the oil asset sales, however, was the cash benefit, and all other objectives were secondary (Vickers and Yarrow, 1988, p. 428; Abromeit, 1988, p. 83; Swann, 1988, p. 316; Whitfield, 1983, p. 39). Philip Shelbourne, the chairman of BNOC, spelt out the government's priority: 'The government was even more keen to raise money than we were.' This money enabled the government to maintain spending and eventually offer tax cuts to their supporters. In addition, both Labour and the Liberals opposed privatisation which, as Nigel Lawson pointed out, 'is not a bad thing because it helps to keep your own in line. If they think others are opposed, there must be a good reason to support it'.

In terms of the oil privatisation, the sales also enabled the Conservatives to direct benefits to specific supporters, namely the oil industry and the financial community. These were two groups of traditional Conservative supporters, and two industries courted by the Conservatives. During the 1979 election campaign and into the Conservatives' first term, the management of some private oil companies complained that BNOC was a time-consuming and costly irrelevance, while others charged that BNOC was unfair and threatened their rights. The Conservatives responded by declaring their opposition to the state-owned oil company starting in 1975 (*Times*, 19 September 1975). These well-known views are why civil servants thought 'BNOC was doomed once the Conservatives came to power'.

The support of the oil companies was crucial to the Conservatives, but also to any British government because development of the North Sea depended on private investment and expertise. In the early 1980s, there was a lull in North Sea investment (see Chapter 5). One way the Conservative government tried to encourage more industry involvement was to guarantee less government involvement in the industry. Nigel Lawson explained the oil companies' reaction to the proposed sale of BNOC:

> They were pleased to see it [the privatisation of BNOC] in the sense that the Conservative government had only been in office for three years at that point and was unpopular so they had concerns in the back of their minds as to how a future Labour government might use BNOC. But because the rump remained and it was perhaps something a future Labour government could use it didn't matter as much.

Thus, the sale of BNOC was only an indication of the Conservatives' intentions and did not address the most important factor for the oil companies, which was the tax regime. But because the oil companies' push for lower taxes on oil from the North Sea clashed directly with the government's need to address its financial problems, the sale of BNOC was a much easier way to try and appease the oil companies (C. Robinson, 1981, pp. 29–30). The retention of the trading portion of BNOC, however, reveals the lower priority ministers assigned to appeasing the oil companies.

The financial press supported the government's plans to sell its oil assets. A typical statement from the *Economist*, for example, described BNOC as 'a free-spending drain on the public purse [which] was given excessive privileges by its socialist creators' (*Economist*, 12 June 1982). The benefits to the financial community were through privatisation in general and not specific to the oil sales, as they helped the City of London, as well as advertising and public relations firms, through a lean time (Chapman, 1990, pp. 67–9; Whitfield, 1983, p. 39). The payments for such services for the oil sales alone, however, were substantial, with the government spending at least £224 million (see Chapter 3, Table 3.1).

In addition to the benefits to supporters, the oil sales also targeted costs to their opponents in the short term. The Conservatives' privatisation programme wrong-footed the Labour Party, undermining their already weak opposition. Traditional Labour Party disagreement on the nationalisation–denationalisation issue made it a divisive issue within the Party and hampered the formulation of a convincing alternative programme (Abromeit, 1988, p. 72). The fact that Labour ministers had been the first to privatise oil assets made it additionally difficult for the Shadow Cabinet to oppose the Conservatives' policy on BP. One minister admitted that 'the BP sale set the tone for the Conservative government in 1979, and it was hard to argue with the accounting practice we had set up, which also gave the Conservatives the grounds for further privatisation'. Lawson (1992) also noted: 'The previous Labour government had inadvertently paved the way with its 1977 BP share sale. So the official Opposition could hardly complain with much conviction' (pp. 199–200). Another minister recalled gleefully, 'the Conservatives taunted Labour with it later'.

Disagreement in Labour's ranks also emerged in public over the first Britoil sale. The shadow energy spokesman, Merlyn Rees, stated in November 1981 that a Labour government would buy back Britoil at its market price. Shortly thereafter, Tony Benn made a speech contradicting Rees' statement saying the government would confiscate Britoil (*Times*, 11 November 1981). As Lawson (1992) described it: 'The Conservative benches had been on the defensive for so long over unemployment and the economy that they were hugely cheered by Labour's obvious discomfiture' (p. 212). In addition, the Conservatives were able to diffuse the effectiveness of Labour's opposition against Enterprise Oil by recalling the fact that Labour had tried to separate the oil assets of the BGC so they could be given to BNOC in 1975, but the Labour government had retreated in the face of BGC's protests. Pointing to this attempt, the Minister of State for Energy Alick Buchanan-Smith asserted that even the Labour government found it questionable that BGC should be involved in oil exploration (R. Bailey, 1978, p. 329; and *Hansard Parliamentary Debates (Commons)*, 13 March 1984).

Though privatisation was used as a means to break a trade union stronghold in some cases (Lawson, 1992, p. 437; Ranelagh, 1991, p. 223; Dobek, 1993, pp. 36–8), the trade unions were not a factor with the oil sales because unions were not prominent in the capital intensive oil industry. The employees of BNOC and BGC, however, proved to be strong opponents of privatisation. The Conservatives sought to diffuse employee opposition by making employee ownership easy and profitable (Pirie, 1988, pp. 187–93). A DEn minister pointed out:

> There was never any representation from the work force to be nationalised again. In fact many employees increased their share. To ensure that the British people got a reasonable way to participate, we made a special provision for those who worked in the industry, and limited the percentage holding by institutions.

Realising the short-term benefits, yet fearing some of the costs were concentrated towards their opponents (boxes 5 and 7 of Figure 7.6), the Conservatives decided to proceed cautiously but sought to avoid criticism wherever possible. The sensitivity of Conservative ministers to public opinion is evident in many of the specifics of the sales, as strong opposition was purposely avoided, according to DEn ministers, by implementing measures to limit the acquisitions that the sales threatened security of supply (also see *Times*, 20 October 1981; Lawson, 1992, p. 217).

The largest public outcry against privatisation occurred when a radical CPRS report was leaked to the *Economist*. The public outcry over severe privatisation measures, including privatising the National Health Service, caused the Conservatives to recoil. Hugo Young (1991) described the Cabinet debating the options:

> After three years of intense unpopularity [overall], they could not persuade themselves there was any wisdom in even privately discussing a serious assault on such sacred parts of the British way of life as health and public education (p. 302).

Because the CPRS report was so politically unpopular, Thatcher denied ever requesting or considering it (Keegan, 1989, p. 193). When extreme measures were proposed, the intensity of middle-of-the-road opinion was raised, and proved to be a constraint to privatisation. The concern over how privatisation was implemented and the reaction to the CPRS report indicated that politicians were responsive to public opinion and were not free to implement an elite agenda.

With the potential for such public outcries in mind, the government sought to avoid raising any of the privatisation issues outside the region of acceptability. Responding to strong public concern for security of supply for oil, the government adapted its privatisation methods accordingly. The government split BNOC and only sold the production portion, thus retaining the trading operation and the participation agreements and royalty in-kind arrangements. As a Treasury civil servant pointed out, 'queues for petrol were the quickest way to lose office. BNOC gave a guarantee [of supply]'. On a more personal level, a civil servant related a story involving the Secretary of State for Energy, David Howell:

> There was a hiccup in supply in 1980, with the result of local shortages. Howell found this very embarrassing with a North Sea oil surplus. At the time, Howell went to fill up his car in a local garage in Wales, where the owner came over and said: 'Not a very good start Mr. Howell'.

The civil servant thought this experience was what convinced Howell to retain the participation agreements, the thinking being that the situation could have been worse without the agreements.

Another measure was to create a 'golden share', which would allow foreigners to invest in BNOC, yet prevent them from gaining a controlling share (*Times*, 21 October 1981 and 3 February 1982). As one minister explained:

> a golden share was put in to protect British interests, to prevent the take-over by a foreign power. You couldn't do this today because of European Community (EC) regulations. We were not worried about a US take-over, but rather German or French, that is, through Demenex, Elf, Total or Petrofina. [Also see discussion in Chapter 3.]

From BNOC's perspective, one executive explained:

> golden shares are political measures. Even though I have worked on many privatisations since, we still don't have it right, don't know if they really do anything. At that stage [when assets sold] free market forces should work. But they [golden shares] were the vogue, the fashion.

One Britoil executive complained that the golden share was a last minute response to political concerns and was not worked out, and therefore later proved to be the cause of major problems for the company as it faced takeover bids from BP and Atlantic Richfield (see Chapter 3).

Another response, according to a DEn civil servant, was to re-enact the assurances agreed with oil companies in the wake of the 1974 oil crisis. In July 1985, the *Financial Times* published a letter from BP to the government, assuring the government that they would meet United Kingdom oil demand, providing they could raise prices as necessary, as discussed in Chapter 2. In response to this revelation, a BNOC executive claimed, the Secretary of State for Energy would only say that 'the arrangements between the government and oil companies are confidential'.

The evidence suggests that the decision to sell the oil assets was a pure political calculation, rather than one due to ideological conviction or economic efficiency goals. Civil servants reinforced the political nature of the decision: 'The government kept BNOC out of political convenience, not any conviction.' Others pointed out that there was no quantitative analysis on how BNOC ensured security of supply or the impact of a sale. It was a matter of political perception. In addition, the government's sales were expedient. They only sold the companies that were easy to sell, particularly those already operating as private companies, rather than those which were public monopolies or met any ideological criteria. With huge consequences for the future, civil servants also felt that the sales were undertaken without any thought to the regulatory implications.

With the case of BP, by 1983 the government realised that instead of having costs concentrated in the short term (box 9), they were in the ideal case where the majority of costs are dispersed and spread over the long term, while the benefits are concentrated and immediate (box 11), in which case they should and did act fast. The financial distribution of costs and benefits for the BP case is illustrated in Figure 7.7. The government received almost £7 billion by 1987 in share sale proceeds while they would have had to wait until at least after 2005, 17 years later, for BP's dividend proceeds to have exceeded the sale proceeds. This is also a conservative estimate because this graph does not take into account the net present value of money, the benefit of having cash in hand versus the promise of future revenues, which is especially important for oil companies whose dividends, due to the nature of the industry, are notoriously unstable. Nor does it take into account the cost to the government of subscribing to new BP issues in order to maintain their shareholding. Thus, the costs of privatisation were propelled into the future – after most of the current politicians would have retired.

The alternative explanation for the Conservative politicians' actions is that they were preference shaping, implementing policies to shape demand

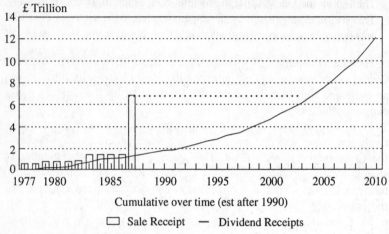

Figure 7.7   The Value of BP: Sale versus Dividend Receipts

and increase Conservative support. Conservative politicians, in fact, claim that they shifted public opinion to favouring privatisation, for example, Nigel Lawson (1992) claimed: 'Wider share ownership was an important policy objective and we were prepared to pay a price for it' (p. 238). For example, in the sale of Enterprise Oil, the government turned down offers of a trade sale of BGC's oil assets. They decided to float the company on the stock exchange because, according to one civil servant, the 'Conservatives had the view that capitalist shareholders would not vote for Labour'. That being said, the sale was not widely advertised and no effort was made to target new shareholders.

There was a limit to the scope of the Conservatives' wider share owner-ship, which was demonstrated by the rejection of Howell's suggestion to give all United Kingdom citizens shares in BNOC. Lawson (1992) in fact claims that no one in the party was prepared to support this proposition (p. 218). There are in fact several general advantages to 'people's capital-ism' noted by academics, including: building up a capital market, wider share ownership, a wider constituency than a tax-cut, state-owned indus-tries having more autonomy, relieving the state of future investment burdens, and that individuals can choose their own portfolio of risk (Aharoni, 1986, pp. 336–7). Yet these advantages were rejected by the Conservatives, which indicates that their primary motive was the cash up front and rewards to Tory voters rather than long-term electoral gain. As one minister explained, based on his experience in the United States:

The link in the US was that the owning class voted more conservatively. This was underestimated by those who wanted to give it away. The link was between private share-owners and Conservative voters.

The electoral impact of privatisation, in terms of converting Labour to Conservative voters, was not felt until the 1987 election, and then it was an estimated shift of only 1.6 per cent, controlling for the range of socio-economic factors correlated with privatisation (McAlister and Studlar, 1989, p. 173). A key reason why the Tories' policy stance converted relatively few voters was that many of the new shareholders already supported the Conservatives (McDonald, 1989, p. 8). And while the number of shareholders in Britain dramatically increased from 5 per cent of the electorate in 1979 to 23 per cent in 1989, shareholders remained a minority of the population (McAlister and Studlar, 1989, p. 166; Chapman, 1990, p. 8). Even after the 1987 election, the median voter was not a shareholder. Thus, privatisation might better be seen as a policy which rewarded loyal Conservative supporters rather than one which converted voters close to the median.

Determining the Conservatives' Position on Privatisation

Once the costs and benefits were favourably assessed and the Conservatives adopted privatisation, the position and intensity of Conservative voters' opinion on privatisation determined the party's position. The key here is the importance of Conservative Party members rather than the overall electorate. In the Conservative Party, members are influential as they determine candidates' selection, mobilise local support and attend Conservative Party conferences. Rather than using the directional theory of voting which emphasises the role of elites to determine positions and then predicts voters' response, or the median voter model which only takes into account proximity of position, I suggest an alternative way of incorporating position and intensity as a means of creating demand for a policy. Adapting Figure 7.3's picture of overall voter demand for privatisation, I extrapolate and incorporate additional descriptive evidence and hypothesise the distributions of position and intensity on privatisation of Conservative voters (see Figure 7.8).

The majority of Conservatives, like the overall population, were closest in position to the status quo, though there were many who favoured more denationalisation (line). In terms of intensity (diamond-dotted line), those at the neutral position did not feel strongly about the issue (point A), while those favouring more denationalisation felt more strongly (point C). The

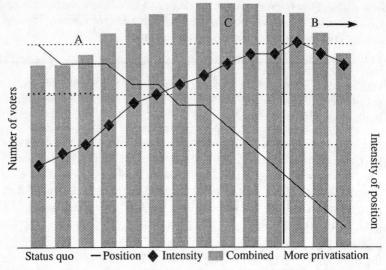

Status quo   — Position ◆ Intensity ▨ Combined More privatisation

Figure 7.8   Hypothesis of the Distribution of Public Opinion towards Privatisation

number of those with extreme intensity declined, possibly because being outside the region of acceptability (B, to the right of the solid line) they perceived their position to be unrealistic.

Instead of parties arbitrarily moving to an extreme position, there is an interchange between voters and candidates. Voters can influence policy positions by threatening to vote against the party on that issue or by threatening to decide their vote based on another issue, which is more likely when intensity is low. Therefore, when determining the most advantageous position to select, politicians must take into account how many voters occupy a position and how intensely they feel about the issue. By simply multiplying the position by the intensity, I determine the electoral impact of a position (bars in the background). The highest point of the bars (point C) is where the most voters will vote according to this issue. At the lower points in the bar either the intensity is less so some voters will select another issue or the intensity is stronger but there are insufficient numbers of voters to make the radical position worthwhile. Outside the region of acceptability, gains in extreme votes are cancelled out by negative votes from the centre.

The Conservative Party started close to the median position in 1979. As they realised the benefits from the policy, which involved the cost-benefit analysis above, and the existence of strong opinions among Conservative voters, they moved to a more extreme position. A high degree of intensity from the extreme position holders led politicians further to the right. For example, Lawson records his amazement and relief at receiving a standing ovation at the 1982 Conservative Party convention after changing the subject of the energy debate from rising gas prices (which were receiving heavy criticism) to the privatisation of Britoil (Lawson, 1992, p. 176).

CONCLUSION

Privatisation in Britain can be divided into three phases. In the first phase, the policy was possible but was only advanced by policy entrepreneurs. In the second phase, the government was committed to the policy but only proceeded on a case by case basis according to the costs and benefits. In the third phase, privatisation was accepted in general terms and evolved into an ideological project in its own right. The oil asset sales occurred during the first two phases, while most explanations of privatisation focus on the third. Therefore, I argue that the traditional explanations of privatisation are less helpful for this case.

The public demand for privatisation was weak and uncertain over time. Opposition was greater to specific privatisations than to the concept in general, over which the population was fairly evenly divided. Because privatisation did not figure highly on any of the voters' rankings of issues, it did not feature in their voting decisions. It was low intensity rather than the parties' failure to offer sufficient stimulus, as the directional theory predicts, which explains the low public demand. Voters did not feel strongly about the privatisation of the oil assets, in part because the policy did not affect them directly. The government, therefore, could proceed without electoral risk. This low intensity and lack of concern gave the political parties a wide range for choice in terms of developing the privatisation issue and selecting their policy position.

Rather than being a 'lottery', I argue that these decisions were determined by specific supply-side factors, namely personal political advantage and party political demand. The effect of these two factors is illustrated in Figure 7.9. Personal political advantage was an important factor because a policy entrepreneur was important to the development and promotion of the policy. Within party political advantage, the distribution of costs and benefits in the short and long term determined whether privatisation was worthwhile to adopt at all, while the distribution of position and intensity

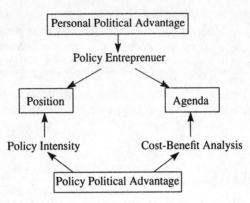

Figure 7.9　Supply Factors

of Conservative Party members, rather than the general public, determined the optimal position for the government to select.

In terms of policy options, the political parameters faced by the government can be illustrated in Venn diagrams where policies to raise taxes, increase the budget deficit and sell assets are represented by points A, B and C respectively (see Figures 7.10, 7.11 and 7.12). The parameters included public demand, personal credibility and electoral success as represented by circles 1, 2 and 3 respectively. In 1974, the issues of taxes and budget deficits were not intensely held opinions; no politicians had staked their career on them and there were no severe electoral risks for selecting any of the policies. As a result, the options available to politicians were large (points A, B and C are in all three circles), as represented in Figure 7.10. Because asset sales were untried and risky, other more traditional policies offered less resistance, and were therefore chosen. In 1977, following the 1976 balance of payments deficits and the IMF crisis, politicians could not afford to allow a repeat situation, therefore, an increase in the budget deficit due to electoral considerations was no longer possible (point B excluded from circle 3), as illustrated in Figure 7.11. Similarly, due to the already high tax rate, Labour politicians feared they would face electoral punishment by raising taxes (point A no longer inside circle 3). Thus, of the three options, only asset sales remained possible (only point C remains in the intersection of three circles).

By 1982, the situation had changed again with the election of the Conservative government in 1979. Public opinion continued to allow politicians a wide range of options, but the Conservative leadership had

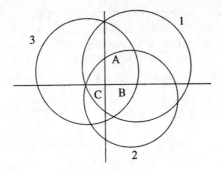

Figure 7.10   Policy Process Parameters, 1974

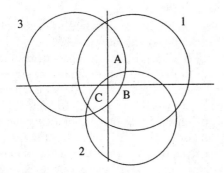

Figure 7.11   Policy Process Parameters, 1977

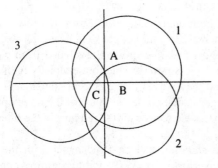

Figure 7.12   Policy Process Parameters, 1982

staked their career credibility on their economic policy, including no new taxes while reducing the budget deficit. As such, they also faced electoral risk if they strayed from these commitments. Thus, only an asset sale was possible (point C is the only option inside circles 2 and 3 and the only option that remained in the intersection of the three circles), as illustrated in Figure 7.12.

8 Explaining State Disengagement

Most scholars of politics, from whatever their viewpoint, have assumed that states and governments grow larger over time, and that it is normal, logical and 'rational' for those who control government power to seek to push outward their scope of influence. Pluralists see groups, including bureaucrats, as always demanding more services and government responding by building greater capabilities to meet these demands (Dahl, 1961; Halperin, 1974). Elite theorists assume that the state is a means for elites to enhance or protect their position and thus expect elite demands to increase the scope of the states (Mills, 1956). Public choice theorists, whether focusing on the bureaucrat or the politician, have assumed that public officials have self-interested reasons for increasing the size of the government (Niskanen, 1971). Even from the perspective of international relations, scholars have accepted the realists' premise that states are power maximisers continuously seeking to increase their wealth and control, and thus their size (Keohane, 1984a; Waltz, 1954 and 1979). This includes scholars from the international political economy perspective who regard states as only one of many actors in the international arena (Strange, 1985; Krasner, 1985b).

Though it is not necessarily intrinsic to these theories, the government growth assumption has persisted (Hood, 1991, pp. 43–5). In part, this can be understood by the fact that most governments have steadily grown, especially since the Second World War, the period in which most of these theories were developed. There has thus been no reason to question the growth assumption. In fact, government growth seemed to be the one constant that political theory had to be able to explain. The idea and practice of 'rolling back the frontiers of the state' which developed in Britain under the Thatcher government, and the effort to disengage government from many spheres of economic and social life, initially raised few doubts about the fundamental premise. A common first response was to be sceptical about whether anything had really changed.

But the longer and more complete a process of state disengagement becomes, the less plausible it is to suppose that nothing of substance has happened, and the more important it becomes to examine the possibility that public officials, groups, elites or states have acted to reduce state power or influence in a long-term way, and therefore have in some sense behaved counter-intuitively. The British government's oil asset sales apparently provide just such a case. They stretched over a 10-year period, involved nine separate sales, and affected assets valued by the private market at £8.5 billion. The sales were a particularly final and once-for-all method of readjusting government's role in the energy sector: the scale of receipts made it virtually impossible for any future government to rebuild any equivalent asset portfolio without changing the whole basis of government/market relations in the United Kingdom. The sales were also a serious undertaking in terms of their transaction costs, conservatively estimated at some £223 million.

Because the underlying assumptions of most theorists are inconsistent with these facts, it is important to stand back somewhat from the theories and the detailed narratives reviewed so far, and briefly re-piece the jigsaw of multiple causes involved. Table 8.1 summarises the general motivations for selling an asset, which can be divided into two categories: financial and functional. Though this list is derived from governments selling state assets, perhaps it can more readily be understood using the analogy of a professor with a 10-year-old automobile.

While there are many reasons why a professor might reconsider ownership of a 10-year-old car, there are only a few specific reasons why she

Table 8.1   Why Sell an Asset?

Financial	Functional

Expensive to maintain	Asset changed in terms of:
	    size
	    capabilities
	    output
	and therefore no longer
	provides necessary service

Becomes a financial liability	Needs change in terms of:
	    political
	    ideological
	    social
	and therefore asset no longer
	necessary

Need the money Other arrangements offer greater returns	Better alternatives available

would actually sell it. Initially, financial reasons might motivate a sale. For instance, the car is expensive to maintain because it breaks down so often, or it has become a financial liability as the make and age of the car increase the likelihood of accidents which have repercussions in the form of an enormous insurance liability. In other scenarios, she needs money for more important priorities, such as to pay her child's school fees, or she has realised that leasing a car is more economical. In addition to financial motivations, there are also functional reasons why a professor might sell her car: Either the asset has changed so that it no longer performs as well, or her needs have changed and she no longer needs the same service or a better alternative now exists. For example, the car has become so run-down it is no longer the reliable mode of transportation it once was, or the professor has grown out of her idealist beliefs and a 10-year-old Russian Lada does not fit with her new conservative image. A final possibility is that the public transport link from her home to university has recently been completed and the 45-minute drive can now be done in 20 minutes on the underground. Of course, she will act faster to dispose of the car the more she needs the money or the more embarrassing it is to have a Lada parked in her driveway.

Given these numerous 'rational' reasons to sell an asset in general, I now turn to the evidence of this case and review which rationales applied to the sales of BP, BNOC and BGC's oil assets from the perspective of the four levels of influences analysed in this book: international, company, bureaucracy and political process. I first examine the international level and consider the theoretical implications for using this level for domestic policy decisions. Then I turn to the domestic actors, the managers of BNOC, BGC and BP, the civil servants and then the elected politicians and review their role in the asset sale decision. In the third section, I consider the broader implications of this analysis for understanding or predicting the extent of privatisation in other contexts. Next I review the prominent role institutions play and the consequences for public choice theory. I then conclude by returning to an overview of this case and the implications of a multi-level approach.

INTERNATIONAL FACTORS IN STATE DISENGAGEMENT

At the international level I argue, in contrast to the realists, that rather than determining a state's behaviour, international factors set parameters to politicians' policy choices. With two variables, an aggregate political variable and an economic issue specific variable, it is possible to predict a country's vulnerability to international pressures in different cases. In Britain's case, it was clear that the British government would be more susceptible to international financial pressures than international oil pressures. In fact, pressures on Britain's finances in the form of the 1976 IMF crisis were the only international forces that directly affected the government's decision to sell its oil assets. Changes in the structure of the international oil industry from a cartel to a free-market industry did not force the sales in the late 1970s or the 1980s, but they were significant in that they diminished the consequences of relinquishing ownership and this made the sales possible. In response to neoliberal claims, the third variable examined in this case was Britain's membership in the EC and the IEA. The evidence revealed that the international organisations per se had little effect on the government's decision to sell its oil assets. The interdependence that led to the creation of the organisations, however, was an important factor. The economic links though can be revealed through issue analysis, rather than specific organisational studies, as was the case with the IMF in the financial issue analysis.

Recalling Table 8.1, the international level was the primary determinant of the government's functional motivations for selling its oil assets. In the case of Britoil, Enterprise Oil and Wytch Farm and BP, and even in the case of winding down BNOC's trading operation, the changes in the structure of the international oil industry were such that the services that the oil assets provided were no longer needed in Britain. Specifically on the demand side, as the global oil industry became increasingly controlled by the free market, numerous sources of oil were developed and state-ownership was no longer necessary to ensure security of supply. On the supply side, the changes were such that BNOC trading and BP were no longer able to provide the services they once did. Due to the extent of free-market competition, a single state could not influence oil prices through a state trading company, especially a relatively small company like BNOC and with Britain's relatively modest reserves. Similarly, though BP could once be relied upon to favour Britain, as the company sought to adapt to the changing international structure, it was no longer possible for BP to discriminate between customers.

The approach used in this case contributes to general knowledge of the role international factors play in policy-making analysis, but it also contributes to understanding of the theoretical underpinnings of international relations theory. This case suggests that international factors can be incorporated as setting parameters in the same way that institutional public choice theorists have considered domestic institutions or game theorists have identified different 'rules of the game' for different situations. While this seems especially obvious in cases of privatisation, which is often referred to as part of an international trend, international factors are also useful in general to domestic policy-making analyses. This case, in fact, helps to illustrate how few truly 'domestic' issues there are, especially for states in weaker international political and economic positions.

In terms of broader international relations theory, the British oil asset sales question one of the basic assumptions regarding the state. International relations has evolved beyond realism to neorealism and neoliberalism, as well as other avenues, such as international political economy (IPE). But in the two mainstream areas, neorealism and neoliberalism, the central assumptions have remained – the state is the primary actor, the international system is basically anarchic and states seek power. This case, with many others in the IPE genre, shows that there are important issues which a state-centred approach cannot adequately address.

The most fundamental criticism of the neorealist approach is that they treat the state's preferences as a given. They assume that the agents and actors of the state are unitary, only the state's capabilities affect the system, and that international institutions play a minimal role (Krasner, 1985b). Neoliberals only challenge the latter two problems and argue that factors such as interdependence and institutionalisation of international rules (international organisations or regimes) are also important. Indirectly they question the pre-eminence of the state, but they do not deny that it is an important international actor (Krasner, 1985b). Only IPE scholars have pointed out that there are other actors such as firms and groups and other constructs such as markets that matter (Strange, 1988; Keohane and Nye, 1979). Some also highlight the complexity of the state and show that it is not a homogeneous actor but rather a compilation of political parties, interest groups, politicians and voters (Milner, 1988; Cohen, 1989; Frieden, 1991; Golich, 1992).

This redefinition of the state cannot be understated; its significance has far-reaching implications. For example, states with different parties in power will have the same capabilities and face the same international parameters, and therefore have many of the same policy choices. But the outcomes may still be different because politicians have different constituents, different party structures and different political strategies. These factors not only affect their policy choices, they in turn affect the state's resources. In the British case, the change of the party in power from Labour to the Conservatives in 1979, and the ensuing interests and strategy changes including voter base, credibility and supply of policy entrepreneurs, resulted in the complete sale of the state's oil assets and a redefinition of the state's position.

THE DOMESTIC ACTORS' CALCULUS

This section reviews the functional and financial motives of the domestic actors involved in the decision-making process, and then examines which were dominant factors.

The Three Main Actors

At the *company* level, by examining the level of organisational autonomy, financial control and success in achieving the company's mission, it was possible to explain the differing actions of BP, BNOC and BGC. Because BP was organisationally autonomous and had financial control, it sought to maintain that status. Due to its considerable size and financial success, BP was effective in persuading the government to sell its holding. By contrast, BNOC and BGC depended on government ownership for their national interest mandate, which they resented losing. But as autonomous and independent companies, they also resisted any measure that would split their companies. Due to its enormous size and financial success, BGC was effective in delaying the sale of Wytch Farm for over two years, but ultimately could not stop either of its oil assets being sold. BNOC was the least successful in defending its interests as the government was able to appoint a new company chairman favourable to privatisation.

Opposition from the managers of nationalised industries was most easily avoided by replacing the top executive with a manager who does not have any allegiance to the company and was favourable to the government's change in policy. When that was not possible, or when opposition continued, the most effective means to appease concern and gain cooperation was to sell the company in one piece. Though this undermined attempts to increase competition and efficiency in the case of monopolies, it increased the value of the company as well as the proceeds to the government. Because a government's time horizon is only the next election, measures that facilitate a sale so that it is achievable during the party's time in office are most desirable, and the consequences of a private monopoly will immediately be no different than from a public monopoly. Only in the long term will disregard for the public interest become apparent, and measures can be implemented subsequently to break the monopoly.

At the *bureaucracy* level, British civil servants were motivated by interesting work that was defined in part by the career opportunities that privatisation presented. One traditional public choice view of bureaucrats is that they are budget-maximisers. Depending on whether there is movement within the bureaucracy and whether bureaucrats choose to act individually or collectively, though, three other types of action are possible: self-maximising, bureau-shaping and career-maximising. This traditional view is especially misguided because collective action is rare. In this case, because British civil servants moved between divisions and departments regularly, their allegiance was to the central government rather than to a particular department or division. Thus, their interests focused on interesting work and career advancement rather than defending the functions of their current division or department.

A strong/weak department–personal affect typology explains why collective action was possible in strong departments where policies were perceived negatively; otherwise individual strategies were more rational. Because the structure of the British civil service was so secure, very few policies were interpreted by civil servants as personally negative. Collective action, therefore, would have been unusual. And because the Department of Energy was a relatively weak department, the lack of collective action in this case is not surprising. However, the fact that collective action was evident in the Treasury suggests that civil servants do react when they perceive a policy shift that threatens them personally and that they are capable of doing so collectively. It also suggests that there are more ways to react in a stronger department; no other department, for example, could realistically promote sales of other departments' assets.

At the *political process* level, traditional public choice models, such as the median voter model, focus on the demand for policies and predict that politicians will select policy positions that appeal to the largest number of voters. This case lends support to the view that, for some issues, there is no strong demand and policy decisions are made primarily according to supply factors. In the case of privatisation in Britain there was little demand in the early stages of policy development. The deciding factors were, therefore, from the supply side: personal political advantage and electoral political advantage. Privatisation provided the ideal electoral advantage where benefits were concentrated towards Conservative supporters in the short term and costs were dispersed in the long term. Originally the Conservative leadership hesitated about selling oil assets, fearing that privatisation would concentrate short-term costs to supporters and opponents alike. But a policy entrepreneur emerged to push the policy through the early stages of internal resistance, especially from the managers of BNOC and BGC and doubters within the Cabinet, and undertook the cost of educating the Prime Minister and other party members of the international changes and the distribution of party members' position and intensity. In other words, Lawson argued that there would be no short-term costs from the sales, that ownership of oil assets would not change Britain's oil situation, even in a crisis, and that the proceeds from the sale would provide immediate cash to distribute to supporters. Once the Conservative leadership accepted this distribution of costs and benefits in the short and long term, they proceeded quickly.

When looking at the three sets of domestic actors, company managers, civil servants and politicians, their reactions towards privatisation were quite different. The managers of BNOC and BGC were opposed while the managers of BP were enthusiastic. The civil servants in the DEn were initially sceptical but were cooperative while those in the Treasury were eager. Among the politicians, most were initially reluctant while a few policy entrepreneurs were enthusiastic. These variations can be explained by the differences in the actors' constraints, but also by their goals and motivations. The importance of looking closely at constraints is illustrated by the variations just between the managers of BP and BNOC. Both were state-owned oil companies and yet their reactions to privatisation were completely different. Thus, even slight variations in structure can produce widely different outcomes. This also highlights the problem of assuming bureaucratic structures to be similar, not only between countries, but within them – as many public choice theorists do.

Despite the differences, calling attention to the constraints reveals new sets of generalisations about actors: they seek to maximise their utility in the short term, and their strategies are influenced by both the constraints of the institutions in which they function and by their own capabilities. In other words, neither constraints nor individuals are generic. Individuals pursue goals as they become possible within the existing structures, and as they are able. For example, a civil servant in a flexible bureaucracy who is not an effective manager may choose to stay in his or her current bureau or department and not seek promotion. As a result of this choice, the civil servant will then pursue self-maximising strategies in that department. Without knowing the structure of the bureaucracy and the individual's abilities, it is difficult to predict such behaviour. Only upon careful examination of actors and their particular constraints can we understand their actions.

The Calculus

In deciding to sell the oil holdings, all three sets of actors as public officials can technically be described as decision makers. But in this case, only the politicians were able to make the final decisions to sell assets, albeit under the influence, not only of the company managers and civil servants, but also of public demand as well as international pressures. The analysis of the calculus (recalling Table 8.1), therefore, focuses on the political level.

The numerous political reasons for selling each oil asset are summarised in Table 8.2. The reasons were surprisingly similar between sales, though the priorities in each case differed according to the company and other external pressures. For all the sales, the financial motivations were pre-eminent. The need for money was of primary importance to the government and the attractiveness of a sale was enhanced because the politicians could raise large amounts of money immediately. According to political short-term calculations, this was a more advantageous financial arrange-ment than the returns in the form of profits and dividends spread over the longer term. In the case of BNOC's trading operations, while there was no option to sell the organisation, the financial liabilities that it represented were the trigger to motivate politicians to close it down.

Functional motivations were also important. In the case of BNOC and BGC, the Conservatives' needs had changed so that state-ownership was no longer consistent with their free-market ideology nor their image as champions of the private sector and small government. There was also a better alternative available to state ownership, namely private ownership

Table 8.2 Political Motivations for Selling Oil Assets

	Britoil	*BGC's Oil Assets*	*BP*	*BNOC Trading*
Party Political	Financial need	Financial need	Financial need	Financial liability
	Other arrangements offer greater returns	Other arrangements offer greater returns	Other arrangements offer greater returns	Ideologically inconsistent
	Ideologically inconsistent	Ideologically inconsistent	Expensive to maintain	
Personal Political	Inconsistent with image	Inconsistent with image	Inconsistent with image	Inconsistent with image
	Prestige from sale	Prestige from sale	Prestige from sale	

and the ensuing prestige from the sale and from governing over a larger private sector.

Though the factors in each case were similar, the priorities differed. In the case of Britoil, the personal prestige factor for Nigel Lawson was the most important factor, followed by the fact that a sale offered an immediate cash return whereas continued ownership meant variable profits into the future. Of underlying importance was the government's need for money, as well as the way it fit with the Conservatives' free-market ideology and the Conservative leadership's image as defenders of the private sector.

In the case of BGC's oil assets, the most important factor was the improved financial arrangement that privatisation offered. It was superior in terms of immediate cash up front, and because the sales also reduced the strength of the remaining BGC, an important objective for the government, which had been frustrated in its struggle to control BGC's profits. The political prestige from the sales was also important, though not as strongly associated with one individual after Lawson moved to the Treasury and not realised in the Wytch Farm case because of the long duration of the sale. As in the Britoil case, the need for money and the inconsistency in both ideology and image were important as secondary factors.

The BP case is more complicated because there were several sales, though they can be divided between Labour's 1977 sale and the subsequent sales by the Conservatives. For the 1977 sale, the most important factor was the need for money and the fact that the sale would raise immediate cash without lessening the government's control over the company. Raising money in this way was more consistent with Labour's image than cutting spending. The maintenance expenses and the prestige, however, were not factors in 1977. For the Conservatives' sales, in contrast, the prestige was of primary importance, as were the enormous proceeds up front versus the expense of maintaining a stake in BP. Though the image of having companies under state-ownership was a factor for the Conservatives, ideological consistency was not an issue as it was in the other cases because BP was not subjected to government intervention and was already functioning efficiently in the private sector.

Finally, the case of the BNOC trading operations offers a slightly different perspective. Though the trading operation did not fit with the Conservatives' free-trade ideology nor with their image of themselves as efficient managers, there were overriding factors that made the operation worthwhile to maintain, such as national security. But as the company began to lose money, which in turn had to be covered by grants made expressly by Parliament, it highlighted the incompatibility of BNOC with the government's programme ideologically or politically and hastened its demise.

EMPIRICAL IMPLICATIONS FOR OTHER PRIVATISATIONS

While the findings are understandable for this case, the real test is whether they can be applied to cases beyond privatisation in Britain. Extrapolating from the findings, I create a list of probing questions to reveal whether these factors exist in other countries and therefore whether privatisation is likely. If adding the pieces together to explain privatisation is a truly viable approach, it should be able to identify general conditions under which privatisation is possible (Savas, 1987, pp. 278–9). Based on the findings of this British case, a series of general questions can be asked of any country which can determine whether and when privatisation is a realistic policy outcome.

The questions in Table 8.3 are designed to reveal whether obstacles exist in other cases. While not designed to discover the intricacies that contributed to our understanding of the British case, these questions may be useful in obtaining a first approximation assessment.

A 'no' to any one of these six questions can prevent privatisation from occurring. The first precondition for a sale is whether there is anything to sell. In some countries the government never created or nationalised industries, therefore there is little to sell. In other countries, where financial markets are small and undeveloped, having something to sell means having assets that are attractive to international investors. The

Table 8.3   Anticipating Privatisation

---

1. Does the country have assets that can be sold?
2. Due to international or political pressures, does the government need money quickly?
3. Will the company managers cooperate, and if not, does the government have the means to circumvent them?
4. Will the bureaucrats in the relevant departments cooperate, and if not, does the government have the means to circumvent them?
5. Can the governing party implement the sale without electoral punishment, ie is public opinion opposed and intense on the issue?
6. Are there other options that will provide greater political advantage for the politicians in power?

---

second question determines whether there is a pressing need for money. If time is not crucial, there may be other more feasible options. Question 3 focuses on the managers of the state-owned industries. Privatisation can proceed only if they cooperate or the government has the means to override or replace them. Question 4 addresses a similar consideration in regard to the government's civil servants; privatisation can only proceed if they cooperate or the government has the means to circumvent or replace them. Question 5 considers the electoral implications of a sale. If the public is opposed on the grounds of national interest, strategic security, financial or even sentiment and votes accordingly, privatisation is not worthwhile for a politician to pursue and the policy will halt. Finally, if politicians have other options which provide greater personal or party political advantage, they will be selected instead of privatisation. Over time, questions 3 to 5 may be altered by political means, which is part of the job of a political entrepreneur. The other questions depend on structural factors and alternative options which for the most part are external to the political process.

To explore the usefulness of these questions beyond the case of Britain, I apply them to the case of Argentina, one of the few cases where a government has decisively moved on and successfully completed an extensive privatisation programme, including its energy assets. In fact, it is the only government besides Britain to dispose of its oil assets completely. (There are, however, a few countries whose governments never owned their oil assets, such as the United States.) Argentina's energy assets include Hidronor, the country's principal hydro-electricity generator, YPF, the national oil company, and the federally held gas and electricity companies. Equally remarkable is the fact that these energy assets were sold in 15 months, from March 1992 to July 1993 and raised $6.65 billion (*Financial Times*, 12 July 1993).

The Argentinian case passes the six hurdles for privatisation set forth in Table 8.3. In terms of question 1 and having assets to sell, as a developing country, Argentina's energy industry was one of the few state-owned resources that would sell, because energy is an internationally traded commodity, and therefore attractive to both domestic and foreign investors. With Argentina's small indigenous investment market, appeal to international investors was crucial. In terms of question 2 and need, because the government of Argentina in 1990 was facing 200 per cent inflation and a fiscal deficit of 22 per cent of GDP, they were desperate for money quickly, particularly foreign exchange, in order to repay their international debt and to stabilise their shaky economy. Privatisation proved to be successful in meeting this need as well, as it ended $2.1 billion annual subsidies to nationalised companies, generated additional taxes from some companies now operating profitably in the private sector, transferred $1.5 billion in liabilities to the private sector, added $5.4 billion in cash to the Treasury, and enabled them to retire $12.5 billion in government debt through equity swaps (*Wall Street Journal*, 12 November 1994).

In terms of question 3 and company managers, the government was able to overcome management opposition to privatisation by hiring an oil industry veteran from the private sector expressly to oversee the privatisation of YPF (*Wall Street Journal*, 12 November 1994). In relation to question 4 and the bureaucracy, President Carlos Menem, with the powers of the Presidency behind him, had the authority and therefore was able to overcome any opposition from government bureaucrats (*Financial Times*, 12 July 1993).

In terms of question 5 and the electorate, the government was able to avoid electoral punishment by convincing the public in two distinct ways that the sales were economically essential. First, the government bought the support of the politically important old age pensioners by allocating a substantial portion of the share offerings to them in order to make good billions of dollars in unpaid bills. There may be electoral repercussions in the future, however, because 30–5 per cent of the shares were subsequently purchased in the market by foreign investors (*Financial Times*, 25 June 1993; *Wall Street Journal*, 12 November 1994). Second, the Argentinian government demanded safeguards including investment and other requirements from the investors, so that ministers argued that they were able to ensure Argentina's energy security. The electorability question may not be as important in the Argentinian case because the Constitution then allowed Presidents to serve only one term in office. Menem, therefore, did not have electoral considerations to weigh, and thus he could pursue the policy without repercussions. Subsequently, however, he altered the Constitution to allow himself another term.

In relation to the last question, number 6 and alternatives, there were few options and privatisation was the least painful compared to tax increases and strict monetary policy. Especially in comparison, privatisation proved to be very successful, and particularly for Menem personally as he was widely credited with stabilising the economy (*Financial Times*, 27 May 1993). This achievement did not hurt his future career aspirations and may have been the impetus needed to alter the Constitution and grant him another term in office.

Looking beyond the case of Argentina, despite the *Economist's* claim that 'Everybody's doing it', privatisation has in fact been a limited phenomenon. Many states have considered sales and other means to reduce the size of their government debts. Also many leaders have proposed such actions; few have been implemented. Given the multiple and complex conditions affecting the privatisation decision, as illustrated by the complex nature of the levels analysed in this book and represented by the hurdles in Table 8.3, it is surprising that so many governments have chosen privatisation at all and have been able to implement their privatisation plans.

THE TENSION BETWEEN INDIVIDUAL CHOICE AND INSTITUTIONAL DETERMINATION

Because institutional public choice theory is more dependent on structures for many of its models than was possibly originally realised, many of its models are difficult to transfer across countries where the actors remain nominally the same, but the structure in which he or she operates is different. The findings from this case clearly reveal the problem. In response, the new typologies presented have attempted to incorporate possible structure variation. Two questions are raised by this approach: how extensively can and should institutions or structures be recognised and incorporated? and can institutional variation be usefully incorporated?

The first question requires consideration in terms of both breadth and depth of the incorporation. In terms of breadth, this case study addressed a wide range of institutions by virtue of its multi-level approach, including both domestic and international levels. Though considered in a more general way in the final section, from a public choice perspective, the theory was robust enough, and its basic assumptions simple and clear enough to be applied to the full range of variables considered. Though it could incorporate the international dimension, no specific international public choice theory looks likely. In terms of the domestic variables, however, the public choice approach was robustly adaptable to a variety of levels, actors and situations.

In terms of depth, however, the emphasis on institutions raises a more fundamental question: does an overt focus on institutions detract from the power of public choice theory, rationality of the individual? In other words, if institutions are so important in determining outcomes, has this taken over from the individual's rational choice? The recognition of the role of institutions in the models developed in this book runs very close to the line. However, I argue that this is no different from public choice theorists who focus on game theory, carefully establishing which game is being played and explicitly identifying the 'rules' of that game. However, when the rules of the game chicken, for example, are changed, it becomes another game, not a variation of chicken. So while better terminology might need to be developed to differentiate between the regulations actors must play by, game theory clearly demonstrates the importance of correctly identifying the 'rules'. The rationality assumption of public choice theorists does seem to leave little room for individual choice, however, once the parameters of their situation are established. This is the nature of the theory; and more 'choice' does not emerge if we choose to be ambiguous in our analysis. Finally, public choice theory recognises possibly one of the most important factors that cannot be determined by institutions: risk. Though the odds are altered by institutional structures and an individual's place in them, they do not determine who is willing to take risks. Though institutions were much more fully incorporated into the models in this case, the actors of this case demonstrated a wide range of choice. We have yet to determine, for example, why one person is willing to take the role of policy entrepreneur and others are not.

The incorporation of institutional variation into public choice theory models is a more straightforward question. The typologies in this case, such as those for managers of state-owned industries and civil servants, demonstrate that not only is the recognition of institutional variation necessary to compare across countries, but that it is necessary to compare across companies or departments. The institutional complexity of one country is sufficient to warrant addressing variation. Whether the most important variations are addressed, parsimoniously, is a matter for further empirical testing.

The usefulness of the civil servants' Strategies and Structures typology (Figure 6.1) can be demonstrated with a discussion of the design of an optimal governmental structure, and issues raised initially by David Osborne and Ted Gaebler's *Reinventing Government* (1992). In a recent interview, David Osborne emphasised that the changes rest on carefully defining bureaucracies' business, mission and customers (Carver and Vondra, 1994, p. 133). This is supported by the Structures and Strategies typology and evidence from the role of civil servants in the British asset sales. The public choice approach also reveals how difficult an accurate definition is to create, and that a generalised approach may negate the intended effect.

The example Osborne and Gaebler herald as a success illustrates my point. A unit within the US Department of Defence in charge of all defence installations has simplified its charter to a one-page sheet that defined their business, mission and customers: 'To provide for our customers – the soldiers, sailors, marines, and airmen who defend America –

excellent places to work and live, and excellent base services' (p. 134). In the words of the Deputy Assistant Secretary of Defence of Installations, 'our policy is to provide excellent barracks, not minimum barracks' (p. 135). By identifying the army personnel as their customers, it is easy to see how their job is simplified and satisfaction is readily measured. The drawbacks of such an approach, however, are that the taxpayer may be paying for higher standards than they think are appropriate and the local communities may not be receiving the consideration they should while the unit's loudest customer is getting more new accommodation. According to some, this does not meet the overall definition of good government. Therefore, more attention needs to be paid to the department's direct contacts, recognising that they may be separate from whom they are meant to serve.

Applying Osborne and Gaebler's streamlined mission to the Oil Division of the Department of Energy, the objective might be to provide for efficient licensing and regulation of the North Sea. If their customers are identified as the oil companies though, which was effectively the case in the 1980s, the meaning of efficient was quite different from where the customers are British oil consumers or taxpayers. There is no right answer and these decisions are not easy to make. Most importantly, if the decision is left to the civil servants, they may select the group with whom they come into the most contact and who are most able to complain to their political masters if they are displeased.

Osborne and Gaebler do recognise that setting up corresponding structures and rewards are necessary in order to sustain the desired changes (Carver and Vondra, 1994, p. 140). But these points too need careful attention. As the finding in this case highlighted, civil servants have distinct sets of motivations. Therefore, some of Osborne and Gaebler's recommendations that are adapted from business are not likely to work with civil servants. For example, they suggest that introducing competition into the bureaucracy and holding out deregulation as a reward for individuals will improve performance. But civil servants who have purposely chosen government service because it offers a secure environment may not respond as Osborne and Gaebler suggest. In fact, such measures may decrease the sense of being part of the government policy making and reduce access to ministers, thereby diminishing two of the main factors that make work 'interesting' for civil servants, and in turn reducing their incentive to cooperate or even stay in the civil service. The structure would then compete with the private sector for employees, and attract civil servants on the basis of salary on which the government is notoriously uncompetitive. Instead, a superior's recognition or additional responsibilities may be simple measures that will more directly achieve the goals of greater efficiency and higher quality service. These changes will be most effective in flexible bureaucracies where individuals are career-maximisers and thus responsive to interesting work and career advancement opportunities.

Other suggestions that may have unintended effects are the decentralisation of government, and the allocation of more power to those dealing directly with the public (Osborne and Gaebler, 1992, Chapter 9), measures advocated by the Conservative government and being implemented via quangos and decentralised agencies and authorities. Such specialist units would presumably have permanent staffs and organisational autonomy yet little financial independence. As such, the officials would not have the option to move to other governmental departments. Using the findings of how civil servants in inflexible bureaucracies and managers in state-owned industries act, it is possible to hypothesise that the officials will be very committed to their organisation and seek to increase the organisation's financial independence as part of a strategy to direct the agency's resources to increase their own well being. They will also pursue other self and budget-maximising strategies to enhance their current situation, but will be concerned with the long-term implications of their actions because they may still be there and called to responsibility in the long term. They will proceed without regard for broader governmental implications, such as expense or conflict with other departments, because those are beyond their realm of responsibility.

Studies such as Osborne and Gaebler's focus on bureaucracies, when instead the real problem concerns the short-term horizons of their political leaders. As Neal Peirce, a leading United States columnist on state and local government notes:

> Indeed, there are not a few cynics who say that legislature and future planning mix like oil and water. The reasoning is that legislators' lives revolve around the election cycles. Politics forces them to be preoccupied with district and regional problems, to go for fast short-term payoffs instead of thinking and acting long-term (as quoted in Osborne and Gaebler, 1992, p. 235).

Neither bureaucrats themselves nor reform of the bureaucratic system alone can transform short-term policies into efficient and effective long-term practices. Even though these studies highlight the importance of leadership, they do so only in connection with motivating bureaucrats (Osborne and Gaebler, 1992, pp. 235–49; and Dilulio, Garvey and Kettl, 1993). The problem is more than just bureaucratic leadership; it is the policies that bureaucrats are given to implement. And politicians have little incentive to change this situation as they have been successfully elected under the current system.

Though considerable thought has been given to this problem, there are few satisfactory solutions (Dunleavy, 1991, pp. 235–49; Osborne and Gaebler, 1992, pp. 136–44). The findings from this British case study suggest three areas where more work can be done on long-term political accountability. These include the role of policy entrepreneurs, how to bring forward the long-term costs of politicians' party political calculations, and how to improve the quality of public demand to incorporate long-term needs.

CONCLUSION

A government voluntarily relinquishing control of valuable national assets is not a rational act – at least when examined as a whole from the macro level. But when the act is broken down into pieces, and factors are isolated at different levels of analysis, the pieces of the process can be understood as rational. Incorporating several aspects of the micro level is important as a one dimensional analysis is insufficient. For example, normally policy entrepreneurs are politicians, or leaders of interest groups (Olson, 1971), but by only focusing on the politicians, it is possible to miss the fact that policy entrepreneurs can also be business executives and officials in international organisations. For example, BP managers and the IMF top officials were the entrepreneurs during the 1977 BP sale. The changes in structures from the international level to the company level to the bureaucracy all were able to affect the policy outcome. This illustrates that it is not possible to predict rational policy outcomes from a macro level as these level-specific factors resist generalisation.

In their own way, each set of actors along with the changes in the corresponding structures set the parameters for the government's decision to sell its oil assets. The connection of these influences can be illustrated with Venn diagrams where each circle represents the overlap of factors at its level. For example, circle 1 represents the area where the parameters from the international financial arena overlapped with the international oil industry and membership in international organisations. While the levels and influences exist in three dimensions, imagine them being placed on top of each other as if looking down from the top of a funnel. The location of these parameters are illustrated for 1974, 1979 and 1982 (see Figures 8.1, 8.2 and 8.3). Circles 1–4 in descending size respectively represent the combined factors of the international, company, bureaucracy and political process levels. The

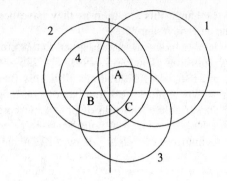

Figure 8.1   Combined Policy Parameters, 1974

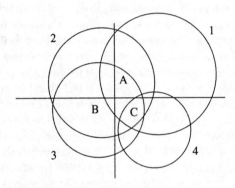

Figure 8.2   Combined Policy Parameters, 1977

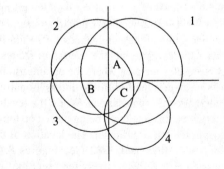

Figure 8.3   Combined Policy Parameters, 1982

points represent specific policy options: point A to increase taxes, point B to increase the budget deficit and point C to sell oil assets.

In 1974, just after the 1973 oil crisis and before North Sea oil was in production (and before BNOC was even created), the structures of the international oil industry and public demand were such that a sale of oil assets was not possible (as represented by the exclusion of point C from circles 1 and 4) as represented in Figure 8.1. In 1977 the situation had changed so that asset sales were within the international and policy parameters while the option of a budget increase was prevented by the IMF and the international financial community (point B excluded from circle 1), while a policy of new taxes was restricted by domestic political opposition (point B excluded from circle 4), as represented in Figure 8.2. An asset sale was thus the only one of these three policies possible (only point C in overlap of circles 1–4). In 1982, again the options changed, where all three options were possible at the international, company and bureaucracy levels (points A, B and C in circles 1–3), but only assets sales fit the Conservatives' political supply-side factors (only point C in circle 4), and again, an asset sale was the only one of these three policies possible (only point C in overlap of circles 1–4) as represented in Figure 8.3.

Looking at all four levels provides a much richer and more accurate understanding of the purpose and the effect of asset sales in Britain. Though the multilevel approach is perceived as the struggle of the modern political scientist, the importance of including layers of analysis is not new. In fact, returning to the original study of states as actors, closer examination reveals that Thucydides' greatest contribution with *The History of the Peloponnesian War* may be the importance of multiple perspectives to enhance knowledge about politics, and his legacy to realists may be misinterpreted. Laurie Bagby and others have argued that Thucydides' emphasis on the state has been overemphasised and that scholars have ignored the depth of his account which includes significant recognition of the role of specific national and individual factors (Bagby, 1994, pp. 131–53).

While many authors have made laundry lists of factors that cause privatisation, few if any are melded into coherent theories (Vickers and Wright, 1989; Sulieman and Waterbury, 1990; Heald, 1989; Dunleavy, 1986; Savas, 1987). By incorporating constraints more systematically into our analysis of individual actors, hopefully I have moved beyond March and Olsen's (1984) first step:

The institutionalism we have considered is neither a theory nor a coherent critique of one. It is simply an argument that the organization of political life makes a difference (p. 747).

Adopting a public choice framework and focusing on the individual while also assimilating the constraints they face at four levels, I propose a more systematic way of incorporating several variables at the same time. This approach also suggests a logic for focusing on the most significant policy determinants. Though losing the parsimony of a single level analysis, this approach retains consistency by focusing on the individual unit throughout. The depth of understanding gained in the trade-off is worthwhile, as no other approaches have satisfactorily explained state disengagement.

This case of Britain's oil asset sales has also demonstrated that despite much work in the field of public choice theory, some of the basic assumptions still need to be refined in order to recognise that bureaucrats are not just budget-maximisers in pursuit of pecuniary benefits, but rather that they also value other factors such as interesting work, and that they pursue career-maximising strategies. Furthermore, it must be emphasised that policies are led by supply as well as demand factors. This case reveals that there are still important areas that have not been fully addressed, including the role of international factors, the role played by the managers of nationalised industries, the use of individual strategies by bureaucrats, and the contribution of political supply-side factors to policy making, including policy entrepreneurs, cost-benefit analyses and demand of party supporters.

Appendix I Chronology of Events

1908:   Oil is discovered in Persia by a syndicate of the Burmah Oil Company, the Anglo-Persian Oil Company (APOC)
1911:   United States Supreme Court orders the dissolution of Standard Oil Trust
1914:   The British government purchases a majority holding in APOC
1914–18: World War I and the mechanisation of the battlefield
1920–23: The British government considers selling its holding in APOC
1922–28: Negotiation of the 'Red Line' and the 'As-Is' agreements
1932–33: Shah Reza Pahlavi cancels Anglo-Iranian Oil Company's (AIOC) concession; AIOC wins it back
1934:   AIOC and Gulf gain joint concession in Kuwait
1938:   Mexico nationalises its oil companies
1939–45: World War II
1950:   Fifty-fifty (participation) agreement between Aramco and Saudi Arabia
1950:   Mohammed Mossadegh nationalises AIOC assets in Iran
1951–53: Korean War
1953:   Mossadegh is overthrown and the Shah returns to power. The management of Iraqi oil operations is contracted to an international consortium and AIOC obtains a 40 per cent majority stake
            Reports surface that the Conservative government is to dispose of its 56 per cent holding in AIOC
1956:   Colonel Gamal Abdel Nasser of Egypt announces the appropriation of the Suez canal
1957:   European Economic Community established
1960:   Organisation of Petroleum Exporting Countries founded in Baghdad
1964:   First round licences are awarded for exploration in the North Sea by the Department of Trade and Industry
1965:   British Petroleum (BP) discovers gas in the North Sea
1965:   Britain imposes sanctions against Rhodesia
1967:   Six Day War, Suez canal closes
1967:   Government's shareholding in BP drops below the 50 per cent mark to 48.2 per cent
1968:   Oil is discovered on Alaska's North Slope
1968:   Prime Minister Harold Wilson announces the end of British military presence in the Persian Gulf, completed by 1971
1969:   Oil is discovered on the Norwegian side of the North Sea
1970:   Oil is discovered on the British side of the North Sea by BP
1972:   Gas Act creates the British Gas Corporation from the Gas Council
1973:   Britain joins the European Community
1973–74: AOPEC countries cut back supplies to the United States and the Netherlands

Shell and BP refuse to give Britain preferential treatment in the supply of oil
1974:   The Department of Energy is established
         International Energy Agency is founded
1975:   Government's shareholding in BP increases from 48 per cent to 68 per cent through the purchase of Burmah's holding in BP
         First North Sea oil lands in Britain
1976:   The British National Oil Corporation is established
1977:   First sale of oil assets: British government sells 17 per cent in BP, reducing its shareholding from 68 per cent to 51 per cent
1979:   Government sells another 5 per cent shareholding in BP, reducing its holding to 46 per cent
         Iranian revolution – Shah Reza Pahlavi goes into exile and Ayatollah Khomeini takes power
1980:   Iraq launches war against Iran
1981:   British oil production in the North Sea surpasses domestic consumption
1982:   OPEC agrees to first quotas
         BGC is instructed to sell its stake in the onshore oil field, Wytch Farm
         Oil and Gas (Enterprise) Act enabled the government to sell BNOC and BGC's oil assets
         BNOC split: production half becomes Britoil, 51 per cent is sold to the public
1983:   Britain becomes the sixth largest oil producer in the world
         BGC's oil assets are sold as Enterprise Oil
         Government sells another 15 per cent shareholding in BP, reducing its holding to 31.5 per cent
1984:   BGC's interest in Wytch Farm is finally sold
1985:   Government sells remaining stake in Britoil
         BNOC is disbanded, replaced by the Oil and Pipelines Agency
1986:   Oil price collapses
1987:   Government sells its remaining shares in BP in the midst of the October stock market crash
1988:   BP takes over Britoil
         Ceasefire in Iran–Iraq War
1993:   Department of Energy re-merges with the DTI

Appendix II The Bradbury and Bridges Letters

THE BRADBURY LETTER

Treasury, Whitehall, S.W.
20th May 1914

Gentlemen,

With reference to the Financial Agreement which has been duly settled on behalf of His Majesty's Government and sent to your company for signature, I am directed by the Lords Commissioners of His Majesty's Treasury to offer the following observations regarding the provisions of the amendments proposed to your Articles of Association:

1. By the Article 91A it is provided than an ex officio director shall have the right to negative any resolution which may be proposed at a board or committee meeting, but that the other directors, or a majority of them, shall have the right to appeal there from to His Majesty's Government, which, for the purpose of the Article, is defined as meaning the Treasury and Admiralty. His Majesty's Government, which, for the purpose of the Article, is defined as meaning the Treasury and the Admiralty. His Majesty's Government are of opinion that it would not be prudent, or, indeed, practicable, to qualify the generality of the right of veto. On the other hand, it is felt that the ordinary directors (meaning by that expression the directors other than the ex officio directors), and incidentally the members of the company, should have some safeguard in the matter. It is thought that the right which is to be given by the new Article to the ordinary directors of appealing to the two Departments will afford the requisite safeguard. The ordinary directors will, by appealing to the Departments, be in a position to ensure in regard to any particular question that the right of veto is not exercised until the question has been considered and adjudicated upon by the Departments.

I am to add that His Majesty's Government do not propose to make use of the right of veto except in regard to matters of general policy, such as –
(1) The supervision of the activities of the company as they may affect questions of foreign, naval or military policy;
(2) Any proposed sale of the company's undertaking or proposed change of the company's status;
(3) The control of the new exploitation, sites of wells, etc.;
(4) Sales of crude or fuel oil to foreigners, or such exceptional sales to other persons on long contracts as might endanger the due fulfilment of current Admiralty contracts;

194

and that their interference (if any) in the ordinary administration of the company as a commercial concern will be strictly limited to the minimum necessary to secure these objects. Further, in the case of any such interference, due regard will be paid to the financial interest of the company in which, under the proposed arrangements the Government have themselves so large a stake.

While His Majesty's Government are not prepared to enter into any binding agreement in regard to the exercise of the veto, you are at liberty to treat the above as an assurance as to the general lines upon which they will act in the matter, not only in regard to the Anglo-Persian Company, Limited, but also in regard to the subsidiary companies.

2. By the word added to Article 96 it is provided that the ex officio directors shall be members of every committee of the board. His Majesty's Government do not, however, contemplate that both the ex officio directors should always be present at committee meetings. Occasions may arise when it may be desirable that both the ex officio directors should be present, but as a general rule the presence of only one of them would be necessary. Indeed, at some meetings it may not be necessary that either of them should be present.

3. You are at liberty to make such use of this letter as you may think fit at the proposed meetings of the shareholders.

I am, Gentlemen,
Your obedient Servant,
(signed) John Bradbury

Messrs. The Anglo-Persian Oil Company, Limited

Winchester House, Old Broad Street, London E.C.

(As reprinted in Hansard, House of Commons 1928–29, 26 March 1929, Vol. 226, col. 2263–4.)

THE BRIDGES LETTER

12 April 1951

Gentlemen,

I am directed by the Lords Commissioners of H.M. Treasury's concern to recent developments on Persia and their possible effect on the Anglo-Iranian Oil Company. H.M. Government have in mind not only their own large financial interest in the Company, but the vast importance of the Company's operations to the economy of the United Kingdom, and indeed to the Sterling area as a whole.

The relationship between H.M. Government and the Company forms the subject of the letter sent by Sir John Bradbury to the Company on the 20th May, 1914, following the signature of the Financial Agreement between H.M. Government and the Company of the same date. H.M. Government do not feel that it is necessary to amend the terms of Sir John Bradbury's letter. While recognizing the close co-operation that has existed between H.M. Government and the Company, they feel sure that the Company will appreciate that it is more than ever necessary, particularly in the present critical circumstances, for H.M. Government to be kept in close touch with the development of the Company's general policy and above all that there should be mutual consultation in good time, and at the appropriate levels, about any developments likely to affect substantially the Company's position in Persia or in other territories where it has a concessionary interest.

I am, Gentlemen,
Your Obedient Servant,
(signed) Edward Bridges

(As reprinted in Hansard, House of Commons, 16 February 1977, Vol. 926, col. 270–1.)

Appendix III List of Interviews

Interview with Robert Adam, 6 August 1992.
BP 1950–83; Director, BP Trading, 1973–75; Director, Sohio, 1972–76 and 1978–83; Managing Director Finance, BP, 1975–83 and Deputy Chairman 1981–83.

Telephone interview with Sir Lawrence Airey, 3 February 1993.
HMG 1949–79, HM Treasury, 1958–79, Second Permanent Secretary 1977–79; Member, BNOC, 1976–77; Chairman, Board of Inland Revenue, 1980–86.

Interview with Sir Fred Atkinson, 22 February 1993.
HMG 1949–79: Treasury, 1955–62 and 1963–69; Foreign Office, 1962–63; Ministry of Technology, 1970; Chief Economic Adviser, DTI, 1970–73; Assistant Secretary General, OECD, 1973–75; Deputy Secretary and Chief Economic Adviser, Department of Energy, 1975–77; Chief Economic Adviser, Treasury, and Head of Government Economic Service, 1977–79; Co-author: *Oil and the British Economy*, 1983.

Interview with Dr Leslie Atkinson, 7 October 1992.
Seconded from BP to CPRS October 1977 to August 1979.

Interview with Lord Joel Barnett, 4 March 1993.
MP (L) Heywood and Royton, 1964–83; Member Public Accounts Committee, 1965–71, and Chairman, 1979–83; Opposition Spokesman on Treasury matters, 1970–74; Chief Secretary to the Treasury, 1974–79; Cabinet Member, 1977–79; House of Lords, 1983–; Opposition spokesman on the Treasury in House of Lords, 1983–86.

Telephone interview with Sir Kenneth Berrill, 15 July 1993.
Adviser to the Treasury, 1967–69 and 1973–74; Head of CPRS, Cabinet Office, 1974–80; Chairman, Vickers de Costa, 1981–85; Chairman, SIB, 1985–88; Deputy then Chairman Robert Horne Group, 1982–90; and Chairman, Commonwealth Equities Fund, 1990–.

Interview with Penny Boys, 11 June 1993.
HMG 1969–89: Department of Energy, 1973–78; seconded to BNOC 1978–80; Head of International Unit, Department of Energy 1981–85; seconded to Treasury, 1985–87; Director of Personnel, Department of Energy, 1987–89; Deputy Director General, Office of Electricity Regulation, 1989–.

Interview with Dr John Buchanan, 30 April 1993.
BP executive, seconded to CPRS 1976–77.

Interview with Graham Campbell, 8 February 1993.
HMG 1949–84: Ministry of Fuel and Power, 1949–65; Under Secretary, DTI, 1973; Under Secretary, Department of Energy, 1974–84.

Interview with Ian Clark, 9 April 1992.
Member BNOC 1976–82, trading, participation, Joint Managing Director, Britoil 1982–85.

Letter from Gerry Corti, 11 May 1992.
   Departments of Energy, mid-1970s; executive, BNOC, early 1980s; Author, *A Nation's Oil:*
Interview with Lord Croham, 29 April 1992.
   HMG, 1939–74; Treasury 1960–64, Department of Economic Affairs, 1964–68; Permanent Secretary, Treasury, 1968–74; Head of Home Civil Service, 1974–77; Deputy then Chairman, BNOC 1978–85; adviser to the Bank of England, 1978–83; Chairman, Guinness Peat Group, 1983–87.
Interview with Roy Dantzic, 23 April 1992.
   Samuel Montagu 1974–80; Member for Finance, BNOC, subsequently Finance Director, Britoil 1980–84; Director, Wood Mackenzie, 1985–89; Chairman Saxon Oil 1984–85; Part-time Director, BNFL, 1987–91.
Interview with Derek Davis, 27 July 1993.
   HMG 1967–: Secretary, Energy Committee, 1977–79; NEDC Energy Task Force, 1981; seconded to NCB, 1982–83; Under Secretary, DTI (formerly Energy) 1987–.
Interview with Edmund Dell, 2 March 1993.
   MP (L) Birkenhead, 1964–79; Paymaster General, 1974–76; Chairman, Public Accounts Committee, 1973–74 (Acting Chairman, 1972–73); Director, Shell Transport and Trading, 1979–; Chairman and Chief Executive, Guinness Peat Group, 1979–82; Founder Chairman, Channel Four TV, 1980–87.
Interview with Sir Eric Drake, 17 October 1991.
Letter from Sir Eric Drake, 24 October 1991.
   BP, 1935–75: Chairman, 1969–75; Court of Governors, LSE, 1963–74; and Hon. Petroleum Adviser to the British Army, 1971–.
Interview with Jeremy Evans, 20 March 1992.
   HMG 1960–76: Ministry of Technology, 1970–74; Department Director of Offshore Supplies Office, 1973; Department of Energy, 1974–76; seconded to BNOC, 1976–78; Managing Director, BNOC 1978–82, Member, Board of Directors, 1981–82; Director, Britoil, 1982–88; British Rail, 1990–.
Interview with Sir Alistair Frame, 1992.
   UKAEA, 1964–68; RTZ, 1968–91: Chief Executive and Deputy then Chairman, RTZ, 1978–91; Director, Britoil, 1983–84.
Interview with Patrick Gillam, 16 September 1992.
   BP 1957–91: General Manager, Supply Dept 1974–78; Director, BP International, 1978–88; Managing Director, BP, 1981–91.
Interview with Ian Goskirk, 28 July 1992.
   Shell International Petroleum, 1956–74; Anschutz Corp, 1974–76; BNOC 1976–85: Managing Director, BNOC Trading, 1980–82; Chief Executive, BNOC, 1982–85; Director, Cooper and Lybrand, 1986–90, Partner, 1990–.
Interview with Lord Hamish Gray, 7 June 1993.
   MP (C) Ross and Cromarty, 1970–83; Asst Government Whip, 1971–73; Lord Comr, Treasury, 1973–74; Opposition Whip, 1974–75; Opposition Spokesman on Energy, 1975–79; Minister of State, Department of Energy, 1979–83; Scottish Office, 1983–86; Government Spokesman on Energy, House of Lords, 1983–86.
Interview with Alan Gregory, 29 July 1992.
   BP 1971–78: Director, UK and Ireland Region, 1980–85; Director, BP Chemicals International, 1981–85; Director of Government and Public Affairs, 1975–85.

Interview with John Guinness, 1 September 1993.
    HMG, 1962–: CPRS 1972–75 and 1977–79; Foreign Office then Foreign and
    Commonwealth Office 1962–72; Home Civil Service, 1980; Department of
    Energy: Under Secretary 1980–83, Deputy Secretary 1983–91; and Second
    Permanent Secretary 1991; British Nuclear Fuels, 1992–.
Interview with Peter Harding, 27 July 1993.
    HMG 1948–91: Department of Energy, 1974–91, Under Secretary, 1989–91.
Interview with Charles Henderson, 23 July 1993.
    HMG 1973–: Department of Energy 1974–88, Heads of Arts and Libraries
    1989–92; Head of Energy within DTI, 1992–.
Interview with David Howell, 25 May 1993.
    MP (C) Guilford, 1966–: Minister of State, Department of Energy, 1974;
    Secretary of State for Energy, 1979–81; Secretary of State for Transport, 1981–83.
Interview with Williams Jewers, 19 August 1992.
    Regional Gas Boards, 1946–68; Director of Finance, Gas Council, 1969–73; BGC:
    Director of Finance, 1973–76, and Managing Director for Finance, 1976–87.
Interview with David Jones, 11 June 1993.
    HMG, 1947–82: Ministry of Power and later Ministry of Technology and DTI,
    1947–52 and 1963–73; Cabinet Office, 1976–77; Department of Energy,
    1978–82; Director, Long Term Office, IEA, 1982–88.
Interview with Sir Philip Jones, 26 May 1993.
    HMG 1955–83: Ministry of Technology, 1967–71; DTI 1971–73; Department
    of Energy 1974–83; Member BNOC, 1980–82; Chairman, Electricity Council,
    1983–90; Chairman, Total Oil Marine, 1990–.
Telephone interview with Lord Kearton.
    Courtaulds, 1946–75, Chairman, 1964–75; Part-time Member, UKAUE,
    1955–81; Chairman and Chief Executive, BNOC, 1974–80.
Interview with Sir Peter Kemp, 6 May 1993.
    HMG 1967–93: Ministry of Transport, 1967–73; Treasury 1973–87; Permanent
    Secretary, Cabinet Office, 1988–93.
Telephone interview with Mr. Khakee, 28 January 1994.
    Accountant, DTI, 1983; on loan to Department of Energy since 1986.
Interview with Sir Christopher Laidlaw, 22 September 1992.
    BP 1948–81: Managing Director, 1972–81, Chairman BP Oil, 1977–81, and
    Deputy Chairman, 1980–81; Chairman, ICL, 1981–84; Chairman, Bridon,
    1985–90; and Director, Amerada Hess, 1983–.
Interview with Gavin Laird, 11 June 1992.
    Amalgamated Engineers Union, 1972–; General Secretary (Eng Section),
    1982–; Member, Executive Council, 1979–82; Part-time Government Director,
    BNOC 1976–86; Director, Bank of England, 1986–.
Interview with Lord Nigel Lawson, 15 February 1994.
    MP (C) Blaby, 1974–90; Opposition Spokesman on Treasury and Economic
    Affairs, 1977–79; Financial Secretary to the Treasury, 1978–81; Secretary of
    State for Energy, 1981–83; Chancellor of the Exchequer, 1983–89; House of
    Lords, 1992–.
Interview with Lord Harold Lever of Manchester, 6 April 1993.
    MP (L) Manchester 1945–79: Paymaster General, 1969–70; Member, Shadow
    Cabinet, 1970–74; Chairman, Public Accounts Committee, 1970–73; Chancellor of
    the Duchy of Lancaster, 1974–79; House of Lords, 1979–95.

Interview with John Liverman, 15 March 1993.
HMG 1947–80: Member, BNOC, 1976–80; Deputy Secretary, Department of Energy, 1974–80.
Telephone interview with Christopher Lucas, 4 February 1993.
HMG 1946–80: Treasury, 1950–70; Cabinet Office, 1970–72; Secretary, NEDC, 1973–76; Under Secretary, Community and International Policy Division, Department of Energy, 1976–80.
Interview with Dickson Mabon, 11 May 1993.
MP (L and Co-op) 1955–81, (SDP) 1981–83: Minister of State, Department of Energy, 1976–79; Chairman RGC (Offshore) 1979–82; Chairman, Indigenous Technology Group, 1984–.
Interview with John McCall, 26 March 1992.
Solicitor, Freshfields, on leave to BNOC from 1976–79.
Interview with Lord John Moore, 22 June 1993.
MP (C) Croydon Central, 1974–91: Vice-chairman, Conservative Party, 1975–79; Parliamentary Under Secretary, Department of Energy, 1979–83; Economic Secretary, HM Treasury, 1983; Financial Secretary, HM Treasury, 1983–86; Secretary of State, Department of Transport, 1986–87; Secretary of State, Department of Social Services, 1987–88; Secretary of State, Department of Social Security, 1988–89; House of Lords, 1992–; Chairman, Credit Suisse Asset Management, 1992–.
Interview with Sir Alistair Morton, 15 October 1993.
Chairman and Chief Executive, Draymont Securities, 1972–76; Managing Director, BNOC, 1976–80; Chairman, Thames Oil and Gas, 1981–83; Chief Executive, Guinness Peat Group, 1982–87: Director, New London Oil, 1986–; Chairman, Eurotunnel, 1987–.
Interview with Robert Priddle, 26 May 1993.
HMG 1960–: DTI, 1973; Department of Energy, 1974–85; Under Secretary, DTI, 1985–89; Deputy Secretary, Department of Energy (now DTI), 1989–.
Interview with Sir Denis Rooke, 4 August 1992.
Gas Board then Gas Council then British Gas Corporation then British Gas plc: Deputy Chairman 1972–76, Chairman 1976–89; Member: Advisory Council for Energy Conservation 1974–77, and BNOC 1976–82.
Interview with David Sarre, 13 May 1992.
BP 1957–82: Secretary of the Board, 1973–82; Legal Adviser, 1970–78; and Director of Personnel, Safety and Environment, 1979–82.
Interview with Sir Philip Shelbourne, 18 October 1991.
Chief Executive the Chairman, Drayton Corp, 1971–74; Chairman and Chief Executive, Samuel Montagu, 1974–80; Chairman and Chief Executive, BNOC, 1980–82; Chairman, Britoil, 1982–88; Chairman, Henry Ansbacher Holding, 1988–91.
Interview with Sir David Steel, 24 March 1992.
BP, 1950–81: Managing Director, 1965–75, Deputy Chairman, 1972–75, BP Chairman, 1975–81; Director, Bank of England, 1978–85; Director, Kleinwort, Benson, 1985–.
Interview with Ron Utiger, 23 April 1992.
British Aluminium, 1961–82, Chairman, 1979–82; Member BNOC, 1976–80; Chairman, 1979–80; TI Group, 1979–89, Chairman 1984–89; Director, British Alcan Aluminium, 1982–.

Interview with Dr Paul Vaight, 30 September 1992.
  BP executive, seconded to CPRS, 1979–82.
Interview with David B. Walker, 10 June 1992.
  BP, 1959–85: Chief Executive, BP Petroleum Development, 1980–82; Chief Executive, Britoil, 1985–88; President, UK Offshore Operators Association, 1982; Chairman, Sun International Exploration and Production Co., 1988–.
Interview with Sir Douglas Wass, 28 April 1993.
  HMG 1946–83: Alternate Executive Director, IMF, and Financial Counsellor, British Embassy, Washington DC, 1965–67; Treasury: 1968–83, Permanent Secretary 1974–83 and Joint Head of the Home Civil Service, 1981–83.
Interview with Julian West, 2 July 1992.
  Department of Energy, 1974–83; Private Personal Secretary to Nigel Lawson, 1983; seconded to start Enterprise Oil; Enterprise Oil, 1984–, Member of the Board, 1991–.
Interview with Christopher Wilcock, 27 May 1993.
Telephone interview, 21 January 1994.
  HMG 1962–: Department of Energy, 1974–; seconded to Shell UK Ltd, 1982–83; Head of Finance, Department of Energy, 1984–86, Director of Resource Management, 1986–88; Head of Electricity Division, 1991–.

Bibliography

OFFICIAL PUBLICATIONS

Beveridge, W.A. and Margaret Kelly, 'Fiscal Content of Financial Programs Supported by Stand-By Arrangements in the Upper Credit Tranches, 1969–78', IMF Staff Papers, Vol. 27, No. 2, June 1980.

Central Statistics Office, *Financial Statistics*, May 1983 and May 1987.

—— *UK Balance of Payments*, 1985.

—— *The Government's Expenditure Plans*, 1977–90.

Civil Service Department, *Civil Service Yearbook* (London: HMSO), 1982–92.

Department of Energy, *Development of the Oil and Gas Resources in the United Kingdom*, 1974–91.

—— 'About Britoil', 1978.

Gas Act 1965.

Gas Act 1972.

Hansard Parliamentary Debates (Commons and Lords), survey of all references to BP (including APOC and AIOC), BNOC, Britoil, Wytch Farm, Enterprise Oil as cited in the annual index, 1911–88.

Hemming, Richard and Ali Mansoor, 'Privatization and Public Enterprises', IMF Occasional Paper No.56, January 1988.

HM Treasury, *Civil Service Statistics*, 1980–90.

House of Commons Energy Select Committee, First Report, BP/Britoil Job Losses and Asset Sales, *British Parliamentary Papers*, 1989–90, Vol. XX.

—— 'Department of Energy's Estimates for 1981–82', Second Report, *British Parliamentary Papers*, 1981–2, HC 231.

Third Report, North Sea Oil Depletion Policy, *British Parliamentary Papers*, 1981–2, HC 337.

—— 'Wytch Farm (Disposal of BGC Assets) Memorandum by British Gas Corporation', First Report, Disposal of the British Gas Corporation's Interest in Wytch Farm Oilfield, *British Parliamentary Papers*, 1981–2, HC 138.

House of Commons Nationalised Industries Select Committee (Sub-Committee B), 'Testimony by Frank Kearton, Chairman of BNOC', Seventh Report, Reports and Accounts of Energy Industries, *British Parliamentary Papers*, 1977–8, Vol. XXXIX.

House of Commons Public Accounts Committee, First Report, North Sea Oil and Gas, *British Parliamentary Papers*, 1972–3, Vol. XIX.

House of Commons Treasury and Civil Service Select Committee, Sixth Report, Budgetary Reform, *British Parliamentary Papers*, 1981–2, HC 137.

International Energy Agency, *Energy Balances of OECD Countries*, 1970/85 and 1980/90 (Paris: IEA/OECD, 1987 and 1991).

—— *Annual Oil and Gas Statistics and Main Historical Series* (Paris: IEA/OECD, 1978–9).

—— *Energy Statistics 1970/1985*, Vol. 2 (Paris: IEA/OECD, 1987).

—— *Energy Statistics of OECD Countries*, 1989–90 (Paris: IEA/OECD, 1992a).

—— *Energy Prices and Taxes* (Paris: IEA/OECD, 1992b).

—— *Digest of Energy Statistics, 1960–75* (Paris: IEA/OECD, 1976).

—— *International Energy Agency* (Paris: IEA/OECD, 1983).

International Management and Engineering Group of Britain Limited, Department of Trade and Industry, *Study of Potential Benefits to British Industry from Offshore Oil and Gas Development* (London, HMSO, 1972).

International Monetary Fund, *International Financial Statistics Yearbook*, 1976–1990.

—— *Manual on Government Finance Statistics*, 1977 and 1986.

Lawson, Nigel, 'Privatisation in the United Kingdom', Speech by the Chancellor of the Exchequer to the Adam Smith Institute, 27 June 1988; in *Privatisation in the United Kingdom: Background Briefing* (London: HM Treasury, 1990).

Mansoor, Ali, 'Budgetary Impact of Privatization', IMF Working Paper, 15 October 1987.

Moore, John, 'Why Privatise?' (Speech by the Financial Secretary at the Treasury and the government minister responsible for coordinating the programme) 1 November 1983; in *Privatisation in the United Kingdom: Background Briefing* (London: HM Treasury, 1990).

Oil and Gas (Enterprise) Act 1982.

Oil Taxation Act 1975.

Oil Taxation Bill 1983.

Petroleum and Pipelines Act 1975.

Rampton, Jack, Department of Energy, 'National Energy Policy', Energy Paper No. 41, August 1979.

Supply Estimates, Class IV: Industry, Energy, Trade and Employment, *British Parliamentary Papers*, 1976–93.

COMPANY DOCUMENTS

British Gas Corporation, *Annual Reports and Accounts*, 1981–8.

—— 'The Work of the Financial Division', internal memo, early 1980s.

—— 'Report to Employees', 1981–2.

BP, 'The Road to Persia: A Brief History of BP', BP Briefing Paper (London, April 1989).

—— *Our Industry Petroleum* (London: British Petroleum Company, 1970).

—— 'The World of BP' (London, April 1990).

—— *Statistical Review of World Energy* (London: June 1990 and July 1989).

—— *BP Statistical Review of the World Oil Industry* (London: 1980, 1989 and 1990).

—— *Financial and Operating Information*, 1985–89.

—— *Annual Reports and Accounts*, years 1955–90.

—— 'Offer for Sale', by N.M. Rothschild on behalf of HM Treasury, September 1987.

—— 'Offer for Sale by Tender', by Bank of England on behalf of HM Treasury, September 1983.

—— 'Offer for Sale', by Bank of England on behalf of HM Treasury, October 1979.

—— 'Offer for Sale', by Bank of England on behalf of HM Treasury, June 1977.
British National Oil Company (and later Britoil), *Annual Report and Accounts*, 1976–85.
Britoil, 'Offer for Sale', by S.W. Warburg & Co and N.M. Rothschild & Sons on behalf of the Secretary of State for Energy, November 1982.
—— 'Reject BP's Inadequate and Unwelcome Offer', 28 January 1988.
—— *Annual Reports and Accounts*, 1982–8.
Enterprise Oil, *Annual Report and Accounts*, 1984.
—— 'Offer for Sale', by Kleinwort Benson Limited on behalf of the Secretary of State for Energy, September 1984.
Shell Briefing Service, 'The Oil Majors in 1980', No. 5, 1981.

NEWSPAPERS, MAGAZINES AND OPINION POLLS

The Economist, 1913–90.
The Financial Times, 1982–94.
Gallup polls, 1978–1989.
MORI polls, as reported in *British Public Opinion*, 1976–88.
Petroleum Economist, 1980–8.
The Statist, 'Navy and Oil Fuel', 30 May 1914; and 'Anglo-Persian Oil Company', 15 November 1913.
The Times, The Sunday Times, The Guardian, The Independent and *The Daily Telegraph*, 1973–94.
The Wall Street Journal, 1990–94.

BOOKS, JOURNALS AND CONFERENCE PAPERS

Abromeit, Heidrun, 'British Privatization Policy', *Parliamentary Affairs*, Vol. 41, 1988.
Aharoni, Yair, *The Evolution and Management of State Owned Enterprises* (Cambridge, MA: Ballinger Publishing, 1986).
Allison, Graham T., *Essence of Decision: Explaining the Cuban Missile Crisis* (Boston: Little, Brown and Company, 1971).
Anderson, J.R.L., *East of Suez: A Study of Britain's Greatest Trading Enterprise* (London: Hodder & Stoughton, 1969).
Arnold, Guy, *Britain's Oil* (London: Hamish Hamilton, 1978).
Avery, William, 'U.S. Agriculture and Two-Level Bargaining in the North American Free Trade Agreement', presented at the annual meeting of the International Studies Association, 25 March 1993.
Bagby, Laurie M. Johnson, 'The Use and Abuse of Thucydides in International Relations', *International Organization*, Vol. 48, No. 1, Winter 1994.
Bailey, Martin, *Oilgate* (London: Coronet Books-Hodder and Stoughton, 1979).
Bailey, Richard, 'Unequal Shares in the North Sea', *Energy Policy*, December 1978.
Baker, A.W. and G.H. Daniel, 'BNOC and Privatisation – The Past and the Future', *Journal of Energy and Natural Resource Law*, Vol. 1, No. 3, 1983.

Barnes, John and David Nicholson, eds, *The Leo Amery Diaries*, Vol. I 1896–1929 (London: Hutchinson, 1980).

Barnett, Joel, *Inside the Treasury* (London: Andre Deutsch, 1982).

BBC1, 'Thatcher: The Downing Street Years', 9:30 p.m., 20 November 1993.

Bending, Richard and Richard Eden, *UK Energy: Structure, Prospects and Policies* (Cambridge, Cambridge University Press, 1984).

Benn, Tony, *Against the Tide: Diaries 1973–76* (London: Hutchinson, 1989).

—— *Conflict of Interest: Diaries 1977–80*, Ruth Winstone, ed. (London: Hutchinson, 1990).

Black, Robert, 'Plus ça Change, Plus C'est la Même Chose: Nine Governments in Search of a Common Energy Policy', in Helen Wallace, William Wallace and Carole Webb, eds, *Policy Making in the European Communities* (London: John Wiley & Sons, 1977).

Blackstone, Tessa and William Plowden, *Inside the Think Tank: Advising the Cabinet 1971–1983* (London: Mandarin, 1990).

Blair, David, 'The International Energy Agency: Problems and Prospects', in Curt Gasteyger, ed., *The Future for European Energy Security* (London: Frances Pinter, 1985).

Blais, André and Stéphane Dion, eds, *The Budget-Maximizing Bureaucrat: Appraisals and Evidence* (Pittsburg, PA: University of Pittsburg Press, 1991).

Bourgeois, B., 'Energy', in Willem Molle and Riccardo Cappellini, eds, *Regional Impact of Communities Policies in Europe* (Aldershot, Hants: Avebury, 1988).

Brittan, Samuel, 'The Politics and Economics of Privatisation', *Political Quarterly*, Vol. 55, No. 2, April/June 1984.

Browning, Peter, *The Treasury and Economic Policy 1964–1985* (London: Longman, 1986).

Budge, Ian, David McKay, Rod Rhodes, David Robertson, David Sanders, Martin Slater, Graham Wilson, *The Changing British Political System: Into the 1990s*, Second Edition (London: Longman, 1988).

Bulpitt, Jim, 'The Discipline of the New Democracy: Mrs Thatcher's Domestic Statecraft', *Political Studies*, Vol. XXXIV, 1986.

Burda, Michael and Charles Wyplosz, *Macroeconomics, A European Text* (Oxford: Oxford University Press, 1993).

Burk, Kathleen and Alec Cairncross, *'Goodbye Great Britain,' The 1976 IMF Crisis* (London: Yale University Press, 1992).

Buxtem, Neil, *The Economic Development of the British Coal Industry* (London: Batsford Academy, 1978).

Callaghan, James, *Time and Chance* (London: Collins, 1987).

Cameron, Peter D., *Property Rights and Sovereign Rights: The Case of North Sea Oil* (London: Academic Press, 1983).

Campbell, Colin and Donald Naulls, 'The Limits of the Budget-Maximizing Theory: Some Evidence from Officials' Views of Their Roles and Careers', in André Blais and Stéphane Dion, eds, *The Budget-Maximizing Bureaucrat: Appraisals and Evidence* (Pittsburg, PA: University of Pittsburg Press, 1991).

Carr, E.H., *The Twenty Years' Crisis, 1919–1939: An Introduction to the Study of International Relations*, Second Edition (New York: Harper and Row, 1964).

Carrer, Todd and Albert Vondra, 'Reinventing the Business of Government: An Interview with David Osborne', *Harvard Business Review*, May–June 1994.

Castle, Barbara, *The Castle Diaries 1974–76* (London: Weidenfeld & Nicolson, 1989).

Chapman, Colin, *Selling the Family Silver: Has Privatization Worked?* (London: Hutchinson Business Books, 1990).

Chester, Edward, *United States Oil Policy and Diplomacy* (London: Greenwood Press, 1983).

Churchill, Winston, *The World Crisis 1911–1914* (London: Thornton Butterworth Limited, 1923).

Cohen, Benjamin, 'European Financial Integration and National Banking Interests', in Paolo Guerrieri and Pier Carlo Padoan, eds, *The Political Economy of European Integration, States, Markets and Institutions* (London: Harvester Wheatsheaf, 1989).

Cohen, Robin John, 'British Energy Crisis Management: A Comparative Study in the 20th Century', London School of Economics, PhD dissertation in Economics, November 1986.

Collins, C.D.E., 'History and Institutions of the EC', in Ali M. El-Agraa, ed., *Economies of the European Community*, Second Edition (Oxford: Philip Allan, 1985).

Confederation of British Industry, *Company Law and Competition* (London: Mercury Books, 1989).

Conservative Party, 'The Conservative Manifesto 1979', 1979.

—— 'The Challenge of Our Times', Conservative Manifesto, 1983.

—— 'The Next Moves Forward', Conservative Manifesto, 1987.

Corley, T.A.B., *A History of the Burmah Oil Company*, Vol. II, 1924–1966 (London: William Heinemann, 1988).

Cornett, Linda and James Caporaso, 'Interests and Forces in the European Community', in James Rosenau, ed., *Governance without Government: Order and Change in World Politics* (Cambridge: Cambridge University Press, 1992).

Corti, Gerry and Frank Frazer, *The Nation's Oil: A Story of Control* (London: Graham & Trotman, 1983).

Cosgrave, Patrick, *Carrington, A Life and a Policy* (London: J.M. Dent, 1985).

Crafts, N.F.R. and N.W.C. Woodward, 'Introduction and Overview', in N.F.R. Crafts and N.W.C. Woodward, eds, *The British Economy since 1945* (Oxford: Clarendon Press, 1991).

Curwen, Peter J., *Public Enterprise: A Modern Approach* (London: Harvester Wheatsheaf, 1986).

Dahl, Robert, *Who Governs? Democracy and Power in an American City* (New Haven, CT: Yale University Press, 1961).

Deese, David and Linda Miller, 'Western Europe', in David Deese and Joseph Nye, eds, *Energy and Security* (Cambridge, MA: Ballinger Publishing, 1981).

Dell, Edmund, *A Hard Pounding: Politics and Economic Crisis, 1974–76* (Oxford: Oxford University Press, 1991).

Devereux, M.P. and C.N. Morris, 'Budgetary Arithmetic and the 1983 Budget', in John Kay, ed., *The Economy and the 1983 Budget* (London: Institute for Fiscal Studies, 1984).

Devereux, M.P., A.W. Dilnot, V. Fry, J. Hills, J.A. Kay and C.N. Morris, *Budget Options for 1984; the IFS 'Green Budget'* (London: Institute for Fiscal Studies, 1984).

de Vries, Margaret Garritsen, *The International Monetary Fund, 1972–1978: Cooperation on Trial. Vol. I Narrative and Analysis* (Washington, DC: International Monetary Fund, 1985).

Dilulio, John, Gerald Garvey and Donald Kettl, *Improving Government Performance: An Owner's Manual* (Washington, DC: Brookings Institution, 1993).

Dobek, Mariusz Mark, 'Privatization as a Political Priority: The British Experience', *Political Studies*, Vol. XLI, No. 1, March 1993.

Donoughue, Bernard, 'The Conduct of Economic Policy, 1974–79', in Anthony King, ed., *The British Prime Minister*, Second Edition (London: Macmillan, 1985).

—— *Prime Minister: The Conduct of Policy Under Harold Wilson and James Callaghan* (London: Jonathan Cape, 1987).

Dowding, Keith, *Rational Choice and Political Power* (Aldershot: Elgar, 1991).

Downs, Anthony, *An Economic Theory of Democracy* (New York: Harper and Row, 1957).

Drewry, Gavin and Tony Butcher, *The Civil Service Today*, Second Edition (Oxford: Basil Blackwell, 1991).

Dunleavy, Patrick, 'Explaining the Privatization Boom: Public Choice Versus Radical Approaches', *Public Administration*, Vol. 64, Spring 1986.

—— 'The Architecture of the British Central State, Part I: Framework for Analysis', *Public Administration*, Vol. 67, Autumn 1989a.

—— 'The Architecture of the British Central State, Part II: Empirical Findings', *Public Administration*, Vol. 67, Winter 1989b.

—— *Democracy, Bureaucracy and Public Choice* (London: Harvester Wheatsheaf, 1991).

Dunsire, Andrew, 'Bureaucrats and Conservative Governments', in André Blais and Stéphane Dion, eds, *The Budget-Maximizing Bureaucrat: Appraisals and Evidence* (Pittsburg, PA: University of Pittsburg Press, 1991).

Eden, Sir Anthony, *Full Circle* (London: Cassell, 1960).

—— *Facing the Dictators, the Eden Memoirs* (London: Cassell, 1962).

El-Agraa, Ali M., 'Basic Statistics of the EC', in Ali M. El-Agraa, ed., *The Economics of the European Community*, Third Edition (Oxford: Philip Allan Publishers Limited, 1990).

El-Agraa, Ali M. and Y.S. Hu, 'Energy Policy', in Ali M. El-Agraa, ed., *The Economics of the European Community,* Second Edition (Oxford: Philip Allan Publishers Limited, 1985).

Engler, Robert, *The Politics of Oil: A Study of Private Power and Democratic Direction* (New York: Macmillan, 1961).

Ferrier, R.W., *The History of the British Petroleum Company: The Developing Years 1901–1932* (London: Cambridge University Press, 1982).

Financial Times, *Financial Times International Yearbook, Oil and Gas, 1992* (Harlow: Longman, 1992 and 1993).

Fraser, Robert and Michael Wilson, *Privatization: The UK Experience and International Trends* (Harlow, Essex: Longman, 1988).

Frey, Bruno, 'Public Choice View of International Political Economy', *International Organization*, Vol. 38, No. 1, Winter 1984.

Frieden, Jeffrey A., 'Invested Interests: The Politics of National Economic Policies in a World of Global Finance', *International Organization*, Vol. 45, No. 4, Autumn 1991.

Fry, Geoffrey, *The Changing Civil Service* (London: Allen & Unwin, 1985).

Gamble, Andrew, *The Free Economy and the Strong State: The Politics of Thatcherism* (London: Macmillan Education, 1988).

Gardner, Nick, *Decade of Discontent, The Changing British Economy Since 1973* (Oxford: Basil Blackwell, 1987).

Garner, M.R., 'British Airways and British Aerospace: Limbo for Two Enterprises', *Public Administration*, Vol. 58, Spring 1980.

Ghadar, Fariborz, 'Oil: The Power of an Industry', in Raymond Vernon, ed., *The Promise of Privatization: A Challenge for U.S. Policy* (New York: Council on Foreign Relations, 1988).

Gilpin, Robert, 'The Richness of the Tradition of Political Realism', in Robert Keohane, ed., *Neorealism and its Critics* (New York: Columbia University Press, 1986).

Glade, William, 'Sources and Forms of Privatization', in William Glade, ed., *State Shrinking: A Comparative Inquiry into Privatization* (Austin, Texas: Institute of Latin American Studies, University of Texas at Austin, 1986).

Golich, Vicki L., 'From Competition to Collaboration: The Challenge of Commercial-Class Aircraft Manufacturing', *International Organization*, Vol. 46, No. 4, Autumn 1992.

Goodin, Robert, 'Rational Politicians and Rational Bureaucrats in Washington and Whitehall', *Public Administration*, Vol. 60, Spring 1982.

Gourevitch, Peter, 'The Second Image Reversed: the International Sources of Domestic Politics', *International Organization*, Vol. 32, No. 4, Autumn 1978.

Graham, Cosmo and Tony Prosser, 'Golden Shares: Industrial Policy by Stealth?' *Public Law*, Autumn 1988.

Grant, Robert M., *The Oil Companies in Transition 1970–1987* (Milan: Franco Angeli, 1991).

Grant, Wyn, 'Business Interests and the British Conservative Party', *Government and Opposition*, Vol. 15, Spring 1980.

—— 'Large Firms and Public Policy in Britain', *Journal of Public Policy*, Vol. 4, Fall 1984.

Gregory, Roy, *The Miners and British Politics 1906–1914* (Oxford: Oxford University Press, 1968).

Grieco, Joseph, 'Anarchy and the Limits of Cooperation: A Realist Critique of the Newest Liberal Institutionalism', *International Organization*, Vol. 42, No. 3, Summer 1988.

Guerrieri, Paolo and Pier Carlo Padoan, 'Two Level Games and Structural Adjustment: The Italian Case', paper presented at the international conference on global and domestic factors in international cooperation, Trento, 3–4 April 1989.

Haas, Ernst, *Beyond the Nation-State: Functionalism and International Organization* (Stanford, CA: Stanford University Press, 1964).

Hall, John A. and G. John Ikenberry, *The State* (Milton Keynes: Open University Press, 1989).

Halperin, Morton, *Bureaucratic Politics and Foreign Policy* (Washington, DC: The Brookings Institution, 1974).

Ham, Adrian, *Treasury Rules, Recurrent Themes in British Economic Policy* (London: Quartet Books, 1981).

Hamilton, Adrian, *North Sea Impact, Off-Shore Oil and the British Economy* (London: International Institute for Economic Research, 1978).

Hann, D., 'The Process of Government and UK Oil Participation Policy', *Energy Policy*, June 1986.

Harrison, R.J., 'Neo-functionalism', in A.J.R. Groom and Paul Taylor, eds, *Framework for International Co-operation* (London: Pinter Publishers, 1990).

Hartshorn, J.E., *Oil Companies and Governments, An Account of the International Oil Industry in its Political Environment* (London: Faber and Faber, 1962).

Heald, David, 'UK Energy Policy: Economic and Financial Control of the Nationalized Energy Industries', *Energy Policy*, June 1981.

—— 'The United Kingdom: Privatisation and its Political Context', in John Vickers and Vincent Wright, eds, *The Politics of Privatisation in Western Europe* (London: Frank Cass, 1989).

Healey, Denis, *The Time of My Life* (London: Michael Joseph, 1989).

Henig, Jeffrey, Chris Hamnett and Harvey Feigenbaum, 'The Politics of Privatization: A Comparative Perspective', *Governance: An International Journal of Policy Administration*, Vol. 1, No. 4, October 1988.

Hennessy, Peter, *Whitehall* (London: Secker and Warburg, 1989).

Hill, Christopher, *Cabinet Decisions on Foreign Policy: The British Experience, October 1938–June 1941* (Cambridge: Cambridge University Press, 1991).

—— ed., *National Foreign Policies and European Political Cooperation* (London: Allen & Unwin, for the Royal Institute of International Affairs, 1983).

Hillman, Judy and Peter Clarke, *Geoffrey Howe: A Quiet Revolutionary* (London: Weidenfeld & Nicolson, 1988).

Hitiris, T., 'Trade Policies', *European Community Economics*, Second Edition (London: Harvester Wheatsheaf, 1988).

Hogwood, Brian and B. Guy Peters, *Policy Dynamics* (Brighton: Wheatsheaf Books, 1983).

Holmes, Martin, *The First Thatcher Government 1979–83: Contemporary Conservatism and Economic Change* (Brighton: Wheatsheaf Books, 1985).

Hood, Christopher, 'Stabilization and Cutbacks: A Catastrophe for Government Growth Theory?' *Journal of Theoretical Politics*, Vol. 3, No. 1, 1991.

Hood, Christopher and Andrew Dunsire with Meg Huby, *Cutback Management in Public Bureaucracies: Popular and Observed Outcomes in Whitehall* (Cambridge: Cambridge University Press, 1989).

Hood, Christopher and Andrew Dunsire with K. Suky Thomson, *Bureaumetrics: the Quantitative Comparison of British Central Government Agencies* (Farnborough, Hants: Gower, 1981).

Howell, David and Sir Geoffrey Howe *et al.*, *The Right Approach to the Economy: Outline of an Economic Strategy for the Next Conservative Government* (London: Conservative Central Office, 1977).

Ikenberry, G. John, *Reasons of States: Oil Politics and the Capacities of American Government* (Ithaca, NY: Cornell University Press, 1988).

—— 'The International Spread of Privatization Policies: Inducements, Learning and "Policy Bandwagoning"', in Ezra N. Suleiman and John Waterbury, *The Political Economy of Public Sector Reform and Privatization* (Oxford: Westview Press, 1990).

Ikenberry, G. John and Charles A. Kupchan, 'Socialization and Hegemonic Power', *International Organization*, Vol. 44, No. 3, Summer 1990.

Ikenberry, G. John, David Lake and Michael Mastanduno, 'Introduction: Approaches to Explaining American Foreign Economic Policy', *International Organization*, Vol. 42, No. 4, Autumn 1988.

Inglis, K.A.D., 'The International Oil Industry – Government Involvement Through Regulation and Participation', in Maurice Scarlett, ed., *Consequences of Offshore Oil and Gas – Norway, Scotland and Newfoundland* (St Johns, Nfld: Institute of Social and Economic Research, 1977).

Jacoby, Neil H., *Multinational Oil: A Study in Industrial Dynamics* (London: Collier Macmillan, 1974).

James, Simon, *British Cabinet Government* (London: Routledge, 1992).

Jenkin, Michael, *British Industry and the North Sea* (London: Macmillan Press, 1981).

Jenkins, Peter, *Mrs Thatcher's Revolution, The Ending of the Socialist Era* (London: Jonathan Cape, 1987).

Jevons, H. Stanley, *The British Coal Trade* (New York: Augustus M. Kelley, Publishers, 1969).

Jewers, Bill, 'Required Rate of Return, Test Discount Rate, Pricing Policies and Financial Targets', Seminar on the Financial Target of Public Corporations, 30 January 1979.

—— 'We're Not As Different as Private Industry Thinks', *Accountancy Age*, 23 June 1983.

Johnson, Christopher, *The Economy Under Mrs Thatcher 1979–1990* (London: Penguin Books, 1991).

Johnson, Ronald and Gary Libecap, 'Agency Growth, Salaries and the Protected Bureaucrat', *Economic Inquiry*, Vol. XXVII, July 1989.

Jones, Geoffrey, *The State and the Emergence of the British Oil Industry* (London: Macmillan Press, 1981).

Jones, G.W., 'A Revolution in Whitehall', *West European Politics*, Vol. 12, No. 3, July 1989.

Jones, Peter Ellis, *Oil: A Practical Guide to the Economics of World Petroleum* (Cambridge: Woodhead-Faulkner, 1988).

Katzenstein, Peter, *Between Power and Plenty, Foreign Economic Policies of Advanced Industrial States* (Madison, WI: University of Wisconsin, 1978).

Kearton, Frank, 'The Oil Industry, Some Personal Recollections and Opinions', in David Hawdon, ed., *The Changing Structure of the World Oil Industry* (London: Croom Helm, 1985).

Keegan, William, *Mr Lawson's Gamble* (London: Hodder & Stoughton, 1989).

—— *Mrs Thatcher's Experiment* (London: Penguin Books, 1984).

Kegley, Charles and Eugene Wittkopf, *American Foreign Policy: Pattern and Process*, Fourth Edition (Basingstoke: Macmillan Education, 1991).

Keohane, Robert O., 'State Power and Industry Influence: American Foreign Oil Policy in the 1940s', *International Organization*, Vol. 36, No. 1, Winter 1982.

—— *After Hegemony, Cooperation and Discord in the World Political Economy* (Princeton, NJ: Princeton University Press, 1984a).

—— 'The World Political Economy and the Crisis of Embedded Liberalism', in John Goldthorpe, ed., *Order and Conflict in Contemporary Capitalism* (Oxford: Clarendon Press, 1984b).

—— 'Theory of World Politics', in Robert Keohane, ed., *Neorealism and Its Critics* (New York: Columbia University Press, 1986a).

—— 'Realists, Neorealists and the Study of World Politics', in Robert Keohane, ed., *Neorealism and its Critics* (New York: Columbia University Press, 1986b).

—— 'Neoliberal Institutionalism: A Perspective on World Politics', in Robert Keohane, *International Institutions and State Power* (Boulder, CO: Westview Press, 1989).

Keohane, Robert O. and Joseph Nye, eds, *Power and Interdependence: World Politics in Transition* (Cambridge, MA: Harvard University Press, 1979).

—— *Power and Interdependence,* Second Edition (Boston: Little, Brown, 1989).

King, Anthony, 'Margaret Thatcher: The Style of a Prime Minister', in Anthony King, ed., *The British Prime Minister*, Second Edition (London: Macmillan, 1985).

—— 'Margaret Thatcher as a Political Leader', in Robert Skidelsky, ed., *Thatcherism* (London: Chatto & Windus, 1988).

Klapp, Merrie Gilbert, *The Sovereign Entrepreneur: Oil Policies in Advanced and Less Developed Capitalist Countries* (Ithaca: Cornell University Press, 1987).

Knopf, Jeffrey W., 'Beyond Two-Level Games: Domestic-International Interaction in the Intermediate-Range Nuclear Forces Negotiations', *International Organization*, Vol. 47, No. 4, Autumn 1993.

Krapels, Edward, *Oil Crisis Management: Strategic Stockpiling for International Security* (London: Johns Hopkins University Press, 1980).

Krapels, Edward and Sarah Emerson, *Storage in the International Oil Market*, Special Report No. 1117 (London: The Economist Intelligence Unit, 1987).

Krasner, Stephen D., 'State Power and the Structure of International Trade', *World Politics*, Vol. 28, April 1976.

—— *Defending the National Interest: Raw Materials Investment and U.S. Foreign Policy* (Princeton: Princeton University Press, 1978).

—— *Structural Conflict: Third World Against Global Liberalism* (Berkeley: University of California Press, 1985a).

—— ed., *International Regimes* (Ithaca, NY: Cornell University Press, 1985b).

Labour Party, 'The Labour Way is the Better Way', The Labour Party Manifesto, 1979.

—— 'The New Hope for Britain', Labour's Manifesto, 1983.

—— 'Labour Manifesto', June 1987.

Lake, David, *Power, Protection and Free Trade: International Sources of U.S. Commercial Strategy, 1887–1939* (Ithaca, NY: Cornell University Press, 1988).

Lantzke, Ulf, 'The OECD and Its International Energy Agency', *Daedalus*, Fall 1975.

Lawson, Nigel, *The View from No. 11: Memoirs of a Tory Radical* (London: Bantam Press, 1992).

—— 'Energy Policy', in Dieter Helm, John Kay and David Thompson, eds, *The Market for Energy* (Oxford: Clarendon Press, 1989).

Lesser, Ian O., *Resources and Strategy* (London: The Macmillan Press, 1989).

Letwin, Oliver, *Privatising the World: A Study of International Privatisation in Theory and Practice* (London: Cassell Educational, 1988).

Levy, Brian, 'World Oil Marketing in Transition', *International Organization*, Vol. 36, No. 1, Winter 1982.

Likierman, Andrew, *Public Expenditure: The Public Spending Process* (London: Penguin Books, 1988).

Lynn, Laurence E., 'The Budget-Maximizing Bureaucrat: Is There a Case?' in André Blais and Stéphane Dion, eds, *The Budget-Maximizing Bureaucrat: Appraisals and Evidence* (Pittsburg, PA: University of Pittsburg Press, 1991).

March, J.C. and J.P. Olsen, 'The New Institutionalism: Organizational Factors in Political Life', *American Political Science Review*, Vol. 78, 1984.

Marsh, David, 'Privatisation Under Mrs. Thatcher: A Review of the Literature', *Public Administration*, Vol. 69, Winter 1991.

Maull, Hanns, 'Oil and Influence: The Oil Weapon Examined', in Klaus Knorr and Frank Trager, eds, *Economic Issues and National Security* (Lawrence, KA: Regents Press, 1977).

Mayer, C.P. and S.A. Meadowcroft, 'Selling Public Assets: Techniques and Financial Implications', *Fiscal Studies*, Vol. 6, No. 4, 1985.

McAlister, Ian and Donley Studlar, 'Popular Versus Elite Views of Privatization: The Case of Britain', *Journal of Public Policy*, Vol. 9, No. 2, 1989.

McBeth, B.S., *British Oil Policy 1919–1939* (London: Frank Cass, 1985).

McCall, John, 'The Lawyer's Role in the Oil Industry – A Look at the British National Oil Corporation and its Legal Department', *International Business Lawyer*, 1979.

McDonald, Oonagh, *Own Your Own: Social Ownership Examined* (London: Unwin Paperbacks, 1989).

McInnes, David, 'Policy Networks within the Department of Energy and Energy Policy', Essex Papers in Politics and Government, No. 82, July 1991.

McKenzie, Richard B. and Dwight R. Lee, *Quicksilver Capital: How the Rapid Movement of Wealth Has Changed the World* (New York: Free Press, 1991).

Meltzer, Alan, 'Monetarism', in David Henderson, ed., *The Fortune Encyclopedia of Economics* (New York: Warner Books, 1993).

Melzer, A.H. and S.F. Richard, 'Why Government Grows, and Grows, in a Democracy', *Public Interest*, Vol. 52, Summer 1978.

Middlemas, Keith, *Power, Competition and the State. Volume Three: The End of the Postwar Era: Britain Since 1974* (London: Macmillan Academic and Professional, 1991).

Mikdashi, Zuhayr, *Transnational Oil: Issues, Policies and Perspectives* (London: Frances Pinter Publishers, 1986).

Mills, C. Wright, *The Power Elite* (Oxford: Oxford University Press, 1956).

Milner, Helen V., *Resisting Protectionism: Global Industries and the Politics of International Trade* (Princeton, NJ: Princeton University Press, 1988).

—— 'Domestic and International Sources of Cooperation: Oil Politics in the 1940s and 1970s', paper given at the Ford Foundation conference on the domestic and international sources of international economic cooperation, Milan, 3–4 April 1989.

Minet, Paul, *Full Text of the Treaty of Rome: An ABC of the Common Market* (London: C. Johnson, 1961).

Mitchell, B.R., *Economic Development of the British Coal Industry 1800–1914* (London: Cambridge University Press, 1984).

Moran, Theodore, *Multinational Corporations and the Politics of Dependence: Copper in Chile* (Princeton, NJ: Princeton University Press, 1974).

Morgenthau, Hans, *Politics Among Nations* (New York: Knopf, 1948).

Morris, C.N., 'Budgetary Arithmetic and the 1982 Budget', in John Kay, ed., *The 1982 Budget* (Oxford: Basil Blackwell, 1982).

Moyer, H. Wayne and Timothy Josling, *Agricultural Policy Reform: Politics and Process in the EC and USA* (Hemel Hempstead: Harvester Wheatsheaf, 1990).

Mueller, Dennis, *Public Choice II* (Cambridge: Cambridge University Press, 1989).

Murdock, Clark A., 'Economic Factors as Objects of Security: Economics, Security and Vulnerability', in Klaus Knorr and Frank Trager, eds, *Economic Issues and National Security* (Lawrence, KA: National Security Education Program, Regents Press, 1977).

Murray, Patricia, *Margaret Thatcher* (London: W.H. Allen, 1980).

Nelsen, Brent, *The State Offshore Petroleum, Politics and State Intervention on the British and Norwegian Continental Shelves* (London: Praeger Publishers, 1991).

Newman, A.M., *Economic Organization of the British Coal Industry* (London: Routledge, 1934).

Niskanen, William A., *Bureaucracy and Representative Government* (Chicago: Aldine-Atherton, 1971).

Nordlinger, Eric, *On the Autonomy of the Democratic State* (Cambridge, MA: Harvard University Press, 1981).

—— 'The Retreat of the State: Critiques', *American Political Science Review*, Vol. 82, No. 3, September 1988.

Odell, John and Thomas Willett, eds, *International Trade Policies: Gains from Exchange Between Economics and Political Science* (Ann Arbor: University of Michigan Press, 1990).

Odell, Peter, *Oil and World Power* (New York: Penguin Books, 1986).

Olson, Mancur, *The Logic of Collective Action: Public Goods and the Theory of Groups* (Cambridge, MA: Harvard University Press, 1971).

Osborne, David and Ted Gaebler, *Reinventing Government: How the Entrepreneurial Spirit is Transforming the Public Sector* (New York: Addison-Wesley, 1992).

Palan, Ronen, 'The Political Process in International Relations: Domestic and Global Structures', paper presented at the annual conference of the British International Studies Association, 17–19 December 1990.

Parkinson, Cecil, *Right at the Centre: an Autobiography* (London: Weidenfeld & Nicolson, 1992).

Pearson, Lynn, *Organization of the Energy Industry* (London: Macmillan, 1981).

Peltzman, Sam, 'The Growth of Government', *Journal of Law and Economics*, Vol. 23, No. 2, October 1980.

Peters, B. Guy, 'The European Bureaucrat: The Applicability of *Bureaucracy and Representative Government* to Non-American Settings', in André Blais and Stéphane Dion, eds, *The Budget-Maximizing Bureaucrat: Appraisals and Evidence* (Pittsburg, PA: University of Pittsburg Press, 1991).

Pirie, Madsen, *Privatization* (Aldershot: Wildwood House, 1988).

Plano, Jack and Milton Greenberg, *The American Political Dictionary*, Eighth Edition (New York: Holt, Rinehart and Winston, 1989).

Pliatsky, Leo, *Getting and Spending: Public Expenditure, Employment and Inflation* (Oxford: Basil Blackwell, 1984).

—— *The Treasury Under Mrs Thatcher* (Oxford: Basil Blackwell, 1989).

Polak, Jacques, 'The Changing Nature of IMF Conditionality', Essays in International Finance, No. 184 (Princeton, NJ: International Finance Section, Department of Economics, Princeton University, September 1991).

Political and Economic Policy Industry Group, *Report on the British Coal Industry* (London: Political and Economic Planning, February 1936).

Porter, Michael, *The Competitive Advantage of Nations* (New York: Free Press, 1990).

Powell, Robert, 'Anarchy in International Relations Theory: The Neorealist-Neoliberalist Debate', *International Organization*, Vol. 48, No. 2, Spring 1994.

Prior, Jim, *A Balance of Power* (London: Hamish Hamilton, 1986).

Prodi, Romano and Alberto Clo, 'Europe', *Daedalus*, Fall 1975.

Putnam, Robert D., 'Diplomacy and Domestic Politics: The Logic of Two-Level Games', *International Organization*, Vol. 42, No. 3, Summer 1988.

Pym, Francis, *The Politics of Consent* (London: Hamish Hamilton, 1984).

Rabinowitz, George and Stuart Elaine MacDonald, 'A Directional Theory of Issue Voting', *American Political Science Review*, Vol. 83, No. 1, March 1989.

Ranelagh, John, *Thatcher's People: An Insider's Account of the Politics, the Power and the Personalities* (London: Harper Collins, 1991).

Redwood, John, *Going for Broke ... Gambling with Taxpayers' Money* (Oxford: Basil Blackwell, 1984).

Rees, Judith and Peter Odell, *International Oil Industry: An Interdisciplinary Approach* (London: Macmillan Press, 1987).

Richardson, Jeremy, ed., *Pressure Groups* (Oxford: Oxford University Press, 1993).

Richardson, Jeremy and A.G. Jordan, *Governing Under Pressure: The Policy Process in a Post-parliamentary Democracy* (Oxford: Martin Robinson, 1979).

Riddell, Peter, *The Thatcher Decade: How Britain Has Changed During the 1980s* (Oxford: Basil Blackwell, 1989).

Ridley, F.F., 'Career Service: A Comparative Perspective on Civil Service Promotion', *Public Administration*, Vol. 61, Summer 1983.

Robinson, Colin, 'The Errors of North Sea Policy', *Lloyds Bank Review*, No. 141, July 1981.

Robinson, Jeffrey, *Yamani: The Inside Story* (London: Fontana Paperbacks, 1988).

Rogowski, Ronald, *Commerce and Coalitions: How Trade Affects Domestic Political Alignments* (Princeton: Princeton University Press, 1990).

Rose, Richard, 'British Government: The Job at the Top', in Richard Rose and Ezra N. Suleiman, *Presidents and Prime Ministers* (Washington, DC: American Enterprise Institute for Public Policy Research, 1980).

—— *Understanding Big Government: The Programme Approach* (London: Sage Publications, 1984).

Rosenau, James, 'Towards the Study of National-International Linkages', in James Rosenau, ed., *Linkage Politics* (New York: Free Press, 1969).

—— *Turbulence in World Politics: A Theory of Change and Continuity* (New York: Harvester Wheatsheaf, 1990).

Rowen, Henry and John Weyant, 'Trade-Offs Between Military Policies and Vulnerability Policies', in James Plummer, ed., *Energy Vulnerability* (Cambridge, MA: Ballinger Publishing, 1982).

St John-Stevas, Norman, *The Two Cities* (London: Faber and Faber, 1984).

Savas, E.S., *Privatization: The Key to Better Government* (Chatham, NJ: Chatham House, 1987).

Scharpf, Fritz, *Crisis and Choice in European Social Democracy* (Ithaca, NY: Cornell University Press, Translated Edition, 1991).

Schonhardt-Bailey, Cheryl, 'Lessons in the Lobbying for Free Trade in Nineteenth Century Britain: To Concentrate or Not', *American Political Science Review*, Vol. 85, No. 1, March 1991.

Schumpeter, J.A., *Capitalism, Socialism and Democracy* (London: Allen and Unwin, 1952).

Shelbourne, Philip, 'BNOC's Growth and Prospects', *Coal and Energy Quarterly*, No. 30, April 1981.

Silverman, David, *The Theory of Organizations: A Sociological Framework*, (London: Heineman, 1972).

Skidelsky, Robert, 'Introduction', in Robert Skidelsky, ed., *Thatcherism* (London: Chatto & Windus, 1988).

Smart, Ian, 'European Energy Security in Focus', in Curt Gasteyger, ed., *The Future for European Energy Security* (London: Frances Pinter, 1985).

Smith, Rodney, 'International Energy Cooperation: The Mismatch Between IEA Policy Actions and Policy Goals', in George Horwich and David Leo Weimer, eds, *Responding to International Oil Crises* (Washington, DC: American Enterprise Institute, 1988).

Starr, Paul, 'The New Life of the Liberal State: Privatization and the Restructuring of State-Society Relations', in Ezra N. Suleiman and John Waterbury, eds, *The Political Economy of Public Sector Reform and Privatization* (Oxford: Westview Press, 1990).

Steel, David and David Heald, 'Report: Privatizing Public Enterprise: An Analysis of the Government's Case', *Political Quarterly*, Vol. 53, No. 3, July-Sept 1982.

Stevens, Paul, 'A Survey of Structural Change in the International Oil Industry, 1945–1984', in David Hawdon, ed., *The Changing Structure of the World Oil Industry* (London: Croom Helm, 1985).

Stiles, Kendall W., *Negotiating Debt, The IMF Lending Process* (Oxford: Westview Press, 1991).

Stobaugh, Robert, 'The Oil Companies in Crisis', *Daedalus*, Fall 1975.

Stockil, P.A., 'A Brief History of the British Petroleum Company Limited', in British Petroleum, ed., *Our Industry Petroleum* (London: British Petroleum Company, 1970).

Stourharas, Yannis, *Are Oil Price Movements Perverse?: A Critical Explanation of Oil Price Levels 1950–1985* (Oxford: Oxford Institute for Energy Studies, 1985).

Strange, Susan, *International Monetary Relations*, Volume II, in Andrew Shonfield, ed., *International Economic Relations of the Western World, 1959–1971* (Oxford: Oxford University Press, 1976).

—— 'Cave! Hic Dragones: A critique of Regimes Analysis', in Stephen Krasner, ed., *International Regimes* (Ithaca, NY: Cornell University Press, 1985).

—— *States and Markets* (London: Pinter Publishers, 1988).

Suleiman, Ezra N. and John Waterbury, 'Introduction: Analysing Privatization in Industrial and Developing Countries', in Ezra N. Suleiman and John Waterbury, eds, *The Political Economy of Public Sector Reform and Privatization* (Oxford: Westview Press, 1990).

Swann, Dennis, *The Retreat of the State: Deregulation and Privatization in the United Kingdom and the United States* (London: Harvester Wheatsheaf, 1988).

Taylor, Charles and David Jodice, *World Handbook of Political and Social Indicators. Vol. I: Cross-national Attributes and Rates of Change*, Third Edition (New Haven, CT: Yale University Press, 1983).

Taylor, David, ed., *British Opinion Polls 1960–1988*, Volume I: Subjects and Names Index, alphabetical and Volume II: Subjects and Names Index, date order (Reading: Research Publications, 1990).

Taylor, Paul, *International Organization in the Modern World: The Regional and the Global* (London: Pinter Publishers, 1993).

Tebbit, Norman, *Upwardly Mobile* (London: Weidenfeld & Nicolson, 1988).

Terzian, Pierre (translated by Michael Pallis), *OPEC: The Inside Story* (London: Zed Books, 1985).

Tetreault, Mary Ann, *Revolution in the World Petroleum Market* (London: Quorum Books, 1985).

Thatcher, Margaret, *The Downing Street Years* (London: Harper Collins Publishers, 1993).

Trades Union Congress, *Stripping Our Assets: The City's Privatisation Killing* (London: Trades Union Congress, May 1985).

Tugendhat, Christopher and Adrian Hamilton, *Oil, the Biggest Business* (London: Eyre Methuen, 1975).

Tullock, Gordon, *The Politics of Bureaucracy* (Washington, DC: Public Affairs Press, 1965).

Turner, Louis, 'State and Commercial Interests in North Sea Oil and Gas: Conflict and Correspondence', in Martin Sacter and Ian Smart, eds, *The Political Implications of North Sea Oil and Gas* (Oslo: Universitetsforlaget, 1975).

—— *Oil Companies in the International System* (London: The Royal Institute of International Affairs, 1978 and 1984 editions).

Veljanovski, Cento, *Selling the State, Privatization in Britain* (London: Weidenfeld and Nicolson, 1987).

—— 'Privatization: Progress, Issues and Problems', in Dennis Gayle and Jonathan Goodrich, eds, *Privatization and Deregulation in Global Perspective* (London: Pinter Publishers, 1990).

Vernon, Raymond, *Sovereignty at Bay: The Multinational Spread of U.S. Enterprises* (New York: Basic Books, 1971).

—— *Two Hungry Giants: the United States and Japan in the Quest for Oil and Ores* (Cambridge, MA: Harvard University Press, 1983).

—— 'Introduction: The Promise and the Challenge', in Raymond Vernon, ed., *The Promise of Privatization: A Challenge for U.S. Policy* (New York: Council on Foreign Relations, 1988).

Vickers, John and Vincent Wright, 'The Politics of Industrial Privatisation in Western Europe', in John Vickers and Vincent Wright, eds, *The Politics of Privatisation in Western Europe* (London: Frank Cass, 1989).

Vickers, John and George Yarrow, *Privatization: An Economic Analysis* (Cambridge, MA: MIT Press, 1988).

Wallace, William, *Britain's Bilateral Links within Western Europe* (London: Routledge and Kegan Paul, 1984).

Walters, Alan, *Britain's Economic Renaissance: Margaret Thatcher's Reforms 1979–1984* (Oxford: Oxford University Press, 1986).

Waltz, Kenneth N., *Man, the State and War* (New York: Columbia University Press, 1954).

—— *Theory of International Politics* (Reading, MA: Addison-Wesley, 1979).

Wass, Douglas, 'The Public Service in Modern Society', *Public Administration*, Vol. 61, Spring 1983.

Watson, Sophie, 'Is Sir Humphry Dead? The Changing Culture of the Civil Service', Working Paper 103, University of Bristol, School for Advanced Urban Studies, July 1992.

Webb, Michael G., 'Energy Policy and the Privatization of the UK Energy Industries', *Energy Policy*, February 1985.

Whitfield, Dexter, *Making it Public: Evidence and Action Against Privatisation* (London: Pluto Press, 1983).

Wilson, Ernest J., 'World Politics and International Energy Markets', *International Organization*, Vol. 41, No. 1, Winter 1987.

Wilson, Harold, *Final Term: The Labour Government 1974–1976* (London: Weidenfeld and Nicolson and Michael Joseph, 1979).

Wilson, James Q., *Political Organization* (New York: Basic Books, 1973).

——, *Bureaucracy: What Government Agencies Do and Why They Do It* (New York: Basic Books, 1989).

Winters, Alan, 'Britain in Europe: a Survey of Quantitative Trade Studies', in Alexis Jacquemin and Andre Sapir, eds, *The European Internal Market: Trade and Competition* (Oxford: Oxford University Press, 1989).

Wolfe, Joel, 'State Power and Ideology in Britain: Mrs Thatcher's Privatization Programme', *Political Studies*, Vol. XXXIX, 1991.

Wright, Maurice, 'Big Government in Hard Times: The Restraint of Public Expenditure', in Christopher Hood and Maurice Wright, eds, *Big Government in Hard Times* (Oxford: Martin Robertson, 1981).

Yarrow, George, 'Privatization and Economic Performance in Britain', *Carnegie-Rochester Conference Series on Public Policy*, No. 31, 1989.

Yergin, Daniel, *The Prize: The Epic Quest for Oil, Money and Power* (New York: Simon and Schuster, 1991).

Young, Hugo, *One of Us: A Biography of Margaret Thatcher*, Final Edition (London: Macmillan, 1991).

Young, Oran, 'Critical Variables', in James Rosenau, ed., *Governance Without Government: Order and Change in World Politics* (Cambridge: Cambridge University Press, 1992).

Young, Robert A., 'Budget Size and Bureaucratic Careers', in André Blais and Stéphane Dion, eds, *The Budget-Maximizing Bureaucrat: Appraisals and Evidence* (Pittsburg, PA: University of Pittsburg Press, 1991).

Young, S., 'The Nature of Privatisation in Britain, 1979–85', *West European Politics*, Vol. 9, 1986.

Index